The Writer's File

Caroline Hurry

Website: https://carolinehurry.com

Cover Design: Caroline Hurry

Library of Congress Control Number: TXu002371123

Preface

Welcome to The Writer's File

So here we are. You, me, and two books showing you how to break free from traditional publishing – smouldering under the kindling of subscription models, print-on-demand services, and TikTok reviews – to explore independent release in 2026 and beyond.

We're the innovators, the risk-takers, the creative entrepreneurs redefining what it means to "make it" in publishing. We own our rights, keep our royalties, and connect with the readers who get us.

Had you told me five years ago I'd be writing about AI-powered publishing tools, audiobook empires worth $35 billion, and authors launching from their kitchen tables without courting a single agent, I'd have laughed into my rejection letter file.

Now *everyone* – irrespective of patron or pedigree – is invited to the Renaissance 2.0 publishing party.

Independent publishing can be exhilarating, liberating, and overwhelming. This box set is your GPS to help you cut through the noise and recalculate with gumption.

Each dispatch from the front line was born from the trial-and-error trenches. Crests and troughs become valuable insight when navigating the tempestuous sea of literary autonomy. Perseverance is your compass.

Once upon a time, publishing was a linear affair:

- Write manuscript.
- Send manuscript.
- Collect rejection slips.
- Frame them as wall art.
- Repeat until madness or miracle.

Now, it's more like:

- Write manuscript.
- Format with AI.
- Design a cover on Canva.
- Publish globally
- Market yourself on TikTok or write a newsletter

Book One: WRITE

Your comprehensive guide to everything you need to know about writing and self-publishing on a shoestring budget, Write is equal parts muse, map, and motivational pep talk. You'll learn how to:

- Build sustainable writing habits
- Structure your book so it flows like a river rather than a traffic jam
- Embrace editing as a creative act
- Format and publish using today's most powerful free tools.

Book Two: SPLASH IT!

Practical, punchy, and full of shortcuts for authors, small business owners, or any creative soul launching their Big Thing, the 2026 reboot is all about visibility with vitality. Here's what's new:

- AI-powered prompts to clarify your message, craft pitches, and plan social media
- Short-form storytelling tips for TikTok, Instagram Reels, and Substack
- New templates for podcast pitches, newsletters, and press releases that actually get read - elevate your pitch and build buzz
- A customizable workbook companion so you can go from idea to implementation in minutes

The Bottom Line

The publishing industry is evolving faster than a plot twist in a thriller, and that's a good thing. Creativity thrives on change.

So, dip in anywhere. Bookmark the prompts that speak to you. Customize the templates to suit your needs. Scan the QR codes for bonus downloads.

Use what works, discard what doesn't, and adapt everything else to fit your unique situation.

I hope you find them useful. Moreover, I hope they encourage you to persevere. Writing is hard. Publishing is harder. But the alternative – keeping your unique perspective locked inside - is the hardest of all.

When the waves get rough, rejections sting, the edits overwhelm, or the marketing feels impossible, return to these pages to remind yourself that every author, from Austen to Rowling, has felt that same uncertainty and pressed "publish" anyway.

Welcome to the wild, wonderful world of modern publishing. Find your voice, own your story, and make genuine connections with the people who need your work.

Ready to make something brilliant? You've got this.

Let's go.

Caroline Hurry

Contents

Who Am I

To Write and Publish with Sovereignty?

A TRAVEL HACK WITH no place to go? Check. Too belligerent for full-time employment? Check. I had to do something, but what?

Wait, *I* know!

Instead of pecking at the stale and dwindling corporate media pie crusts with the other moulting crows, why not write and publish a book on Amazon? Pen my reflections into a passive income, surf the royalty swells, and make the million-dollar drop?

Checkity, checkity, *check!*

How hard could it be? After all, I embellished my way into a newspaper gig during the typewriter era that launched a long journalistic career. Step into your best future, right? Bring it!

The book raging inside me burned my keyboard with the fierce heat of 2020 lockdown fury. Bewildered by nurses dry-humping drip stands, neighbours clanging pots at the moon, and politicians turning on the populations they were supposed to serve, jet-setting Jeanette – the old me

– segued from home-alone Harriet into Author Annie.

No longer tethered to travel journalism, I opted for a stay-at-home retreat – barefoot wanderings, hen companionship, and communion with Mother Nature. I dedicated myself to my first love – writing – held my nose and jumped into the self-publishing pool.

I sank like a stone on my first attempt, bobbed up again, and started treading water. At first, I felt like a casual snorkeler encountering a colossal squid and contemplated throwing in the towel more than once.

But here's the thing about starting. Once you begin, momentum builds. Putting out online feelers led to founding the women-only Hygge Queen Coterie – a great tip, right there. Start a group and sound out your future readers.

Their experiences inspired *Reign: 16 Secrets from 6 Queens to Rule Your World with Clarity, Connection, and Sovereignty* – equal parts memoir, self-help manual, and Brave New World travelogue.

Some might call that genre confusion. I prefer 'carving a niche in creative non-fiction' because regret, like thin skin, has no place in a writer's life.

True to my surname, haste trumped consideration when I jumped in, oblivious to lurking crocodile tasks and unforeseen responsibilities.

When I wrote *Handbook for the Huntress* (DoubleStorey, 2011), my traditional publisher handled everything. I only had to attend the occasional TV interview, which I dreaded, being deeply introverted.

An indie author must juggle everything from conjuring captivating covers to promotion. A TikTok twerkathon is fine if you have the confidence and energy to spare. I don't, so I made mistakes, and plenty of them.

I wasted money on self-proclaimed publishing promoters and marketing charlatans. Hint: If anyone unsolicited approaches you to review, publish, or promote your books, hit the delete button, pronto! School fees!

It's all good. The magic, as always, is in the learning. I've never been the type to throw myself a parade, but when your funds are tap-dancing on the edge of a dime, you start thinking creatively.

I followed up *Reign* with *Flow*, a tongue-in-cheek guide to dating, and then whipped up *Splash It!* in under a month.

It got to #1 in three Amazon Kindle categories - Public Relations, Business Writing Skills, and Business Communication Skills.

Lessons learned? Give people something they want or can use. Make it free to download for a few days to boost ratings. Easy peasy! Just kidding.

Putting your work out there takes courage and the constant shedding of redundancies, but it takes just one reader to express what a difference your work has made in their life to make it worthwhile. Writing for its own sake has its exhilarating moments, too.

The trick is to stick at it with all the zeal of a catfisher scamming women on social media with honeyed words. Had I thrown in the towel, as I often felt tempted to do, I would never have experienced the emotional alchemy writing offers.

Your life expands when you put love before money, but there's no reason you can't earn a living from your passion, too.

Today, it's easier than ever to produce books. AI can help organize research, format manuscripts, and even suggest marketing strategies. The tools are there. It's how you choose to use them that counts.

I've channelled this approach into several bestsellers: *Medusa's Musings* explores mythology through a modern lens. Touch wood, it's garnering great reviews!

Written under the pseudonym Stella Firewall, my short cybersecurity guide equips readers with practical protection strategies in *Gone Phishing!*

The Rooster Diaries emerged from the careless cruelty that sparked my entire backyard fowl-keeping venture.

A factory farm is no place for living creatures, but banging the worthy drum kills prose faster than a fox in a henhouse. So Smart Alec, king of the heap, took over as the narrator, offering a riotous version of my ongoing adventures in sustainable living.

From there, AI helped me transform vermiculture notes that didn't make it into *The Rooster Diaries* into *Worm Wrangling* - a 26-page guide penned in a day – another zinger in its category, proving that even your leftover material can find new life with the right approach.

Each book taught me something new and reminded me to persevere. Every crest and trough becomes valuable insight when navigating the tempestuous sea of literary autonomy. Perseverance is your compass in the voyage of exploration.

Self-publishing requires resilience and constant vigilance, but nothing beats the exhilaration of transforming ideas into books, blogs, articles, newsletters, and even graffiti!

Write is my guide to everything you need to know about writing and self-publishing on a shoestring. If you're prepared to approach rocky terrain from different angles and move on from your mistakes, everything's possible.

I hope you find it useful. More than that, I hope it encourages *you* to keep going.

You, Too, Can

Make Literary Magic on a Shoestring

Unless it's a test result for some dread disease, 'no' can be a devastating one-word sentence. Or, it can be the sign you need to self-publish.

You'll cross plains of procrastination and hit some turbulent tides, but taking the reins, letting your creativity soar, and turning your work into a dialogue with the world is the most transformative thing you can do.

If your untold story taps your shoulder, but potential costs prevent you from ruling the indie author realm, you'll find everything you need to succeed – free tools, DIY editing, formatting, insider tips, references, and chatbot prompts to guide your way with minimal outlay.

Take the Hygge highway via five elemental routes – Fire, Water, Air, Earth, and Metal – to incorporate human connection into your work and evolve.

Learn how to grow your community, gather your supporters, garner reviews without learning judo moves, and evolve as an authorpreneur along warm currents of camaraderie.

If you're ready to ignite your passion, make waves, let your words resonate, build a solid foundation, and launch your masterpiece, read on.

The Elemental Sections

Fire – Forge, Ignite, Research, and Expand

With the FUEL and BURN approach. Fan that initial spark of inspiration into a roaring flame. Learn to fuel your ideas, research your market, and expand your reach with a fiery, inextinguishable determination. Fire Hygge is your matchbox chapter.

Water – Write, Adapt, Title, Edit, and Revise.

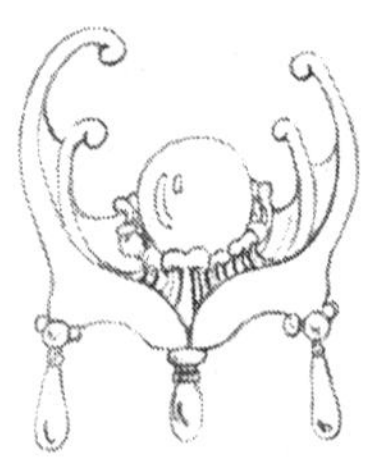

Dive deep into crafting your masterpiece. Will you make waves or ripples? You'll learn to write captivating content, adapt to your audience, choose the perfect title, design a cover, edit, and revise until your work shines like a diamond.

Air – Audio, Inspire, and Resonate.

Discover strategies to amplify your voice through audiobooks, initiating conversations with your readers, or creating content that resonates like a harmonious symphony. Disperse discord and let your words soar. Air represents freedom to share your story in your voice,

Earth – Establish, Author, Reviews, Test, and Hack

your way through challenges. Lay the groundwork, create a structural outline, establish your authorial presence, and test the waters before you release your work. We'll cover formatting, media whispering, and what to plant for fertile growth.

Metal – Market, Engage, Tackle, AI, and Launch.

Metal is about strength and resilience. Learn to market your work effectively, engage with your readers, tackle obstacles head-on, use AI tools to your advantage, and orchestrate a powerful launch without getting out of your pajamas. Go for gold.

Appendix Prompt Vault

Your go-to resource for discovering effective AI prompts across every aspect of writing, publishing, and book marketing. Whether you're crafting a blog post, refining your Amazon description, or brainstorming email subject lines, this vault is designed to save time, boost creativity, and help you get better results from ChatGPT.

At the heart of the Vault is the W.R.I.T.E. framework, a simple yet powerful blueprint for shaping precise prompts that deliver focused, usable output.

Appendix Publishing Platforms

Everything you need to know about setting up an account, uploading your manuscript, royalty rates and distribution options on Amazon KDP, IngramSpark Draft2Digital and Smashwords, Kobo Writing Life, and Lulu for niche print-on-demand projects like journals.

You'll find essential checklists for pre-upload readiness, DIY cover design tips using free tools, best practices for formatting files, an overview of Amazon's promotional features, and QR code integration. Whether you're going wide or staying exclusive, this appendix provides the resources you need to cross platforms.

Appendix Marketing Systems

Set up profiles on Instagram, Discord's VIP reader lounges, Threads, and Bluesky. Learn to create Facebook groups and master email marketing that feels like chatting with friends rather than shouting into the void.

Discover battle-tested strategies, step-by-step setup guides, and insider intelligence. Whether you're choosing the perfect username, crafting bios that make readers stop scrolling, or figuring out how to use AI tools to work smarter instead of harder, this appendix is your permission slip to market authentically without selling your creative soul. Everything is designed for authors working on shoestring budgets who would rather write than wrestle with social media demons.

Fabulous Free Tools

Your secret sauce to self-publishing success is the stash of invaluable free tools and resources in this chapter

I've packed my six-pronged elemental process into a carry-on bag for you. Grab my hand. Let's go!

Contents

One

Fire Section

Forge, Ignite, Research, Expand

Create something new with illumination, heat, and energy. Burn redundancies. Fire inspires you to show up for yourself, pinpoint your focus, set complex ideas aflame, and take action. Learn how to:

- **Forge** Your Foundation: Build unshakeable self-belief. You don't need permission to start. Channel fear and friction into creative fuel. Your voice matters. Cultivate self-discovery.
- **Ignite** Your Authentic Voice: Break free from self-censorship and embrace courageous expression. Trust your unique perspective and transform your experiences into compelling narratives.
- **Research** And Understand: What makes you indispensable to your ideal reader. Transform curiosity into value by addressing their specific needs, crafting irresistible hooks, and creating urgent reasons for them to choose your work over countless alternatives.
- **Expand** Your Reach: Create a website. Personalize content, appraise needs, network and distribute through various platforms.

So summon your writing dragon, and let's light the fuse.

> *"Writers are dragon whisperers. We take our fears, our fury, our fire and burn through silence, scorching the lies."*
>
> Caroline Hurry

Forge

Ahead, Shed Perfectionism, Just Start!

> *One serene and mind-blowing day, you will wake up and realize you are your own dragon. Through depths of despair and spiralling heights of imagination, you will know you have returned to roost in your heart, and your fire will be strong and quell all of your fears before you. Fling your mind forward with a will, for your dragon awaits you!*
>
> Donna White, the Minka series

You've always wanted to write a book, but how can you be sure it will succeed? That's the burning question. What does success mean to you? Is it freedom, visibility, income, or personal healing?

Ryan Hale, the best-selling author of *One for the Money* and the Blake Franklin series, says his desire to 'someday write a book' was weaker than his desire to live his life. "I thought it would be too tricky, too daunting, and impossible to write a full-length book."

And then he wrote his first book and thought: "Why the hell did I wait so long to have this much fun?"

My motivation for writing was sovereignty. My soul clashed with corporate mindsets. I'd lived in limbo long enough. I needed to begin. When I did, the old world melted away. So did many of the people in it.

The myriad me reflections that mourned them died, too. I kept going. I found new friends in scribes and readers who vibe with authenticity.

Bright Spark Case Study

Fiona overcomes her fear:

Stuck in a cycle of apathy, convinced she wasn't talented enough to pursue her passion, Fiona, in her 60s, lacked the confidence to bring her words to life. Haunted by her past, she feared – not without good reason – the judgments, jealousy, and behind-her-back bitching from her social circle.

"Having lost pieces of myself to tragedies, I'd been using what I didn't want as the benchmark for my choices. Battling the overwhelming despair of 'thankless daze,' I was still waiting for my life to begin."

Reading about how the women in *Reign16 Secrets* turned their fear into bonfire fuel and set it alight, she felt a shift. "Talk about all the sizzles! They sparked me to do the same."

Fiona reduced her divorce papers to ash and set to work on her memoir to inspire other women to bounce back after emotional setbacks.

"The terror of being judged for my words – or what those who recognize themselves might say – belongs to another time. I want my work to be light, but it takes dark turns. I'm 30,000 words in. I love the process. I feel myself growing as a human being, which is beyond price."

Hygge Hint:

When former friends hiss from the undergrowth, reach for higher standards. Says Fiona: "I switched off my phone. I became 'super-choosy' about how I spent my time. More sunshine, less stress. Writing became my therapy and salvation. I discovered my most powerful asset was me!"

Fear can be paralyzing and keep you from reaching your full potential. Instead, use it as a motivator to push yourself. Embrace the unknown and take risks. You never know what opportunities might come your way if you're willing to step outside your comfort zone.

Celebrate your successes, no matter how small. Every step forward is a step in the right direction. Staying true to your vision is essential.

Bright Spark Case Study

Artist-author, Kim Parker Defends Her Work:

When a top New York publisher told Kim she couldn't combine design and memoir in the book she'd spent two years compiling, she refused to compromise her vision.

"I stayed true to my instincts. It took me a few deep breaths, but relief replaced fear when I hit the send button to say I couldn't see us collaborating. A few days later, the publisher mailed back to say they'd do it my way."

That book, *Kim Parker Home: A Life in Design*, sold over 13,000 units, went into an almost instant second printing and earned rave media reviews.

Kim took the self-publishing route for her third book, *Interior Gardens: A New York Memoir,* because it put her firmly in the driver's seat with control over the entire process. "I get emails from women worldwide thanking me for inspiring them to follow their creative paths," she says.

Hygge Hint:

Our fears and doubts – analysis paralysis – hold us back. We convince ourselves we're not ready, undeserving of success, or not talented enough. Stop right there with the self-flagellation. Read no further until you're prepared to throw all self-defeating notions into fiery oceans.

Your fire-breathing dragon self subsumes all projected realities and emits splendid dreamscapes in a single shape-shifting puff. You're *so* more than enough.

But, but ... what? Talk to the bot. Burn those 'buts.' Have you planned a cut-off date to stop caring about what anyone else thinks? Self-doubt and worry are a waste of time. Trample your fears underfoot and step into your purpose.

SPARK Your First Draft

- **Set a timer for 15 minutes** and start. Jot down every random idea you have. Get everything out of your head. Don't stop until the timer goes off. You'd be surprised by what emerges when you permit yourself to **write without judgment.**
- **Put your thoughts in order** as you go: Organize but don't censor yourself. Forget about grammar, typos, or self-correcting as you bang out the **random stuff that comes to mind.**
- **Arrange your copy.** Break it up into smaller, more manageable chunks with bullet points or headings.
- **Rough out the contours** as an outline. Writing a foreword into your first draft helps you pinpoint where you'd like your narrative to go. The Earth section will cover structure.

- **Keep going.** Writing can feel emotionally exhausting, so take as many breaks as you need. Recharge. Ground yourself. Take a walk or do whatever sparks joy for you.

I don't know where my ideas come from. Nor does any writer. The only answer is to drink too much coffee and buy yourself a desk that doesn't collapse when you beat your head against it.

Douglas Adams

SCORCH a Foreword

Summarize, Cover, Organize, Relate, Contextualize, Highlight

- **Summarize** your project in three sentences. These should give readers a clear idea of what they can expect from your book.

- **Cover** why you wrote it, who it's for, what it involves, and how **i**t differs from other books on the same subject. Set the tone and establish your credibility as an author.

- **Organize** your copy into an overview of what your readers can expect. Break it into sections or chapters and give readers an idea of what each contains.

- **Relate** to your readers with **information that is relevant to them**. Use examples and anecdotes.

- **Contextualize** your thoughts and ideas You can detail your experience, education, or research, but don't be too self-promotional or overly biased.

- **H**ighlight additional topics, key themes, ideas, or concepts your book explores to pique readers' interest and encourage them to read further. You can also ask an expert in your field to write a foreword for you.

FIRE up a KDP Account

Initially, you'd do best to stick to Amazon's all-in-one publishing platform that handles everything from orders to customer support . Open a free KDP author account. See the Appendix Publishing Platforms chapter for everything you need to know about uploading your book on Amazon.

- Download Your Forge Ahead Worksheet here

Name: Date:

Author's Flame Worksheet

Your Creative Flame – Worksheet

Answer these questions

1. What is your book about in one sentence? *E.g. It's a poetic reckoning for women reclaiming their voice after being silenced.*

2. What fear is holding you back? Burn it here. *Write it. Rip it out. Burn it (safely).*

3. What makes your voice different? *List 3 things you bring to the page that no one else does.*

4. What does success mean to you? *Your soul's definition, please.*

5. What's your publish "Go Live" date? *Set the fire. Circle it in red.*

6. Who is your book for? Who do you want to reach or stir to life? *Name and visualize them reading it - your reader.*

7. What would your future self say if you gave up now? *Write it out.*

Ignite

Flame On! Blaze an Online Trail!

Don't think. Thinking is the enemy of creativity. It's self-conscious, and anything self-conscious is lousy. You can't try to do things. You simply must do things.

Ray Bradbury

Creative fire isn't always constant but you write through it anyway. Set the writing process alight, then let it burn because no flame is ever the same. Some days you're a spark; other days a wildfire. Both are valid. Writing is an infinite cosmic dance you set in motion. You change the steps as you go.

"What I love most about being an independent author is the complete control it gives me over my book. There are no gatekeepers deciding whether my book is worthy of publication," says D.G Torrens, poet and author of 25 books.

"I guarantee its release on my terms. I own the rights, choose the cover design, set my publication date, and manage my own sales dashboard. I can see my daily orders in real time, including where in the world they are coming from. Plus, the royalty share is far more generous compared to traditional publishing. Self-publishing means being your own boss, which is incredibly empowering."

Author Beverley Latimer says she puts her heart into her stories about how choices shape who we become. "But it's also about learning to live with what we can't change, " says Beverley who hit her stride with *Deceit and Reclamation,* illuminating one of Ireland's darkest, most shameful decades regarding young, unwed mothers. After its publication, several women contacted her to share their own experiences of childhood abuse. "It makes you realize that as writers, we can connect on a deeply personal level."

"I write for those who've experienced pain, felt silenced, and sought justice. Writing lets me channel these experiences into something meaningful."

Break the Silence: Write What Scares You

Self-censorship kills creativity. The most powerful writing often comes from truth-telling that makes us tremble.

Fiona told me her desire to please and make herself desirable to her ex-husband translated into tepid prose that lacked heat.

"I was big on self-censorship, fearing to offend anyone with my words. But as flames devoured the paraphernalia of my past, I realized good writing demanded courage to release the words I once kept hidden."

Your Voice, Your Authentic Vibe

When writing *Reign 16 Secrets To Rule Your World With Clarity, Connection & Sovereignty,* I, too, contemplated with trepidation the potential backlash of going against a prevailing narrative.

The potential of words to ignite change comes at a price. The truth is offensive to those who invest in lies, but my sovereignty is not for sale. Is anything more ephemeral than the good opinion of others? So I persevered. And something magical happened.

For every person who left my women's only group in high dudgeon over self-expression being given free rein, more asked to join.

A community of kindred spirits found solace in our shared experiences and collective voice. Our shared stories illuminate truths our overlords would prefer to keep hidden.

Honesty is a captivating key to the heart's door because the most meaningful words come from the places that scare us.

Your stories are reflected in the flames of fearless self-expression in those dark corners.

Blaze through the deadwood of self-doubt and keep the fire in your belly burning. Clear the dark forest of uncertainty. Ignite that flame in your imagination's wilderness and set the world alight with your stories.

Community Grows in Authenticity

I used to fear being seen. Now I fear staying silent. I wrote ***Medusa's Musings*** when I decided to stop apologizing for who I am. When you show up as yourself, even if that truth shakes others, you attract the right people to your work.

If visibility and social media scare you, start where you feel most comfortable (X, Instagram, TikTok) and build at your own pace.

- Download Your Free Visibility Flame Worksheet

Name: Date:

The Visibility Flame

Your Visibility Flame – Worksheet

Answer these questions

1. What's holding me back from posting?

2. What do I most want to say today?

3. Who is my story for? Who does it help?

4. Three hashtags that reflect my vibe:

5. One brave caption to post this week:

6. How can I best illustrate what I want to say?

7. How will I celebrate showing up for myself today?

Research

Reel In Readers With the Burn Approach

> *"Research is formalized curiosity. It is poking and prying with a purpose."*
>
> Zora Neale Hurston

TUMBLING DOWN RABBIT HOLES is your jam, but can you turn it into bread and butter? If curiosity alone fuels you, diving into a topic headfirst can be tempting, but does anyone else want to read it?

Can you turn that curiosity into connection, and ultimately, into sales? If you're anything like my friend Fester, the answer is ... not yet.

Fester's book on meditation was a meticulously researched tome. But sales? Nada. When he begged me to review it for a newspaper, I asked him: "Who are your readers, Fester?"

With an eyeroll, he replied, "Only 25 million people on Amazon."

Yeah... about that. Amazon's millions don't matter unless your message *resonates* – not with everyone, but *someone*. A reader. Not a demographic. A living, breathing, story-seeking soul. Identifying readers is the art of pinpointing kindred spirits whose struggles resonate with your message. And here's the twist: you don't have to guess who they are. You can ask AI to help you find them or construct a reader profile in 90 seconds.

Reel in Your Readers

A reader's number one question is: "What's in it for me?"

That's what you must address first. Figure out how your book can change their situations, cure their pains, and fulfil their desires. Self-help readers don't buy things because of who they are. They buy because of who they want to become. It's the transformation they seek. Not the steak but the sizzle of satisfaction and social proof that it's possible. The most successful infomercials comprise 70% testimonials. Use your own experiences or other real-life stories to convey your message because three more questions readers will ask:

1. Do you (the author) understand your readers' struggles? These may include budget constraints, lack of experience, time management, self doubt, difficulty promoting their work or gaining visibility within a competitive market.

2. Can you (the author) teach others to achieve their desired results? These may include teaching them practical techniques to improve their writing skills, self-publish their work, overcome obstacles, fulfil their ambitions, and achieve success as independent authors *on their terms.*

Reinvention is the watchword and the way out."

Polly Horton, NYPR dynamo

Burn to Learn

Bait, Understand, Research, and Navigate

Bait

Hook them in with relevance. What pain or desire does your book address? Your title, subtitle, and book description should echo those emotional triggers. Your words should inflame the reader's imagination.
AI Prompt: "What's a compelling one-sentence hook for a book about [your topic] that targets [your ideal reader profile]?"

Understand

Dive deep into their psychology: what do they fear, crave, or secretly hope is possible? Use a sense of urgen**cy** to pull readers in.
AI Prompt: "List 10 unspoken fears and desires of [insert audience] related to [your theme]."

Research

Use ChatGPT to identify existing books, trends, communities, and objections. Look at Amazon's most popular genres and emerging trends to see if they fit your book.
AI Prompt: Compare and contrast top 5 Amazon bestsellers in the [genre] space. What tone, promise, and structure do they share?

Navigate

Don't cast a wide net, laser-focus your topic and niche down. Keep it specific.
AI Prompt: Suggest 5 niche subtopics under [theme] that are underserved in the nonfiction market.

Tools You *Actually* Need

- **ChatGPT** – audience research, social content, blurbs, and hooks
- **Publisher Rocket** – Amazon keyword and category research
- **BuzzSumo** – trending blog/social topics by keyword
- **Substack + Reddit** – community-based reader exploration
- **BetaBooks.co** – gather feedback from test readers in your genre

Amazon's 6 Biggest Non-Fiction Niches

1. **Biographies & Memoirs:** True crime, celebrity biographies (Elon Musk, Donald Trump), and compelling life stories.
2. **Business & Money:** Sales, stock market, cryptocurrency (Bitcoin, crypto), CEO leadership, and personal finance.
3. **Health, Fitness & Dieting:** Mental health, meditation, self-improvement, diets (keto, Mediterranean, carnivore), and wellness.
4. **Self-Help & Personal Development:** Books focusing on motivation, productivity, habits
5. **Cookbooks, Food & Wine:** Specialized diets, beginner-friendly recipes, vintage and anti-inflammatory diets.
6. **Parenting & Relationships:** Parenting for dads, pregnancy, ADHD, autism, anxiety, divorce, and self-help for families.

- Kindlepreneur provides info on Amazon keywords and trends
- Research Your Ideal Reader: Download the Worksheet here:

Name: Date:

Map Your Ideal Reader

Open ChatGPT and enter these prompts:

1. Profile someone struggling with [insert problem your book solves]. Include demographics, goals, habits, search behavior, and online communities.

2. List 5 objections my readers might have about a book like mine.

3. Give me 5 social media post ideas to start conversations with this audience.

4. List 5 everyday struggles my readers have.

5. List 5 desired outcomes, my readers want.

6. List 5 examples of their typical vocabulary or slang with definition of each.

7. List 5 ways to overcome my readers' struggles and objections.

Expand

Set Up a Website and Establish Visibility

"Set up your sites. Stop waiting for somebody to give you permission to do anything you want to do."

David White, The Authority Figure

BACK IN THE DAY, as a freelance travel journalist full of stories, I launched a travel website that opened the gate to countless luxury junkets from river cruises to five-star safaris. *Gazes dreamily into the distance.* Yep, those were the days. Then came the travel clampdown and I swapped my suitcase for an ergonomic wishing chair.

Recalcitrant Me sulked. The uphill battle of writing and publishing felt overwhelming, as if I were trapped in a narrow cave with only one way out: forward, into the unknown. Was I ready for this 'authorpreneurial' hike?

I could only try. So, I did. And yes, I'm glad I persevered.

The old me? Burned to ash. Nature's fierce, uncompromising love dissolves and transmutes outdated selves along the path. Ghosting those versions of myself created space for more hygge – joy, if you will.

Individuality, I learned, isn't fixed. I'm more like a shifting frequency, reforming daily with nature's infinite permutations.

Writing is my therapy, helping me navigate this dynamic reality. Publishing has expanded my perspective in delightful, unpredictable ways. It's fun, even when it's hard.

And, if *you* don't take the reins of your destiny, who will?

Yes, you'll traverse the plains of procrastination and spelunk the caves of insecurity. But sovereignty – ruling your realm on your terms – gives your life purpose. Age, sex, or circumstance doesn't matter. What matters is owning your story and sharing it.

Case Study: How David White Spins Websites

Here's something authors never tell you: writing books is just the beginning. The real magic happens when you transform that hard-won expertise into a web presence that builds your authority while you sleep.

After years of writing books, David White, best-selling author of *The Authority Figure,* discovered something revolutionary: each medium demands its own structure.

Books follow one rhythm, websites another. The breakthrough came when he stopped trying to force his book-writing skills onto web pages and started treating each platform as an independent entity. Here is his battle-tested approach to turning expertise into online influence.

The Multi-Platform Strategy

"I have a string of websites, and I write for those," David explains. But here's the clever part. He creates complementary pieces that support the content. David's website copy enhances his video content, which in turn deepens his written material. This approach does two powerful things:

- **Extends your content's lifespan** (one idea can have multiple touchpoints)
- **Builds authority across different learning styles.** (Some people read, others watch, many do both.)

The 'Problem, Agitate, Solution' Structure

After experimenting with the Heroine's Journey structure, David settled on the simple PAS - Problem, Agitate, Solution - structure for his web pages. It works fastest because it mirrors how we make decisions.

"It's what I'm moving towards," admits David, with refreshing candour. "That's the beauty of treating your website as a living experiment rather than a perfect monument."

Sometimes the simplest tools are the sharpest.

How to Structure a Converting Homepage

David uses his Problem-Agitate-Solution blueprint to overhaul his TheA uthorityFigure.com site :

The Hook (Hero Section)

The Headline: "Your Expertise Deserves Better Than Hope-and-Pray Authority Building"

By talking about what his visitor deserves, David shifts from 'me' to 'you,' which makes all the difference.

With a 'bridge-building subhead' David acknowledges their decades of experience and validates their struggle with digital authority, then positions his solution as turning "art into science."

It's smart positioning. He's not dismissing their expertise; he's offering to systematize it.

The Problem (Where It Hurts)

Instead of jumping straight to solutions, David first 'agitates' the problem. He's identified five core frustrations his audience faces:

1. Quality content getting lost in the noise
2. Inconsistent positioning across platforms
3. Zero visibility into authority ROI
4. Losing deals to inferior competitors
5. Authority building is difficult to systematize

An Emotional Hook: "Meanwhile, leaders with identical credentials but better positioning are commanding premium fees, attracting top talent, and securing the opportunities your expertise should earn."

That sentence creates urgency, validates frustration, and hints at the solution without giving it away.

The Solution (The Big Reveal)

David presents "Three Authority Acceleration Systems":

1. **Authority Intelligence Engine** (know where you stand)
2. **Strategic Content Automation** (generate credible thought leadership)

3. **Client Authority Amplification** (turn authority into revenue)

The Social Proof Master Class Move

By sharing testimonials David improved his authority improvement metrics by 67% in 90 days.

"Authority OS gave me a system instead of a hope-and-pray approach. My client acquisition cost dropped 40% while average deal value increased significantly. Numbers prove it works. Stories prove it's real."

Market Education

David creates urgency by highlighting market reality: "Digital-first buyers are making decisions before they ever speak with you. Your reputation is being formed in their minds within minutes of discovering your name."

Some might call it manipulation. David prefers market education. He's not pressuring you to buy; he's helping you understand why waiting costs you opportunities.

The Low-Resistance Entry Point

It's David's secret weapon : "The first thing a visitor must see on arrival to the webpage is an opt-in offer."

Why? Because most visitors won't read everything. They're in a hurry, scanning for relevance. If you make them scroll to find a way to connect with you, most won't bother.

"I am big on making low resistance offers," David explains. "Visitors get is an educational sequence that will lead them to other goodies and services I offer to start to build a relationship with the subscriber."

In short: Don't try to sell the big thing first. Sell the small thing that leads to the relationship, which in turn leads to the big thing.

Forge the Framework

"I map out the structure, consider the flow, and then fill in the blanks," says David. "Structure sets me free. When you understand the framework, you can focus on the message and fill the framework with your unique voice and expertise.

Your Next Move

David's website authority happened through experimentation, learning from what worked, and having the courage to admit what didn't.

The lesson isn't to copy his exact approach, but to develop your systematic method for each platform you use. Whether that's the Problem-Agitate-Solution framework, Hero's Journey, or something else, structure is key. As David discovered, when you stop hoping your expertise will magically translate into online authority and start building systems that make it inevitable, everything changes.

The question is: what structure will you build to ensure they get it?

After writing *Reign* and *Flow,* I started two websites – Carolinehurry.com and Hyggequeen.com to showcase my books and blogs. I realized readers wouldn't materialize out of thin air, so I developed a five-part framework: SPARK – Share, Personalize, Appraise, Research, Kindle.

Kindle the Spark Approach

Share (Set Up a Site)

Setting up a website using keywords from your book title or description is a top marketing move. It gives you a home base for updates, blogs, and newsletters. Plus, it's a great way to build a subscriber list and share your publishing news with future readers.

Six Free Ways to Set Up a Landing Page:

1. **HubSpot Free Landing Page Builder**: Offers real-time analytics, advanced SEO tools, and seamless integration with email and Customer Relationship Management (CRM).

2. **WordPress.com**– Pre-designed templates and blogging features. Beginner-friendly and powerful for customization.

3. **Canva Free Websites**: Canva offers free, simple landing page creation with drag-and-drop design and publishing; perfect for visuals and portfolios.

4. **SITE123**: Recommended for its simplicity and speed. Beginner-friendly, it offers mobile-ready templates and built-in lead capture features. Great to get online fast without a learning curve.

5. **Wix**: Continues to be a top recommendation for free landing pages, offering robust templates, a drag-and-drop editor, built-in marketing and analytics tools, and seamless integrations. It's recommended for both beginners and advanced users

6. **Carrd.io** – Sleek, simple one-page sites with customizable templates. Great for authors.

Personalize (Pinpoint Problems With Pizzazz)

1. **Personal stories and vulnerability build empathy.** Be real, but intentional. You want your readers to scarf your content like hyenas happening on a fresh kill. Sharing your experiences is the fastest way to create an empathetic bond and enthuse others.

2. **Avoid info-dumping or over-sharing.** Sprinkle those innermost thoughts, but don't oversalt the narrative. Let your content feel like a conversation, not a confession. You're a therapist with a keyboard, not just writing content but lifting spirits now, too. So, establish a transformational tone unique to you.

3. **Position yourself as a relatable guide, *not* a guru.** People crave connection, not perfection. Enter the breach by addressing their problems, you're creating a sense of shared experiences, becoming the friend they can rely on, and the confidant who understands their struggles. Go ahead. Put your spin on things. Your readers will thank you for it.

Appraise (Amplify with Insight)

Highlight the consequences of not solving the problem your book addresses but do it with finesse. Don't oversell your work. Under promise and overdeliver on expectations. And for the love of everything holy, don't overshare or info-dump. Your reader is not your therapist or BFF. They seek insights, not a play-by-play of your latest breakdown. Never preach, either. Offer value and end with a clear call to action:

- Follow me
- Comment below
- Join my list
- Rate my book

You're building a two-way street.

Research, (Reciprocate, and Review)

Research what your readers care about and craft content that speaks to their hearts. Use SEO tools (like Google Trends or Ubersuggest) to find relevant keywords.

Reciprocate to amplify: comment on other blogs, support fellow authors, share their work. This goodwill expands your visibility and community reach. The more you give others the recognition you crave, the faster things happen. Reciprocation increases your connectivity flow. Building relationships with other authors expands your reach exponentially.

Review your analytics to double down on what's working.

- Download Your Free Websites Comparison Table Here.

PLATFORM	BEST FOR	NOTABLE FEATURES	FREE PLAN LIMITS
HUBSPOT LANDING PAGE BUILDER	Marketers and CRM Integration	Real-time analytics, SEO tools, email + CRM integration	HubSpot branding, limited templates, feature restrictions
WORDPRESS	Bloggers and Customizable Content	Pre-designed templates, strong blogging features, customizable themes	WordPress branding, limited plugins and storage, no custom domain
CANVA FREE WEBSITES	Visual Portfolios and Creatives	Drag-and-drop design, visual-centric layouts, fast publishing	Limited site structure (one-page), Canva branding, limited analytics
SITE123	Beginners and Quick Setup	Mobile-ready templates, built-in lead capture, no learning curve	Limited customization, storage and bandwidth SITE123 branding,
WIX	Beginners to Advanced Users	Drag-and-drop builder, robust templates, marketing tools, analytics	Wix ads, no custom domain, limited storage and bandwidth
CARRD.IO	Simple, One-Page Websites	Sleek templates, responsive design	One-page, Carrd branding, limited integrations

Fire Hygge

Torch Fears, Fuel Your Inner Flame

Your fire hygge transforms and nourishes your creative spirit, burning away everything that once held you back.

Just as fire transforms wood into heat and light, your fear becomes creative power when acknowledged and released.

Fire consumes what no longer serves and transforms adversity into strength. The writing phoenix demands destruction and renewal. Burn through fear and forge something stronger in its place.

You are the dragon. That's your mantra now. You are the spark, the phoenix, and whatever you imagine yourself to be. Let your fire blaze. After everything you've survived, you're no longer waiting for permission. You don't need to be perfect. Begin as you are now, warts and all. Just start.

Torch your fears, fuel your inner flame, and light the way for yourself. Your fire is self-sustained. It's time to write a new story on your terms. You have your creative spark, experiential fuel, and oxygen. What else do you need?

- *See the Appendix Prompt Vault for more brilliant motivational ideas to keep your creative fire blazing.*

Your Fire Ritual

How do you harness this transformative fire? Start by burning all the things that stifled it.

The Method: Gather your kindling. Write down all your limiting beliefs on pieces of paper. Include:

- Old stories that kept your voice small and held you back.
- Cruel words from internal and external critics that fuel your self-doubt
- Analysis paralysis that leads to endless research but no writing
- Perfectionism that demands flawless first drafts
- People-pleasing patterns that dilute your authentic voice
- The inner "no-can-do" chorus that lists every reason not to write

Read each limiting belief or criticism aloud, then burn it one by one.

Remember Fiona from the Forge section, who reduced her divorce papers to ash and set herself free to pursue her memoir, inspiring other women to bounce back after emotional setbacks?

That's the power of the burning ritual. What will you burn to fuel your creative fire?

Your Next 3 Moves

Channel your inner fire by preparing the path towards your success. XWhen impostor syndrome strikes, write anyway. Just because your readers are not in the room with you right now doesn't mean they don't exist.

1. **Write Raw and Real:** Draft a rough foreword, create an outline, or explore a truth you've been hesitant to share. Honest writing invites connection and builds trust. Vulnerability creates a magnetic connection. *Prompts: What would I do if I were not afraid of? What do I fear I might reveal about myself? How might that be powerful?"*

2. **Open Your Publishing Door:** Set up a KDP account (see the Appendix KDP Guide section) or create a Kobo account. Start building the platform you'll use to share your voice.

3. **Build a Website.** Today' spark can keep tomorrow's "future positioning" bonfires ablaze. Start with a free version from the Expand chapter and start playing!.

Fire Hygge Hints

Tend Your Flame: Self-care is oxygen for your creative fire. Do whatever sparks you. Kindle your strengths with self-compassion.

Keep Going: Persistence is the steady heat of transformation. You don't need permission to be brilliant. You don't need to be perfect to be powerful. You need to keep going.

Ignite. Burn Bright: Morning walks to watch the sunrise. Saying no. Saying yes. Let their silence fuel your fire. Your originality fuels your brand.

Rest and Connect: A fire warms the community. Be at one with nature's principles of undoing and renewing. Your creative fire requires a sacred creative space. Trust the rhythm of expansion and contraction.

It's time to let your words blaze their trail. Let's write the book.

Two

Water Section

Write, Adapt, Title, Edit, Render

Fluid writing carries you on an emotional current. With the resilience of a surfer, you ride the waves and refine your technique.

- **Write** anything from a preface to a press release. Flow with clarity and humor. Weave curiosity and purpose into every line.

- **Adapt** like water to its container. Repurpose successful content and experiment with new formats. Share personal stories that forge emotional bonds.

- **Title** your work with impact. Let your subtitle ground the promise. Sparks curiosity; the right subtitle builds trust.

- **Edit** to engage. Revise and shine. Dissolve what distracts. Cut clutter. Fix flow. Proofread with precision. Good editing lets the message rise from the page like mist from water.

- **Render** a cover that speaks before your words do. Curate imagery, color, and typography to reflect your tone and genre. Your cover is your first impression. Make it feel inevitable.

Let's dive in.

"Eventually, all things merge into one, and a river runs through it. ... Under the rocks are the words, some of the words are theirs. I am haunted by waters."

Norman Maclean, A River Runs Through It

Write

Create Compelling Content

"Writing is the dragon that lives underneath my floorboards. The one I incessantly feed for fear it may turn and devour my ass. Writing is the friend who doesn't return my phone calls; the itch I'm unable to scratch; a dinner invitation from a cannibal; elevator music for a narcoleptic. Writing is the hope of lifting all boats by pissing in the ocean. Writing isn't something that makes me happy like a good cup of coffee. It's just something I do because not writing, as I've found, is so much worse."

Quentin R. Bufogle

I WRITE FOR THE reason I read – to feel like somebody else for a while. The undeniable allure of immersing myself in captivating life stories drew me to journalism, but writing itself has always been a double-edged sword for me. The urge to write things down, accompanied by the crippling fear someone might read my thoughts, is a compulsion only fellow keepers of private diaries will understand.

I've burned more notebooks than I can count.

Some of the best writers like to rearrange circumstances and share a profound suspicion of the status quo. The trick is to make it work for you. Find a way to let writing transform your life as you immortalize your ideas into a legacy. Paper can provide a cathartic sanctuary and transportation to other realms of possibility when the chaos of your world feels overwhelming. Yes, it's an escape, but isn't that what your readers want?

The Truth About Writing for Money

Writing will not pave the path to riches straight away. Oh, sorry, did I forget to mention that? My bad. Like a shoestring, it's relative and depends on your definition of wealth. You're an army of one, so you'll have to stand up and arm yourself against the naysayers because you'll find no shortage of them, either.

Toby Neal, a USA Today bestselling author, recounts how a careless comment: "What – you want to be a writer? You'll never make a living doing that," crushed her ambition for years. "I was 40 before I put that all-too-common myth behind me and grieved for all the time lost. Then, I saw how I had created my life. It wasn't a waste after all," reflects Neal, who identifies four powerful qualities of successful creators:

- A dangerously curious nature
- A keen observer of everything
- A fusion of talent and passion
- An ability to learn from criticism without ever giving up

While these qualities resonate across various fields, they hold particularly true when making your writing shine. Like a skilled sailor navigating rough seas, you must maintain stability, focus, and clarity in your work.

Treat each word as a stand-alone spell capable of casting mesmerizing enchantments without anesthetizing your readers. There's no finite knowledge in the creative realm, only an innate impulse to grow.

Remember, Mother Nature constantly rearranges and redesigns.

Writing is a creative calling and a compulsion. Defy the doubters. Paint vivid images. Captivate with narratives that dance across the page. Amuse your readers and they'll hang on to your every word. Transform your copy from drab to fab with a KICK-ASS approach.

> *"If you find you've written a sentence you're really proud of, there's an excellent chance it needs to come out!"*
>
> Yvonne Aileen, author of Goddesses Stay Sexy

The KICK-ASS Writing Framework

Keep your writing clear, concise, and tight.
Increase engagement with simple, straightforward responses.
Create high-vibrational verbs – 'love' or 'heal' – to inspire connection.
Know and understand the readers' goals.
Add accurate information to build trust and credibility.
Share in a style appropriate to the readers' culture and context.
Soundbites are easy to understand and encourage momentum.

Kick-Ass Writing Approach

K Keep it tight.
I Increase engagement with simple responses.
C Create high-vibrational verbs
K Know and understand the readers' needs

A Add accurate information to build trust.
S Share in an appropriate contextual style.
S Say it in a soundbite!

The more you can make one word do the work of five, or more, the more it can transform worlds. Publishing your musings transforms them into a public dialogue, so present entertaining solutions to struggles if you're writing 'how-to' non-fiction.

Kick self-doubt or perfectionism to the curb. Let your subconscious do the heavy lifting by connecting the dots in the background and invigorating word seeds buried for decades. You might amaze yourself!

Enjoy the transformative powers of writing as a self-discovery process. If you hit a roadblock – no biggie – cut yourself some slack and go around it. Follow your bliss because life becomes one long compromise if you don't. Find magic in the mundane. The money to do what you love will manifest. At least, that's what I experienced.

The Sacred Six: Your Content Foundation

These six key interrogatives must be addressed for a well-rounded satisfying piece that approximates the truth.

1. **Who** did it? Who was there is what you want to share.

2. **Why** did it happen? Illuminate motivation.

3. **What** took place? Describe salient details.

4. **When** did it happen? Capture moments in a timeline flow.

5. **Where?** Show the location.

6. **How:** An anagram of who that will empower your piece.

Apply these to your writing: **who, what, when, where, why,** and **how.** Ask yourself **who** your readers are, **what** you want them to know, **why** you're writing, and **how, where,** and **when** you'd like to debut your masterpiece.

Here's my best tip: Love your process and relish the unknown. Keep going and watch yourself grow as a human being. Catch a current and flow.

Surf Self-Expressive Blog Waves

Like water adapting to its surroundings, infuse your writing with your personality to enable your readers to relate to you and vice versa.

Establish a consistent, easily recognizable conversational tone and style. Build a loyal following and create a sense of community with your blog. Let your readers get to know you.

Blogging requires unique elements that spark interest, so lead in with an attention-grabbing question. How would you know if the person beside you is a human droid composite, for example? You can then segue into your experience or share insights related to your book. The best impromptu blogs are written well in advance.

Whether you're writing about raising backyard hens or turning your sour milk into cheese, the trick is to use phrases your readers will relate to and understand.

Like a strong ocean current, be yourself and deliver the value and engagement readers crave. If you can't think of anything inspiring, share feedback about books you've read or other author podcasts. Research and optimize your content for search engines to rev up your blog traffic.

- **Free SEO Tool**

Boost Your Bio

Your bio is your chance to showcase your unique personality. Highlight what sets you apart from others in your field, using humor, wit, or storytelling to create an irresistible impression.

Social media bios have limited space, so distill yours down to punch ideas. Avoid jargon or technical language and stick to the essentials.

End with a question or prompt with a link to your website, book, or second social media platform.

Captivate with Captions

Visual content is king in the era of clickbait headlines and endless scrolls, but an image without a caption is like a meal without salt. If you show up to a costume party without explaining what you're trying to be, it's a missed opportunity. Captions bridge the visual and the verbal.

Like a sidekick adding a punchline to your image, your attention-grabbing captions bring your pictures to life and keep readers engaged. Never leave editors asking questions.

Transform your captions from forgettable afterthoughts to amusing companions to your graphic design elements. Anchor your photo in time and space. Use descriptive words in the present tense. Instead of labeling the image's subject, add a clever twist or a dash of humor.

Craft a Dynamic Description

Formulating a synopsis as compelling as a movie trailer may seem like climbing Mount Everest, but **an excellent grappling hook** is all it takes. Flex your creative muscles with these **five tips.**

1. Craft your description around readers' wants. Aim for a conversational tone with **inclusive, approachable language**.

2. Explain why only you could have written this book. (Establish your **authority figure status**.)

3. **Add intrigue** and twist the knife.

4. Keep it **short and sweet.**

5. Tweak it like a recipe and **refine it** later.

12 Helpful Headline Hacks

1. **Spark Curiosity:** Raise but don't answer a provocative question. "Is Your To-Do List Is Ruining Your Life?" Intrigue the reader.

2. **Use Powerful Words:** "Unleash," "Unlock," "Discover," "Transform," "Reveal," "Hidden," "Mistake," "Truth," or "Secret" energize headlines and trigger emotional responses.

3. **Promise a Benefit:** Let readers know what they'll gain: insight, entertainment, a solution, or a surprise without spoiling how.

4. **Keep It Short:** Aim for 6–12 words. Brevity: packs more punch.

5. **Highlight Emotional Stakes: I**mply a Story or Struggle. Tease without blowing the ending. "How Writing Saved My Sanity!"

6. **Use Numbers for Clarity and Structure:** Lists are clickable. "7 Lies Writers Tell Themselves" signals easy-to-digest content.

7. **Speak to a Specific Audience:** "For Aspiring Authors Over 50: Why Now Is the Time" builds trust through relevance.

8. **Avoid Clickbait Clichés:** Don't oversell or mislead. "You Won't Believe What Happened Next" is tired and often backfires.

9. **Alliterate for Rhythm:** "Poise, Power, and Publishing"

10. **Don't restate: I**f your article is titled "5 Marketing Hacks," don't say "Here Are Five Marketing Tips ...

11. **Create a Knowledge Gap:** "The One Word That Improved My Writing Overnight" makes readers want to fill that gap.

12. **Test:** Use headline analyzers like CoSchedule or Sharethrough to see how your headline scores in engagement, clarity, and emotion.

Write a Newsy Report

Use the inverted pyramid. Prioritize the Sacred Six – Who, What, When, Where, Why, How – at the top with supporting details to provide the ballast. Readers can decide if they wish to continue.

Maintain objectivity. Fact-check your work for accuracy. Strive to present a balanced view. Ensure your tone is appropriate for the subject matter. Avoid using overly emotional or inflammatory language, especially when discussing controversial topics.

Checklist for News Reports:

- Does your headline grab the reader's attention and accurately reflect the story?
- Does the lead-in provide the most crucial information?
- Have you identified the people involved, described the situation, its motivation, where, and when it occurred?
- Cut to the chase. Adopt a feisty tone to encourage readers to engage with the material
- Be impartial. Your personal opinions are surplus to requirements
- Keep an open mind. Let your understanding of the topic evolve as you report on the story's nuances

As the mainstream media loses credibility and public trust, people instead swipe their smartphone screens to read citizen blogs or listen to podcasters

Alison Hill, Journalist, Writer's Digest

Preface Power

Like a charming chat with the author, a preface provides context, establishes credibility, sets expectations, and acknowledges the writing process. You can introduce why you wrote your book, what inspired you, and what message you hope your readers take away.

First impressions matter, so taking a moment to write that preface will help your reader appreciate your work more. As Robertson Davies, said: "The preface is the fence around your garden, which tells the passers-by that you're a civilized person, with tastes and a sense of order."

Write a Winning Interview Profile

Encapsulate your subject's uniqueness by showcasing many angles from background details to lasting impressions. Open with their connection to any relevant news event and deal later with birth, family, education, career, and hobbies, unless one is the story's focus.

1. **Start with an anecdote,** quote, or detail to build curiosity.

2. **Provide background.** Contextualize their current position with relevant information.

3. **Observe subtleties** – mannerisms, habits, posture, tone, vocabulary, and clothes.

4. **Avoid personal opinions.** Let your subject speak.

5. **Deepen, don't repeat.** Quotes that reflect their thoughts and feelings add authenticity.

6. **Show, don't tell.** Use concrete details. Anecdotal examples reveal a personality better than descriptions like "generous." They slipped the parking attendant $50 because that's how they roll!

7. **Organize your information thematically**. Round out your piece with relevant insights, anecdotes, or alternative perspectives. When contacting sources for quotes, explain who you are, the topic of your article, and why you think they would be helpful.

8. **Ask insightful questions.** Before interviewing experts, research their work to keep the conversation flowing. Based on your research, probe for what motivates them, what they most desire or care about, and how they hope to accomplish something.

9. **Conclude with a lasting impression.** Try a quote, anecdote, or thought-provoking idea that leaves your readers thinking.

When I write, I feel like an armless, legless man with a crayon in his mouth.

Kurt Vonnegut

Take Your Writing From Tepid to Terrific

1. Never use three or more words when one will do.

2. Eliminate unnecessary words and phrases.

3. Bring your prose to life with vivid, sensory details.

4. Choose your words with precision.

5. Read widely and often for inspiration.

6. Hone your skills by writing as often as you can.

7. Cut yourself slack. Writing is a process, and it's normal to experience self-doubt.

Adapt

Echoes of Rebecca, Finding Relevance

> *"If your words don't gut you emotionally – and this is true for fiction and nonfiction – you haven't dug deep enough. You haven't mined for Truth."*
>
> Yvonne Aileen, author of Goddesses Stay Sexy

One of my favorite opening lines is: "Last night, I dreamt I went to Manderley again."

Tossed into a whirlpool of wedlock with a wealthy widower, the unnamed narrator is swept into a ghostly love triangle. Her voice – fragile, overshadowed, but searching – resonates with generations of readers in Daphne Du Maurier's *Rebecca.*

Central to the tale is Manderley Estate and the narrator's journey, from meeting Maxim de Winter to her unsettling encounters with Mrs. Danvers, the ominous housekeeper.

The dark secrets of Rebecca's past and the mystery surrounding her death throw shade over the narrator's marriage.

Rebecca's themes of jealousy, manipulation, and the struggle for identity echo through works like *Mrs. de Winter* by Susan Hill and *Rebecca's Tale* by Sally Beauman. The novel's influence has spanned media, from Ken Follett's WWII espionage in *The Key to Rebecca* to Michael Ondaatje's *The English Patient* and Stephen King's chilling homage in *Bag of Bones.* Even Jasper Fforde's *Thursday Next* series plays with the iconic Mrs. Danvers.

In short, there's no GPS with a predetermined route when you first start writing your own story.

Expecting high seas, you'll wade in with your surfboard only to find the water flatter than glass. When your muse plays hide-and-seek, do something else. You don't always have to dive deep. Let go lightly. Your muse will come to you.

Adapt Content to the Context

Contextually-relevant content refers to specific situations. For example, if your readers struggle to find time to write, you could blog about *Staying Productive When You Only Have 30 Minutes a Day to Work on your Book* or post 25 practical tips for getting things done.

Flow with the most relevant information to create context. Why does it matter? Why should your readers care? Predict what will happen if they don't address their concerns. Use true-to-life examples.

Proffer a slice of reality. If corporate pollution of Mother Nature's waterways troubles you – and it should – post images of yourself cleaning up a riverbed section to create contextual currents. Personal connections and expert perspectives also help establish credibility.

Create a Connective Current

In the Fire section's Research chapter, I showed how easy it is to ask a Chatbot for an in-depth description of your reader based on the location and keywords you input.

When I started on *Write,* I knew who my readers were – others, like me, wanting to take their writing or an existing book to the next level but weren't sure where to start. I understood their sources of angst or pain points – lack of recognition, publisher rejection, a lousy review, writer's block, etc.

That's how I can address their needs from a personal point of view. Be authentic and transparent to build trust and create an emotional bond with your readers. Use self-deprecating humor to share how you moved past the denunciation you experienced to engage your audience.

Reach out to those who share your interests by commenting on their blogs or social media posts. Be opinionated, passionate, and generous with your information. Share applicable hyperlinks to other people's work, comment on their posts, or retweet their opinions. Pay it forward.

Enhance Your Visibility

1. **Serve aces from the start.** Your first chapter should be like an espresso shot – strong, bold, and leaving your reader buzzing.

2. **Create relatable characters.** Give them, or yourself, quirks, flaws, and a backstory.

3. **Take risks.** Readers love to be surprised.

4. **Write with passion.** How else can you expect your readers to be excited about your story?

5. **Show, don't tell.** Use vivid descriptions and sensory smell or taste details. For example, Bornholm, an island in the Baltic Sea, smells like horse dung and herring. (It does, too.)

6. **Edit, edit, edit.** Nothing ruins a great story like poor grammar or typos. Take the time to revise your work until it's polished and error-free.

7. **Find your niche**. Lean into whatever sets your work apart, whether a specific genre or writing style.

8. **Believe in yourself.** Writing is a solitary pursuit but not necessarily lonely. Keep going.

Top Tip

See what other writers in your genre have done, and determine how your book can offer more.

Try Crowdfire for content curation.

Stay Current and Connected

Adjust Your Voice: Tune into your readers' conversations. What keeps them up at night? What makes them laugh? Adapt your tone and examples to match their world. If your audience is drowning in productivity hacks, permit them to be messy. If they're craving authenticity, ditch the corporate speak.

Dive Into What Matters Now: Address the elephant in the room or whatever your readers are dealing with today. Use real situations, not hypothetical scenarios. Share how you failed spectacularly at something everyone thinks you're an expert in. That's the content that gets shared.

Advance Through Connection: Build relationships. Respond to comments. Share your behind-the-scenes moments - the late-night rewrites, the impostor syndrome attacks. People connect with human beings, not brands.

Polish Your Presence: Hook readers from the first sentence. Make them think, "Finally, someone gets it." Create characters (or personal stories) that surprise . Write with energy that jumps off the page.

Tailor With Smart Tools: Use AI as your research assistant and ask it to spot trends or suggest angles you haven't considered. Experiment with formats. Convert that blog post into a video script, or turn a newsletter into a podcast episode.

Bottom line: Stay curious about your readers' changing world and adapt. Trends change, but authentic connection never goes out of style.

REFLECT & ADAPT

1 **Where are you resisting the current?**

Can you identify an area in your writing or where you feel stuck or resistant?

2 **Who downstream awaits your message?**

Describe your ideal reader's emotional state. What do they need to hear today?

3 **How can you flow around a recent obstacle**

What's a new way around a writing block, rejection, or distraction?

4 **What small stone of truth can you drop today?**

Write one vulnerable sentence you'd be willing to share

5 **When are you most creative?**

Can you honor your natural rhythm more intentionally this week?

"We shape our lives with every decision we make. The beauty is that if we don't like the path we're on, we can always make a different choice. It's the same with writer's block. Redirect."

Angie K. Love, the Awakening Series

Title

And Subtitles That Convert

> *"Even before your book is judged by its cover, it will be judged by its title."*
>
> Goodreads Community Wisdom

Your book title can make or break your success. A great title whets appetites and communicates clear benefits. A weak one dooms your book to obscurity, no matter how brilliant the content inside.

My book *Reign: 16 Secrets from 6 Queens to Rule Your World with Clarity, Connection & Sovereignty* started with a different title: *Washing Windows.* I thought it captured my personal purification process. "Life through a clean window beats staring through a glass darkly."

"That will never work," my friend Uscha replied. "It's too obscure. People expect cleaning supplies and ladders. Besides, you're the world's worst housekeeper."

My next attempt? *Romancing the Crone: Miss Havisham's Rebirth.* Noooo, shrieked Uscha, "That's even worse. Nobody wants to admit to their dotage Beside, who the hell is Miss Havisham? An influencer from the Victorian era?"

Then inspiration struck: Rain. Rein. Reign. Nature's sovereignty – dragon breath in the skies, sunlight filtering through trees. Nature wild and free. Everything I longed to be. Everything I could be.

As author Yvonne Aileen wisely noted: "Don't fixate on your vision to your detriment. When people advise you to lose a section of your work, listen. Flexibility can save you from expensive learning experiments."

5 Essential Title Elements

1. **Know Your Book Type** – Let your book's purpose guide your title. A cookbook benefits from words like "recipes," "delicious," or "easy" for discoverability. A memoir needs emotional resonance.

2. **Speak to Your Audience** – What does your demographic crave? Business readers want results and efficiency. Parents want solutions and hope. Make sure your title speaks directly to their needs.

3. **Highlight Your Unique Factor** – What makes your book different from the dozens of others on the same topic? Your personal story, unique approach, or distinctive tone should shine through.

4. **Stay Transparent** – Avoid misleading or clickbait titles. Be honest about what readers will actually find inside. Disappointment kills reviews and word-of-mouth.

5. **Maintain Brand Consistency** – If you have an established platform, ensure your title aligns with your existing style and voice.

The Power and Pitfalls of Wordplay

Wordplay - including puns, alliteration, rhyming, and creative misspellings- can make your title memorable and fun. *The Life-Changing Magic of Tidying Up* transforms a mundane topic into something whimsical and appealing.

The Benefits:

- Creates positive associations and memorability
- Helps your book stand out in crowded markets
- Makes recommendations easier ("You have to read this book with the clever title!")

The Risks:

- Can sound amateurish or cheesy if overdone
- May confuse readers if too obscure (*An Eden of Earthly Delights* sounds like steamy romance, not gardening)
- Might mislead genre expectations

The Rule: Be bold, but never sacrifice clarity for cleverness.

Crafting Subtitles That Convert

Your subtitle should expand and clarify your main title while listing three concrete benefits readers will receive. Think of it as your book's elevator pitch.

Strong Example: *The Suburban Farmer's Manual: Grow Fresh Produce in Small Spaces, Transform Your Balcony into a Garden Oasis, and Reduce Your Grocery Bills*

Subtitle Best Practices:

- Keep language clear and jargon-free
- Showcase specific outcomes or methods
- Match your audience's sophistication level
- Make it easy to say and remember
- Always get feedback from trusted readers
- Click here to download your Title and Subtitle Checklist

TITLE & SUBTITLE CHECKLIST

1	**IMPACT & CLARITY**	Title is clear and easy to understand ✓ Emotional or curiosity-driven appeal is present ✓ Doesn't require too much explanation ✓ Avoids cliches or generic phrasing ✓
2	**KEYWORD & SEO FRIENDLY**	Includes relevant keywords for your niche or genre ✓ Phrases readers might search for are included ✓ Tested using tools like Amazon KDP, Publisher Rocket or ChatGPT for fresh variations ✓
3	**READER RESONANCE**	Title speaks to a need, desire, or pain point ✓ Avoids overly abstract or confusing wording ✓ Genre and tone are clearly reflected ✓ Feedback received from beta readers, or online polls ✓
4	**SUBTITLE STRENGTH**	Subtitle explains or enhances the main title ✓ Clear, benefits are outlined ✓ Easy to pronounce and remember ✓ Matches the tone and promise of the book ✓
5	**SLOSH OUT:**	Titles that are too vague, poetic, or obscure ✓ Subtitles that promise too much or say too little ✓ Misleading, gimmicky, or irrelevant phrasing ✓ Not aligning with your brand or reader expectations ✓
6	**PROMPT CHATGPT**	Generate 5 title and subtitle combinations based on my themes of [insert themes], targeted at [ideal audience], in the style of [humorous, mysterious, inspirational, etc.]

Edit

Reread, Review, Revise and Shine

"If a passage, however beautifully written, does not advance your story or give further information to the reader, take it out to use in another more appropriate piece of work."

Jayne Southern, books editor

Luckily writing isn't brain surgery because few hit the bullseye on their first attempt. Crafting an effortless read requires a strategic mindset, and a steady hand.

If the writing process was a band, editing would be the drummer – keeping rhythm, refining pace, and holding everything together. While writing lets your creativity explode, editing is where you carve clarity by word sculpting from a block of text. It's where good writing becomes great.

The idea that your first draft should be perfect is a myth. Anne Lamott's famous advice to "write shitty first drafts" reminds us that the real magic lies in rewriting, sharpening your words into something unforgettable.

Revision can be a delicious pleasure.

While all writers will tell you the first draft is cr@p, they forgot to tell you to pat yourself on the back for getting this far. Go on, blow yourself a kiss in the mirror! You know you want to!

Think of your first draft as the uncut gem. Editing is the facet work that lets it catch the light and dazzle with brilliance: 'Did I write that? It's good!'

But there are two typos of writers – those who can edit and those who can't! Unless you're a seasoned wordsmith, skimping on the polishing is inadvisable. The editing phase is not the place to cut corners.

A skilled editor bridges inspiration and information, recalibrates your grammar, and infuses charisma into the twirl of your ideas tap dancing across the page. Without one, you might shoot yourself in the foot. Sigh. Yes. I know. Your coffers are running low. But that's why you bought this book, remember?

With a little help from AI, you, too, can reshuffle sentences with a ballroom dancer's grace.

Editing is a marathon, not a sprint. Embrace mistakes like old pals and take more breaks than a world-class procrastinator. But first, let's set the two stages and get into character.

I base mine on UK-based Jayne Southern[1], whose hawk-eye spots syntax errors and grammatical oversights everywhere she goes. A misspelled word on a billboard? She winces. A misplaced comma on her rates bill? A personal affront, dear God!

Don't get her started on apostrophe promiscuity on public signs or the social media horrors. Armed with a red pen and a quick wit, Jayne loves nothing more than whittling away at words with the precision of a Jenga champion. Jayne offers gentle editorial guidance, never raises her voice nor lets rip with profanities. Unlike me.

Grammar & Style: Polishing the Surface

Grammar is a clarity framework to enable your readers to glide through your work, not get distracted by errors. Use **Grammarly** or **Hemingway Editor** to tighten your prose. Your style might break rules for effect. That's okay if done with purpose.

Self-Editing: Let it Rest Before You Wrestle

Give your writing room to breathe. Let it marinate overnight or longer. Come back to it with fresh eyes and a red pen. You know what you meant. Now check: did you say it clearly? Did you repeat yourself? Do your metaphors work? Do your paragraphs wander? Self-editing is about listening to what your writing wants to become. Zoom out. Ask yourself:

- Does this piece deliver on its purpose?
- Is my voice consistent?
- Do the ideas flow logically?

Line Editing

Zoom in. Line by line, seek passive sentences, vague phrasing, or repetition. Read your work aloud. Your tongue will trip where your writing stumbles. Your ear will notice rhythm or the lack of it.

Trim flab, replace overused words. Make each sentence pull its weight. Look at sentence structure and clarity. Trim it to be tight, compelling, and magnetic. Rake and rid your copy of excessive verbiage. Toss the guff like a decluttering pro. Use 'if' instead of 'in the event of' or 'try' instead of 'make an effort to.' Imagine earning a crisp ten-dollar bill for every word or redundant phrase you banish.

6 Tips to Take Copy From Drab to Fab

1. **Streamline and Simplify**
   Unburden your words from excess weight. Distil your prose to the essence. When in doubt, cut it out! Summon verbs. Abandon verbosity. Boot out adverbs and adjectives! Vary sentence structures and pacing. Crush the clichés!

2. **Embrace the Active Voice**
   Lose the complicated words. Nobody cares about your better-than-average vocabulary. Clarity beats excess. Active sentences claim the page with vitality. Use robust verbs.

3. **Break Free From Redundancies**
   Evade the labyrinth of needless echoes. Lose the tautologies like a 'novice without experience' or 'uniquely one-of-a-kind.' Keep your language crisp and impactful. Avoid repetition. Evict mundane words that mooch off your prose without adding value.

4. **Increase Engagement with a Conversational Tone**
   Open with 'Let's consider' or 'Here's the scoop.' Generate casual charm with concise, informal responses. Create a vivid picture with sensory details. Allow readers to engage and use their imaginations to fill in the details for a more satisfying experience.

5. **Know What Your Readers Want**
   Does your copy answer their questions? Add accurate information to build trust and credibility. Check for holes, unanswered questions, and inadequacies in the content.

6. **Double-check Facts**
   Ask yourself: Have I attributed or documented all my facts and figures? Are quotes in context? Is my writing accurate and trustworthy?

Craft Engaging Content: A Editor's Guide

Paint with Vivid Imagery

Sensory details transform abstract concepts into tangible experiences. Specific, concrete descriptions create an immersive world. Present facts as experiences that readers can see, hear, or smell. Build trust through accuracy and transparency. Fill content gaps with information. Address potential confusion before it arises. When featuring real people or specific claims, verify details and seek input from those involved to maximize credibility.

Shape Linguistic Flow

Create rhythm through varied sentence structure. Mix short, punchy statements with longer, more complex constructions to mirror human speech patterns. Connect related ideas smoothly with transitional phrases. Create a seamless progression from one thought to the next. Eliminate unnecessary words and vague expressions. Every sentence should serve a purpose, and every word should earn its place. Brevity is the soul of wit.

Master Parallel Structure

Consistency in grammatical structure creates clarity and elegance. When listing items or presenting concepts, maintain the same grammatical form throughout. "She enjoys reading, writing, and hiking" flows better than "She likes to read, writing, and hiking." Parallel constructions creates a pleasing rhythmic quality. Non-parallel structures confuse and weaken your message's impact. Review your work for these inconsistencies.

Use Concrete Examples

Replace abstract concepts with specific, relatable examples. Specific details help readers visualize and connect with your content. Choose inclusive language that welcomes all readers. This approach creates more welcoming content and often results in clearer, more direct communication.

Cut a Dash or a Hyphen

Dashes create emphasis and set off explanatory information. Use them in pairs to highlight important details: "The solution – though it seemed impossible – proved remarkably simple." Single dashes work well to introduce final emphasis or attribute sources.

Hyphens join words to create precise meaning. "A small-business owner" describes someone who owns a small business, while "a small business owner" might describe a small person who owns a business. Use hyphens with compound adjectives, especially before nouns.

Craft Resonant Conclusions

Strong endings leave readers satisfied yet still musing. Circle back with new perspective to themes you introduced earlier. Create emotional resonance – wonder, satisfaction, or contemplation – that lingers after the final sentence. Avoid simply summarizing what you've already said. Instead, offer a fresh insight or unexpected connection that completes the piece. The most powerful endings leave space for readers' imagination and interpretation.

Refine Through Revision

Common weaknesses include overused adjectives, adverbs that dilute rather than strengthen your prose; overly complex sentences that lose readers; tangents that distract from your main message; inconsistent tone or unnecessary jargon; and poor organization that makes content hard to follow. Read your work aloud to catch awkward phrasing and rhythm problems. If you stumble while reading, your readers will too. Trust your ear. It often catches what your eye misses.

The best writing feels effortless to read precisely because the writer put the effort in. Each revision of your work should make it clearer, more engaging, and more memorable.

Common Grammar Pitfalls to Avoid

Dangling Modifiers

Keep participial phrases close to the words they modify. When a sentence begins with a participle (a verb ending in -ing or -ed), ensure it clearly connects to the intended subject.

"Walking down the street, the trees were in bloom" suggests the trees were taking a stroll. Instead, write "Walking down the street, I noticed the trees were in bloom."

Comma Overload

While commas organize and clarify text, excessive use clutters your writing. Use them to separate items in a series, set off introductory elements, or join independent clauses. Resist the urge to sprinkle them everywhere.

Apostrophe Confusion

Apostrophes serve two purposes: forming contractions (it's for "it is") and showing possession (the writer's desk). That's it.

Double Negatives

These constructions reverse your intended meaning. "I don't want nothing" means you do want something. However, double negatives might reflect authentic speech patterns worth preserving for character authenticity.

There/Their Mix-ups

"Their" shows possession and contains "heir" – think ownership. "There" indicates location and contains "here" -think place. When in doubt, substitute "here" or "belonging to them" to check which fits.

Proofreading: The Final Polish

This is your last line of defence before you hit publish. Typos, missing words, and formatting glitches interrupt the flow so don't proofread right after writing. Come back with fresh eyes. Even a short break helps reset your perspective.

Change your reading medium. If you've been working on screen, print a hard copy. The different format often reveals errors your eyes glossed over digitally. Mark corrections with a pen or highlighter as you go.

Read your work aloud. This technique forces attention to individual words and reveals awkward phrasing, missing words, or rhythm problems. Your ear catches what your eyes miss, especially in dialogue and transitions.

Read backwards, sentence by sentence. It slows your brain down and helps you spot tiny errors.

Use digital tools wisely. Grammar checkers and spell-check catch basic errors, but they miss context-dependent mistakes and sometimes suggest incorrect "fixes." Always review their suggestions with a critical eye.

- **Fab Free Tools Chapter for Digital Editing**

Getting Feedback

Seek outside perspective. Choose people who will give honest feedback. Often, the most valuable insights come from those least invested in sparing your feelings. Don't ask if it was good, ask: What parts confused or bored you? Where did you want more?

Be open. Defensive writers don't grow. Not every piece of feedback needs to be implemented, but consider it all. Every comment is a window into how your work lands. While feedback about problems is usually accurate, suggested fixes aren't always the right answer.

Use their observations to guide your own solutions.

Unlike friends and family, who might hesitate to criticize, beta readers focus on improving your work. Join writing groups on social platforms where members and beta readers exchange honest feedback.

ARC (Advance Review Copy) readers help promote your work after publication through reviews and recommendations. They're typically bloggers, reviewers, or avid readers in your genre.

- Visit the Water Prompt Vault for more feedback tips.

EDIT

- Enhance
  your writing through revision. **Eliminate** redundancies. Recognize that initial drafts are just the starting point; **true magic happens when you revise** and polish your content.

- **D**iversify
  your language and structure. **Delve into line editing** to enhance sentence structure, word choice, and clarity. Emphasize the active voice. **Vary pacing and sentence length.** Dive into the details, tighten your prose, and replace wordy phrases with verbs.

- **I**mprove
  proofreading techniques. Take breaks to gain a fresh perspective. **Read your work aloud for rhythm.** Check for errors by reading your text backward, using grammar tools, and seeking feedback from others. Simplify language, vary sentence structure, and employ specific descriptive words to enhance readability.

- **T**rim
  unnecessary adjectives, adverbs, and clichés. Be ruthless about what serves the piece because when you take the time to revise and shine, it shows in your work.
  Focus on a precise, concise style to enhance your writing's effectiveness.

- Download Your Free Self-Editing Checklist

---

1. Jayne Southern - https://www.bookaholiceditor.com/

 SELF-EDITING CHECKLIST 1

Use this list to polish your work before sharing it. Beneath each heading, you'll find an AI prompt to help you refine your draft using ChatGPT or similar tools.

1 STRUCTURE & FLOW

📌 *Does the piece have a clear beginning, middle, and end? Are transitions smooth?*

AI Prompt: Analyse the structure of this piece. Suggest improvements to the sectional flow .

2 CLARITY & COHERENCE

📌 *Are your ideas expressed clearly? Can readers easily follow your argument or narrative?*

AI Prompt: Highlight any sentences or sections in this text that are unclear or confusing.

3 VOICE & TONE

📌 *Is the tone consistent with your purpose and audience? Does the voice feel authentic?*

AI Prompt: Is the tone appropriate for my intended audience? Suggest adjustments if needed.

4 WORDINESS & REDUNDANCY

📌 *Are there unnecessary words or repetitive ideas that could be trimmed?*

AI Prompt: Identify and revise any wordy or redundant passages in this draft.

5 GRAMMAR & MECHANICS

📌 *Have you checked for grammar, spelling, punctuation, and syntax errors?*

AI Prompt: Proofread this text and correct any grammar, punctuation, or spelling mistakes

Date:

SELF-EDITING CHECKLIST 2

6 **SENTENCE VARIETY & RHYTHM**

Do sentence lengths and structures vary to create an engaging rhythm?

AI Prompt: Can you suggest edits to improve sentence variety and rhythm in this piece?

7 **STRONG OPENINGS & ENDINGS**

Does your beginning hook the reader? Does your ending leave an impact?

AI Prompt: Evaluate the opening and closing paragraphs. Are they compelling and effective?

8 **FACT-CHECKING & CONSISTENCY**

Are names, dates, facts, and formatting consistent and accurate?

AI Prompt: Check consistency in names, dates, terminology, and formatting throughout this text.

9 **PACING & LENGTH**

Is the pacing appropriate for the genre and reader attention span? Is the length right?

AI Prompt: Analyze the pacing and suggest where the narrative might drag or rush.

10 **EMOTIONAL & THEMATIC IMPACT**

Does your writing evoke the intended emotions or communicate key themes?

AI Prompt: Can you enhance the emotional tone and themes in this draft?

Date:

Render

A Cover Design That Speaks Volumes

> *"If you can't find the right color, use the wrong one. Keep experimenting until you're done."*
>
> Donna White, the Minka Series

Experimentation is one of author-artist Donna White's life mantras because, she says, "it can extrapolate to all areas of our lives. The last time I opened an art exhibition with experimentation as my theme, it led to one person in the audience giving up smoking.

"It was just before Christmas, precisely the wrong time to give up anything, and she did it anyway! A few years later, she told me my words had given her the 'wrong push in the right direction.'

"All art is artifice anyway so permit yourself to play. Rules are not rules if they can't be broken."

That's the power of creative risk.

And yet, the prevailing cover-design rule echoes loud and clear: "Don't even think about doing it yourself."

All very well, but what's a scribbler with a gasping budget to do? Answer: You **d**are to design and embrace feedback from any artist whose opinion you respect.

I'm not ashamed to say I have created all my own covers with the exception of *Reign.* I also belong to a helpful Facebook group called Indie Cover Project where member artists scrutinize your creations and give candid but constructive criticism.

You must know the rules to break them. Even though we're told not to judge a book by its cover, who doesn't? A cover grabs attention, signals genre, and sets the tone in seconds.

Your cover should be memorable but not overwhelming, distinctive but not confusing. Every element should enhance, never distract. Your cover is a promise to readers and often the deciding factor between "maybe later" and "add to cart." Make it count.

What Makes a Great Cover?

Great covers *communicate* tone and genre. A **shirtless hero** says steamy romance. **Neon spacescapes** scream sci-fi. **Big, bold text** on a minimalist background? Likely nonfiction or literary fiction. Think of how many covers *Pride and Prejudice* has had. Covers evolve; great design endures. Appropriate imagery, a compelling title, effective color use, and typography are essential cover design ingredients. Your cover should:

- Grab attention at thumbnail size
- Signal your genre and tone
- Make a promise

- Look polished across print, digital, and audio formats

DIY Cover Ingredients

Title + Subtitle + Author Name: Always legible and prominent

Imagery: Relevant and high-quality

Colors: Emotional impact + genre cues

Fonts: On-brand and easy to read

Layout: Balanced and clean

Research the latest design trends to explore ideas, use a high-quality image relevant to your subject and genre.
Consider how your cover will look on your website, Amazon, and other retail platforms. **Use** bold fonts to grab attention. Your cover should pop like a punchline, not fizzle like a flat joke.

- See the Earth Section's Establish and Formatting Chapters.

Five Free Design Resources

DIY BOOK COVERS	**Templates, mockups, tutorials**
CANVA	**Design, templates, mockups**
TEMPLATE.NET	**Customizable templates**
POSTERMYWALL	**Quick, simple designs**
INDY COVER PROJECT	**Facebook community feedback**

Back Cover Essentials

Include a brief book synopsis, blurbs from reviewers, and relevant information about the author. **See it as an opportunity** to provide more information and entice potential readers. **Leave room** for a barcode with your ISBNs for the paperback and hardcover.

ISBNs: Your Key to Global Book Distribution

Just as you need a passport for international travel, your book needs an ISBN to sojourn through bookstores, libraries, and online retailers worldwide. An ISBN (International Standard Book Number) is a unique13-digit code that serves as a distinctive identifier for your book.

This clever little number conveys everything the world needs to know about your book's format, publisher, and edition. Trying to sell your book without an ISBN would be like trying to sell a product without a barcode.

The eBook Dilemma: To ISBN or Not?

While Amazon Kindle Direct Publishing and most e-book retailers don't require an ISBN for e-books, getting one is akin to upgrading from economy to business class. Your book will be easier to find and open doors to libraries and specialty retailers. If you're thinking beyond Amazon's ecosystem, an ISBN becomes your golden ticket.

1. Amazon KDP offers free ISBNs for paperback and hardcover books, but there's a catch. Amazon becomes the official publisher, and you can't use that ISBN anywhere else. It's convenient but limiting.

2. Similarly, the IngramSpark Option offers free ISBNs with the same publisher-of-record strings attached. Great for getting started, but you're renting rather than owning your book's identity.

3. The Independent Publisher Path: Want full control? Buy your ISBN from your national ISBN agency. This makes you the publisher and gives you the freedom to distribute wherever you like.

What's New in 2026: ISBN Updates

New Number Format: All ISBNs are now 13 digits. You'll increasingly see the 979 prefixes as the traditional 978 series reaches capacity. Those old 10-digit ISBNs? Museum pieces now.

Format = New ISBN: Each version of your book requires an ISBN, including paperback, hardcover, eBook, and audiobook.

Geographic Perks: Live in Canada, South Africa, or New Zealand? You may be eligible for free ISBNs from your country's national agency.

Where to Get Your ISBN:

- **United States:** Bowker – myidentifiers.com | Email: support@myidentifiers.com

- **Canada:** Library and Archives Canada – bac-lac.gc.ca | Email: isbn@lac-bac.gc.ca

- **United Kingdom:** Nielsen – nielsenisbnstore.com | Email: isbn.agency@nielsen.com

- **Australia:** Thorpe-Bowker – myidentifiers.com.au | Email: info@thorpe.com.au

- **New Zealand:** National Library – natlib.govt.nz Email: cip@dia.govt.nz

- **South Africa:** National Library – nlsa.ac.za Email: isbn@nlsa.ac.za

The Bottom Line

An ISBN is your book's ticket to professional legitimacy and global reach. Whether you go the free route with platform limitations or invest in your own for maximum flexibility, this 13-digit key unlocks doors that remain firmly closed to unidentified books.

Kindlepreneur offers a free ISBN Barcode Generator that allows you to create a barcode image by entering your ISBN-13 and optional pricing information.

Generate Your Barcode:

1. **Enter ISBN-13**: Input your 13-digit ISBN. Ensure it's correctly hyphenated as per official standards. **Set Price (Optional)**: You can embed a price into your barcode or leave it blank. Entering 90000 will create a barcode with a price placeholder, which is useful if you plan to sell in bookstores but haven't finalized the price.

2. **Select Format**: Choose your preferred file format (PNG or JPG) for the barcode image.

3. **Download**: Once generated, download the barcode and incorporate it into your back cover design.

Note: Amazon KDP and IngramSpark can generate and place a barcode on your cover; however, your own barcode allows you greater control over placement, appearance and distribution.

Pro Tips

- Double-check all details before submitting your ISBN application to avoid delays.
- Keep a record of all ISBNs you assign, including format and publication date, to prevent confusion as your catalogue grows.
- If you change your publishing name, notify your ISBN agency to update your records.
- Assign a new ISBN for each new edition or format to ensure accurate tracking and sales data.

"An ISBN is more than just a number - it's a symbol of your book's legitimacy and professionalism."

- Reedsy

Your design should stop scrollers and whisper, "Pick me up."

RENDER a Book Cover

- **Research:** Study bestseller lists in your genre. What visual themes keep appearing? Notice color schemes, typography, and visual elements that instantly communicate genre.

- **Explore:** Try unconventional fonts, striking color combinations, and creative layouts. Use Canva to draft concepts that honor your genre's visual language. Experiment to get a feel for what you'd like your cover to convey.

- **Nurture:** Move from experimentation to intention. Select imagery that resonates with your narrative. A memoir might feature broken pottery mended with gold. Think visual storytelling: every element should contribute to your cover story. Trust your instincts. Let authenticity lead

- **Develop:** Build your vision by creating three versions –perhaps one bold and graphic, another atmospheric and subtle, and a third that surprises you. Ask for feedback to determine which cover works best.

- **Execute:** Ensure hierarchy by orchestrating the elements: your title commands attention, your subtitle provides context, and your author name establishes credibility. Test at thumbnail size , crucial for online bookstores. Squint at it. Hold it at arm's length. Can you still read the title? Ensure your cover works across digital, print, and audiobook formats.

- **Refine:** Polish until it shines. Obsess over typography – adjust spacing and alignment until everything feels balanced. Good typography is invisible; it just feels right. Balance boldness with clarity.

GENRE	FONT	SAMPLE	WHY IT WORKS	AVOID IN
Romance	Feeling Passionate	Love in the Air!	Curves convey emotional promise	Subtitles or where readability is a concern
HORROR	HELLPRINT	FEAR THE NIGHT	CREEPSTER'S JAGGED EDGES EVOKE A SENSE OF TERROR	Formal documents
SCI-FI	MOKOTO GLITCH 1	TO INFINITY AND BEYOND	MOKOTO GLITCH 1 EVOKES ADVANCED TECH AND DIGITAL SPACE	Historical fiction
ThRiLLER	DRUNKen HOUR	ThE RANSoME NoTE	DRUNKen HOUR's's suGGEsT deliRiUM and LUNacY	Subtitles or text
Non-Fiction	Neue Montreal	Knowledge is power	Neue Montreal's classic design ensures readability for any topic	Creative or whimsical contexts
Children	Chewy	Fun & Games!	Chewy's' playful style appeals to young readers	Business contexts

Water Hygge

Flow, Release, and Renew

Water wears down rock over time. Just as water moves around obstacles, your creativity flows around resistance when you trust the natural current to cleanse what no longer serves and nourish new growth. You are the ocean, the current, the wave, and the depths. You don't have to swim against the tide. Let your truth flow through the filters of doubt and emerge clear.

Your Water Ritual

Writing demands dissolution and release for renewal. You're going to swirl down the plughole all the sediment that's muddying your creative waters.

You need: Running water (shower, sink) and your voice. That's it.

As you stand beneath the shower with the water running, name aloud everything upsetting you. That spiteful one-star review? Procrastination patterns? That perfectionist voice? Rejections that still sting? Fears of not being good enough. Let the running water wash everything away.

Visualize each concern dissolving like sea salt as it gurgles down the drain.

Your creative channels are now clear. The debris that was blocking your flow has been washed away. Trust that, like fresh spring water, your creativity will flow more freely now.

Remember water carves canyons through solid rock, shaping landscapes as it moves with patient persistence? That's the power of the cleansing ritual. What will you wash away to clear your creative channels?

Your Next 3 Moves

1. **Explore uncharted waters:** Share a story that flows from your authentic experience. Honest writing creates ripples. **Prompts:** What story wants to flow through me? How might my vulnerability become someone else's life raft?

2. **Play With Design.** Open a free Canva account and let your artistic side flow free. Using templates, design a cover or two for the book you have in mind. Even if you hire a professional designer, playing with design ideas keeps the creative juices flowing. create ideas. You can also create a few fun social media illustrations.
   Resources: Canva.com for design
   Unsplash, Freepik, and Graphics.co for free visuals

3. **Release and Renew:** Revise everything you've written so far, even if it's just a chapter within your book outline. Flex your editing skills with AI assistance on how to develop core ideas.

Slosh Out

- Author intrusion, phrases like "I feel," or "in my view." Your name is on the book cover. No need to remind readers.
- Extraneous details that muddy your core message. Plagiarism, uncredited work, irrelevant content, and misleading information.
- Loaded words like 'undeserved,' 'whopping,' or 'only'.
- Sensationalism and overhype. Avoid exaggerating or making unrealistic claims about your "world-changing" work.
- Jargon and complex terms or industry-specific vocabulary that create barriers for readers.
- Clichés, unnecessary verbiage, and needless self-reference that interrupt your natural flow.
- Information overload or elements that create chaos such as Illegible fonts, low-resolution images, weak title contrast.
- Words that end in 'ly' – partly, really, happily, hopefully, virtually. Except baby (with the bath water). Obviously.

Water Hygge Hints

You are fluid and intuitive. Let your personality ripple and create currents with your quiet charisma. Every sentence you write is a wave reaching someone's shore.

Own your flow. Your emotional depth is your brand's undercurrent. Show your readers the true tides within you. Let your presence move with grace—calm, powerful, and impossible to ignore.

Use empowering tools that align with your rhythm. Embrace knowledge like rain on dry ground. Protect your energy. Connect, don't chase. Your influence runs deep when you stay true to yourself

Reflect the Source that fuels your creative flow. Write from your deepest wellspring.

Replenish with Self-Care. Morning walks by the water. You don't need to make waves. Say nothing when silence serves. Authenticity is your anchor. Vulnerability can melt the hardest heart.

Rest and Reflect: Trust the dance between movement and stillness. Witness your process. Observe with discernment.

Keep Moving: Persistence is power. Keep flowing, through storms and calm weather alike.

Carve your channel as you go. Curiosity creates insight and a connective current. Your influence ripples outward as you share your work.

Nature's elements are a harmonious whole, worlds away from corporate pressure. You have your intuitive depths, emotional currents, and natural grace. Your flow is self-sustaining. Keep it going.

- Dive into the Water Prompt Vault for more brilliant ideas to maintain your creative flow.

THREE

Air Section

Audio, Initiate, Resonate and Amplify

The air element, like water, has a sense of flow. High-vibrational words can refresh minds in the fire of enthusiasm. When your literary voice finds its authentic frequency, it amplifies the narrative, carrying your words into conversations,

- **Audio:** Consider how to bring your book to life through sound. Choose a narrator who can bring your story to life, read your book yourself, or opt for Amazon's free Virtual Voice technology.
- **Initiate:** Ignite dynamic engagement and unlock the impact of audiobooks through podcasts. These platforms let you connect with listeners and build a community around your work.
- **Resonate:** Revel in linguistic secrets of how words direct energy to shape reality. Focus on performance, delivery, and accessibility. Consider incorporating sound effects to enhance and transform your audiobook into an immersive experience.

Let's take flight!

"Finding common ground, risking vulnerability, validating lived expertise, and integrating knowledge into personal growth rather than hero worship is how we free ourselves from polarizing "discussions" aka social media postulating, obfuscations, and gatekeeping. Now is the time to call out your dragons!"

Jill Woodworth, Conversations With Friends

Audio

Soar onto the Airwaves

"Audiobooks are for people who hate reading and for those of us who love reading."

Matthew Rubery, audiobook historian

Let's face it. Your day is packed tighter than a subway car at rush hour. Between work deadlines, family obligations, and that persistent need to sleep, who has time to sit down with a book?

Welcome to the audiobook revolution, where homemakers sleuth between laundry loads and traffic-bound commuters scale Everest with intrepid explorers. Dusting the blinds becomes more fun when unravelling conspiracies or hearing a motivational pep talk. You can slay villains with every scrub of the loo.

An ancient primal longing draws us to the sound of a measured voice breathing life into worlds of adventure, danger, and romance, with their characters and exploits. The sheer pleasure of being read to harks back to a duvet-snuggling childhood of magical adventures brought to life by a parent's voice.

A skilled narrator's cadence and nuances of inflection add layers of meaning to the text, making long road trips feel like brief detours. Audiobooks allow you to squeeze more literature into sardine-packed schedules and fly with your feet on the ground.

DIY Narration: A Personal Touch

Independent authors can and *do* narrate their books, especially recommended for non-fiction writers. Your natural tone and rhythm can authenticate your work in a way that resonates with readers. The personal connection you establish through your voice creates an intimacy many listeners appreciate.

The line between audiobooks and podcasts continues to blur, with more production elements, multiple narrators, and immersive sound effects creating experiences that traditional books can't match.

The modern audiobook is a way for the perpetually busy (all of us) to consume more books

- A gateway for reluctant readers and those with reading difficulties to access literature

- A creative playground for voice actors, celebrities, and increasingly sophisticated AI

If your wallet could talk, it would tell you to invest in audiobooks. The global audiobook market was $8.6 billion in 2025 - up from $6.5 billion. By 2032, we're looking at a $56.09 billion.

Who's Pressing Play ?

Fiction fanatics: Account for 64.3% of the market

Smartphone addicts: Make up 43.8% of listeners - finally, a healthy relationship with your phone!

Adults: Represent 76.4% of the audience, proving that being read to isn't just for kids anymore[1]

Where Are All These Listeners?

North America: Leading the charge with 43.7% market share. What else will you do during those endless highway stretches?

Asia Pacific: Coming in hot with 26.4% and accelerating faster than a thriller's plot twist

While purists clutch their matte jackets, the democratization of storytelling continues apace. As the book editor Jayne Southern notes, "For some reason, fiction has to be more believable than fact."

This applies to audiobooks too. With advancements in AI narration technology, self-published authors can afford to turn their e-books into audiobooks without mortgaging their homes.

Audiobook Barriers & Breakthroughs

When I tried to create an audiobook with a professional narrator (that trans-Atlantic accent I craved!) in 2021 I hit the ACX eligibility wall.

Despite having a US bank account, I couldn't upload to ACX since I didn't live in one of their eligible countries. Amazon's introduction of a Virtual Voice option for authors has now evened the odds, transforming the audiobook landscape for indie authors.

INaudio

Led by industry veterans, INaudio is now your alternative go-to for reaching the broadest possible audience. Spotify partners with INaudio to keep the distribution doors open. With seasoned industry leaders at the helm of this new venture, the audiobook universe is poised for expansion. So, whether you're a publisher, an indie author, or a retailer, consider this your cue to lean in and turn the page. The future of audiobooks just got louder.

Amazon Virtual Voice

At first, I rolled my eyes at the prospect of AI narration – *quelle horreur* – but I changed my mind when Ken Vernon, author of *Everest '96: A Compelling Expose of Death and Deceit*, told me his book sales quadrupled after he converted it to Amazon's virtual voice. "The reasoning? When I was on Everest (1996) there were a few dozen climbers and a few hundred trekkers. Now there are about 200 000 trekkers a year. All wear headphones and listen to books!"

Encouraged by Vernon's words, I used Amazon's virtual voice technology to convert *Medusa's Musings* into an audiobook in under two hours.

Guess what it costs. Nothing. Zero dollars for your audiobook production. I could have narrated it myself but here's the thing: the virtual voice sounded better than mine and got sentences right in a fraction of the time.

So intuitive is the user interface, even I managed to navigate it, and that's saying something! Medusa is all about AI. Thanks to customization options that enable you to adjust pronunciation, speed, and tone, I thought her virtual voice worked well.

Look, it's not perfect. Accent options are limited to American and English. You can switch between voices every chapter but not *within* the chapters.

Emotional range? Since death scenes and worm composting receive eerily similar treatment, you have to get more creative with your pronunciation efforts. For example, with the word "read," you can ask the AI to pronounce it as "reed" rather than "red."

You can't choose what plays in the preview, so potential listeners might hear about your character's grocery list rather than their car chase, but so far, it sounds passable and the 40% royalties on every sale works for me.

Another plus is that updating is as simple as changing your social media status. Revise the ebook, update the audio, and that's it! Best of all, you can reach readers who prefer listening to traditional text.

Work Magic with KDP's Virtual Voice Studio

Amazon's Virtual Voice has made audiobook creation more accessible to almost any author. You can tweak pronunciation, pacing, intonation, and more using the Virtual Voice Studio. The customization options allow more control over how your words come to life. Here are a few strategies that can elevated your AI audiobook from "robotic" to "listenable."

- **Match Voice to Content:** You can select from American and British AI voices and fine-tune pronunciation, pacing, emphasis, and pauses. For *Medusa's Musings*, I chose an English accent for Medusa and a warm American accent for my own voice.

- **Fix Pronunciation Issues:** Customize tricky names and emphasis**.** Get creative with your words. Learn to spell them in a way the AI will understand like 'led' if you want to describe the metal. For emphasis, either slow down or speed up a word or phrase between 25 and 50%. Commas, dashes, or an ellipse help guide your digital narrator through the emotional landscape of your prose.

- **Adjust Pacing:** Fine-tune the tempo for better conversational flow that's neither rushed nor sedated.

- **Enhance Dialogue:** Use rhythm and pauses to differentiate speakers. Use pauses for emotional inflection or to create differentiation so listeners can tell who is speaking. For male dialogue, I slowed the voice down by 25% to give it more gravitas.

- **Edit for Audio:** Shorten long sentences and clarify transitions. Chop wordy sentences. The beauty is that you can update your books at the same time.

- **Clarify Transitions:** Some words make sense on the page but confuse the ear. For example I asked the AI to pronounce byte as "byte with a y" so readers could differentiate it from bite.

- **Complete Review:** Listen to the entire audiobook before clicking on 'publish audio.'

Production Costs and Royalties

Zero. Creating an audiobook with Virtual Voice is free. You set your price between $3.99 and $14.99, and KDP pays you a 40% royalty.

The production timeline from final approval to global availability is just a few days. Once approved, your audiobook goes live on Audible and Amazon faster than traditional audio production.

Your book is eligible for Virtual Voice on KDP if: It has been live for at least 7 days and is not public domain (sorry, Napoleon Hill). It must be in English with a table of contents. It needs to be audiobook-friendly (so, no coloring or recipe books) and under 240,000 words (roughly 26 hours of narration.)

The Future of Audio is Here

The audiobook landscape has evolved from an exclusive domain requiring expensive equipment, professional narrators, and technical know-how to an accessible format. Whether you choose professional narration, record your own voice, or utilize Amazon's Virtual Voice, audiobooks are essential for serious authors.

While AI narration won't replace the artistry of professional voice actors, it has made audiobook production accessible to authors who would otherwise be priced out of the market. More stories reaching more listeners is a win for everyone.

Compare Extracts on Audible:

1. *Reign,* narrated by Natalia Williams
2. *The Rooster Diaries,* narrated by Stephen Dalton
3. *Medusa's Musings,* virtual voice narration

Further Reading: Virtual Voice Audible audiobooks: A guide for authors https://www.getresponse.com/blog/virtual-voice-audible-audiobooks

Create Audiobooks in Minutes: https://www.toolify.ai/ai-news/create-audiobooks-in-minutes-using-ai-on-amazon-kdp-1402745

> *"The younger demographic is a key driver of audiobook growth, encouraging family adoption, diversifying genre demand."*
> Fortune Business Insights

Bring Your Words to Life

Audiobooks open doors to broader, more diverse audiences who prefer to consume content on the go and expand your reach, increase your visibility, elevate your brand, and foster deeper engagement in a marketplace where attention is hard-won.

When done well, audio storytelling becomes an experience, brought to life with emotion, tone, and voice. Think soundscapes, character voices, and pacing that draws listeners in. The good news? You no longer need a professional recording studio or voice actor to make it happen.

Use Amazon Virtual Voice

Turning your book into an audiobook is now easier, faster, and more affordable than ever. Amazon's Virtual Voice technology enables authors to create professional-quality audiobooks using AI narration without studios, actors, or steep production fees.

What You'll Need

- A polished manuscript (Word, EPUB, or PDF)
- A KDP or ACX account
- About 24 hours for processing

Step-by-Step Process

1. Prepare your manuscript: remove images, tables, and anything that doesn't translate well to audio.
2. Log into KDP or ACX and find your book project.
3. Select "Create Audiobook" and choose "Virtual Voice."

4. Browse AI narrators by tone, accent, and style.
5. Upload your manuscript and preview the result.
6. Use the built-in editor to fine-tune pronunciation and pacing.
7. Approve and submit for Amazon's quality review (typically within 72 hours).

Benefits for Authors

- No need to hire narrators or rent a studio
- Fast turnaround—ready in hours, not weeks
- High-quality, consistent results
- Easy to update later if your manuscript changes

Audiobooks are a powerful way to meet readers where they are. Whether you write fiction or nonfiction, offering an audio edition of your work helps you stay competitive, accessible, and relevant in the modern publishing landscape.

---

1. *Sources: Market.us Scoop, Coherent Market Insights, Straits Research*

Inspire

Podcasts - Share Voices, Sell Books

> *"The landmines of hopelessness are everywhere. It's okay when you fall. We all do. There's no ideal way to do it. It's all perfect right here and now."*
>
> Jill Woodworth, podcast consultant

Ever caught yourself thinking, "Oh, that's something Jill would say!" about a podcaster you've never met? That's the magnetic pull of authentic audio presence. Some podcasters become more companionable than our actual friends. They're in our ears with fresh thoughts, hilarious observations, and brilliant advice that cuts through the noise.

Take Massachusetts-based podcast consultant and story cultivator Jill Woodworth, who delivers sharp, matter-of-fact wit and simplifies complex topics by "sharing deep lived experience across multiple paradigms."

Listening to Jill present in an amusing, relatable way, vital but often ignored subjects like the bio-digital convergence being perpetrated on humanity, inspired me to write *Medusa's Musings*, where my protagonist explores similar themes as a battery repurposed in a smart city.

Jill invites fascinating guests onto her "Conversations with Friends" podcast and gets unstuck in her livestreams with nature riffs, where she is invariably found hiking in the nearby woods.

Her message resonates: "The time is now to boogie, dance, pray, sing, learn to feel your skin, write with your hand on paper, and put your bare feet on the earth. Break the signal. Embrace the weird and goofy. Dance in the woods like a nut."

By speaking her truth in a way that exposes and polarizes corporate deceit that relies on ignorance, Jill embodies sovereignty.

From Self-Conscious to Self-Assured

Starting a podcast is one of the most effective ways to promote a book, but if you're introverted, it can feel like mountain hiking in high heels, right? If you, like me, cringe at the sound of your voice, you're not alone.

Even Jill felt that way, at first. "Listening to myself and editing my takes was excruciating," she admits. "I watched myself with horror and felt uncomfortable for several years. But just like life, podcasting evolves organically."

Jill's transformation came through self-compassion and inner work. "I began caring less about my appearance and more about finding flow state. One day, I realized, 'Damn, you're a rock star pitching from the heart. You've come so far.' Now I cheer myself on, but it didn't start like that."

Her advice? "Practice like a self-absorbed fool. Just keep going and speak out about what you know to be right."

Get Started: No Excuses, No Expensive Equipment

If you're still hesitant about putting yourself out there, Jill has news for you: there's no wrong way to podcast, and you don't need expensive equipment. "Almost every phone has a microphone, and most texting apps let you record and send audio tracks to yourself. Start getting comfortable speaking out loud. Record yourself talking about your children, your forest hike or anything you know well. Just do it. Speak and record. Get used to hearing your voice."

The same principle applies to video podcasts. "Talk about what you're familiar with and go from there. Watch yourself and have compassion for yourself and what you're saying."

Her challenge: "Put up a 30-second video or audio recording on social media. Feel all the fear and judgment that might emanate from family and friends. Do it anyway. Then walk away and forget about it."

The Power of Audio Presence

Jill's growing podcasting success illustrates that when we speak from our experience with vulnerability, we create connections that make our audience feel heard, understood, challenged, and inspired to embrace their sovereignty, too. Her work on her lived experience of special needs parenting has endeared her to thousands of other mothers.

"We're all living and learning here," she reminds us. "Thanks to all the brave humans for standing up and not staying quiet."

That's the real power of podcasting: not just promoting your book but becoming a voice that matters in someone's daily life. A presence that challenges, comforts, and inspires action. Somebody like Jill.

Your voice deserves to be heard, too. Are you ready to let it be?

10 Burning Questions

Podcasting provides a powerful way to connect with readers.

1. Do I need professional equipment to start a podcast?
Not at all. Start with your smartphone. Many phones now rival entry-level microphones. As you gain confidence, you could upgrade to a USB mic and headphones for cleaner sound. But don't let the tech hold you back.

2. **How do I choose a theme or topic?**
Choose themes from your book that can fuel 20 episodes. This "idea endurance test" ensures long-term relevance. Focus on behind-the-scenes insights or conversations with fellow creatives in your niche.

3. **What's the best format for an author's podcast?**
There's no one-size-fits-all. Solo storytelling? Cool. Interviews? Great for networking and variety. Choose what energizes you. Mixing interviews with personal commentary? Yes!

4. **How do I record and edit my podcast?**
Use your phone, computer, or an affordable USB mic. For editing, use free tools like Audacity, GarageBand, or intuitive platforms like Descript and Riverside.fm. AI tools now clean up audio and remove filler words, making post-production faster than ever.

5. **Where do I host and distribute it?**
Use a podcast hosting service such as Spotify for Podcasters, Buzzsprout, or Podbean. These platforms handle distribution to Spotify, Apple Podcasts, Google Podcasts, and more with a few simple clicks.

6. **How do I grow my audience?**
Promote each episode through your email list, social channels, and website. Cross-promote with other podcasters and authors. Consider asking listeners to leave reviews or share episodes.

7. Do I need to script every episode?
Not necessarily. Some podcasters write full scripts; others use bullet-point outlines. Choose what keeps you focused while allowing natural flow.

8. How long should my episodes be?
There's no perfect length, but 20 - 40 minutes is a sweet spot for most beginner podcasts. Short-form content (10 – 15 mins) is trending for busy listeners. Pay attention to analytics and listener feedback, then adjust accordingly.

9. I hate the sound of my voice. What do I do?
Chill. Start by recording just for yourself. With time, you'll get used to hearing yourself and build confidence. As Jill Woodworth wisely says, "Your voice is the connective tissue between your message and your audience." Practice, compassion, and consistency are your best allies. **A good tip:** rehearse the intro and key points, then speak from the heart.

10. Can podcasting help me sell books?
Absolutely. Podcasting boosts your visibility, establishes credibility, and cultivates connections. You can serialize chapters, share the writing experience or feature your characters. It's also a great entry point into guesting on other podcasts, another smart way to reach new readers.

Bonus Tips

- AI is your co-producer: Tools can help you write episode outlines, generate transcripts, and edit audio.
- Short-form podcasts are booming: Bite-sized episodes for time-crunched listeners are gaining traction.
- Video is on the rise: Record both video and audio, then repurpose the content for YouTube Shorts, TikTok, and Instagram Reels.

Resonate

WITH SOUND, MEANING AND WORDS THAT ECHO

"Create an environment where the reader feels as though they can relate to the story you're telling them, that they're in safe hands with you."

Andrea Campbell, author

WORDS INFLUENCE OUR THOUGHTS and shape our realities. It's no coincidence that the linguistic 'morpheme' – the original primitive emoji delivering meaning in bite-sized units – sounds like 'morphine.' Are numbers designed to 'numb us' while words awaken us to deeper truths?

The Mind's Symphony

Imagine your brain as a conductor orchestrating language's spellbinding symphony. Within your mind's auditorium, specific areas direct the harmonious interplay of words to the left hemisphere's linguistic command centers.

Here, the legendary Broca and Wernicke regions – those audition halls of speaking and listening – segue into a cross-border dialogue dance of spoken melodies and profound understanding.

Frenchman Paul Broca unravelled the brain's speech production hub's finesse, partnering with German Carl Wernicke, who pinpointed the language comprehension epicenter. By revealing words to be more than mere communication tools, Broca and Wernicke ignited neurolinguistics.

Linguistic Sorcery

What if word sounds – phonetics themselves – could direct energy and reprogram minds. Has language always been literal magick? The Phoenician alphabet inventors crafted sounds and double meanings to influence the masses and convey insider knowledge to those in the know.

The ancient Greeks called this reality-creating vibration *Logos* – an intermediary agent between god and the cosmos. Egyptian sages harnessed vowel sounds to sculpt their world. Shamans and witches wielded words in rituals, divination, and spells to invoke supernatural forces. The ancient grimoire lives on, encapsulated within the our modern grammar.

Can we escape the linguistic labyrinth lined with double-edged semantics? Consider the paradoxes that bind us: Is "awake" the opposite of "asleep," or a gathering for the departed? Why does "funeral" begin with "fun"? These are breadcrumbs leading us toward deeper understanding.

Words are the birds carrying our messages and the bars confining our thoughts. Our enchanting language pays homage to the Phoenicians and their fiery phoenix of rebirth rising from antiquity's ashes. "Hours" anagrams to Horus, the cyclical solar god; myth lives in our modern speech.

Storm Chasing Lessons from J.K Rowling

Every compelling narrative embodies resilience, transformation, challenges and victories. J.K. Rowling, who faced divorce and financial hardship before the world recognized her brilliance, exemplifies this archetypal pattern. Even when cancel culture attacked her for defending women's rights, the Harry Potter author met every barb with wit and fortitude.

Asked how she sleeps knowing she's "lost a whole audience," she replied: "I read my most recent royalty checks and the pain goes away pretty quickly."

In 2024, Rowling declined a life peerage and a damehood, a testament to her commitment to authenticity over establishment approval.

Her acclaimed Cormoran Strike series, (written as Robert Galbraith) and philanthropy, continue to inspire. Rowling's story is one of enduring relevance. She confronts storms head-on and defines her legacy.

The Architecture of Story

Every compelling story follows mythologist Joseph Campbell's archetypal "monomyth" pattern – the hero's journey that appears across all cultures, a fundamental evolvement blueprint in six pivotal stages.

The Call beckons the protagonist from ordinary existence, often met with initial resistance before acceptance. **Challenges and Trials** emerge as they cross the threshold into adventure, where obstacles test their resolve. **Friends and Enemies** appear – mentors offering guidance, allies providing support, and adversaries forcing growth through conflict.

The Prize awaits. It might be physical treasure or profound realization, earned through facing the ultimate ordeal. **The Return** brings the transformed hero back to ordinary reality. **Resolution** follows as they integrate newfound wisdom into daily life.

Who doesn't love a good underdog story? Growth, struggle, and transformation themes captivate readers because they mirror our own psychological development. When we recognize these stages in our own lives, we create deep emotional resonance with characters who embody our struggles and aspirations.

This archetypal understanding becomes especially crucial for audio storytelling, where the rhythm of language must carry listeners through the transformative journey without visual cues to anchor their attention.

The Seven Pillars of Reader Connection

1. **Embrace Authentic Voice:** If you're writing non-fiction, you *are* the protagonist of your heroine's journey. Lean into this role. Share your experiences, values, and contradictory personalities. Use relatable themes like love, loss, and identity to help readers invest emotionally.

2. **Create Empathy Through Shared Struggle:** Share, with sensitivity and awareness, the obstacles you've faced. Not everyone can relate to missing your first-class upgrade or your housekeeper failing her driver's license again. Focus on universal challenges – fear, rejection, self-doubt – that transcend socioeconomic boundaries.

3. **Master the Rhythm and Flow:** Vary your sentence length. Short sentences create urgency. Longer, more complex sentences allow for deeper exploration of ideas and can mirror the natural breathing patterns of thoughtful conversation. Dialogue reveals character traits while creating conflict and advancing your narrative arc.

4. **Know Your Tribe:** Understand your readers' age range, interests, and expectations with laser precision. Tailor your humor accordingly to avoid unintentional offense. Use cultural references – slang, regional dialect, professional jargon – that resonates with your specific audience while remaining accessible to newcomers.

5. **Paint with Literary Devices:** Deploy metaphors, similes, and figurative language to create vivid mental images. Personification breathes life into abstract concepts. Irony adds complexity and nuance. Rich descriptions help readers feel they're experiencing your story first hand.

6. Cho**ose Active Voice to Vivify Your Prose:** Onomatopoeia and strategic hyperbole add humor and make your narrative voice distinctive. Alliteration and subtle rhyme add a memorable musical quality.

7**. Trust Reader Intelligence:** Maintain consistent tone to create coherence and believability. Use foreshadowing and symbolism to add layers of meaning, but remember, less is more. Don't over-explain or over-describe. Let your readers' imagination fill the gaps.

> *"Spoken English thrives on purposeful redundancy, guiding the mind with each word. In audio, brevity and clarity must dance in a simple listening rhythm, setting the pace for the mind to catch up with associated visual connections.*
>
> Monica Zwolsman, author and English coach

The Alchemy in Action: Words That Transform

Consider how language choice can transform even the most mundane scenario into a compelling narrative. When we write with intentional rhythm and sound, focusing on the musicality of our words, we create what Monica Zwolsman calls that "simple listening rhythm" that allows minds to catch up with visual connections.

We might embellish "The journalist investigated the case and wrote a report," thus: "The wind howled through deserted streets as journalist Jackie Hastings trudged through rain, her heart quickening as she approached the abandoned warehouse where months of tracking the Shadow Stalker would finally converge."

Notice the difference? The second version employs five key principles:

1. Sensory engagement through weather and physical sensation
2. Active voice that places Jackie at the center of action
3. Rhythmic variation in sentence structure
4. Specific details that create visual anchors
5. Emotional stakes embedded in the details.

Three principles apply: Focus on rhythm and sound in your writing. Read everything aloud. Don't fear breaking grammar rules when it serves your artistic purpose. Fragments can create power, repetition can build hypnotic effect. Choose words that elevate rather than merely inform.

RESONATE

- **R**elease lifeless, academic writing that drowns readers in facts but starves their souls. Instead, use words that breathe, pulse, and transform both writer and reader.

- **E**xplore the hidden history of language as power. Ancient civilizations understood that words command. Every sentence carries the potential to influence, inspire, or ignite change.

- **S**tudy the ancients who knew language as magic. Greeks called it *Logos* – the word as creative force. Egyptian hieroglyphs functioned as spells, aligning human consciousness with divine patterns. Their writing shaped reality.

- **O**pen yourself to shamanic wisdom: intention plus vibration equals manifestation. Write so that your words become portals that transport readers to where they need to be.

- **N**avigate the bridge between ancient wisdom and modern craft. Blend timeless principles of persuasive language with contemporary storytelling techniques.

- **A**ttain emotional freedom by recognizing how many words carry contradictory meanings that confuse your message. Be clear about your language, and you'll clean up your impact.

- **T**ap into language's true power source: the realm of myth, metaphor, and imagination. When your writing springs from this deep well, it pulses with an energy readers can't ignore.

- **E**mbrace narrative mastery through transformation. Create stories and characters that mirror your readers' struggles with loss, growth, and becoming. Give them heroes they can emulate.

Air Hygge

Inspire, Broadcast and Elevate Ideas

Air is the element that carries your words beyond the page, across distances, dispersing your message through podcasts, audiobooks, and authentic chats.

You are a breath of fresh air. Your voice carries your unique frequency that no one else can offer – your superpower.

Light, clever, impossible to pin down, your mind dances with ideas. Your presence is clear. Be the zephyr. Let your uniqueness swirl into everything you do.

Use your voice to elevate, expand, spread insights, stir imagination and uplift conversations.

Speaking from curiosity, courage, and compassion is the secret sauce to listener loyalty.

Let your creativity breathe freely. Stop overthinking. Start speaking. You have everything you need to give your words wings. Your voice, your breath and your message are waiting to soar. Let your voice lift others.

The Air Ritual

Ground yourself and clear your mental static. Here's your breathing practice to connect with the air's healing power and calm your thoughts.

Method: Find a quiet space. Breathe deeply with purpose. As you inhale, draw in clarity and confidence. As you exhale, release tension and fear. Conscious breathing increases oxygen to your body, boosts energy, sharpens mental clarity, and centers you like the eye in a hurricane. Focusing on your breath tells your nervous system to shift from a state of stress to one of calm.

Releasing unprocessed emotions through breathwork opens doors to greater self-awareness and inner peace. Breath is the essence of life.

Disperse on the Breeze

- Everything holding you back that keeps your voice small.
- Audiobooks misconceptions: They're no longer too expensive or technical to produce. AI narration and user-friendly platforms now guide you through the entire process.
- Assumptions about needing to be tech-savvy, or extroverted to podcast: You just need a voice and the courage to share a message.

Your Next 3 Moves

Now that you've cleared the mental clutter and dispelled limiting beliefs, it's time to make a podcast. You don't need fancy gear to begin. Start with your phone. Find a quiet, comfortable spot and use your phone's built-in voice recorder. Keep it close (2–4 inches from your mouth) to get clear audio and minimize background noise.

1. **Create a Loose Outline Before Recording**
   A few bullet points help keep your episode focused. Plan your key messages, mentions, and a call to action (such as where listeners can buy your books). This prevents rambling and makes your episodes easier to edit later.

2. **Use Free or Low-Cost Editing Apps**
   After recording, use simple editing apps on your phone or computer (such as Audacity, GarageBand, or Anchor) to trim mistakes, add intros and outros, and polish your audio.

3. **Publish and Share on a Platform**
   Sign up with a podcast hosting service (many offer free plans, e.g., Anchor or Buzzsprout). Upload your episodes and submit your podcast RSS feed to directories like Apple Podcasts, Spotify, and Google Podcasts to reach listeners. Promote your episodes on social media and mention your books in your show to drive sales.

Air Hygge Hints

Breathe Before You Speak: Your nervous system will thank you, and your listeners will hear the difference. Deep breaths anchor you to authenticity. Fear is just stagnant air. Transform it into creative power with breath and direction.

Let Your Voice Flow: Don't over-script. Allow for natural pauses and authentic emotions. The best audio content feels like a conversation with a trusted friend. Be the breeze that lifts stories, spreads insights, and stirs imagination. Let your voice carry your authentic message on the wind, whether it's through podcasts, audiobooks, or authentic social sharing.

Let's take root in the earth element.

Four

Earth

Construct a Grounded Framework

- Establish Your Foundation: A solid framework supports your work. Your message, tone, and theme should be consistent and intentional.
- Author with Intention: Maintain forward momentum. Your Amazon Author Page is your digital storefront. Make it magnetic.
- Release and Refine: Put it on pre-order to address last-minute issues and build anticipation.
- Test and Tweak: Test your keywords and category placements to ensure discoverability. Watch what works and adjust. Small tweaks can unlock big visibility.
- Hack the Media with Hygge: Sharpen your message. Become a media whisperer: follow journalists on social media, understand what they care about, pitch relevant, timely stories and position yourself as an authority figure in your field.

Let's dig in.

"If you have built castles in the air, your work need not be lost; that is where they should be. Now put the foundations under them."

Henry David Thoreau

Establish

Framework & Formatting

> *"Throw it together as only you can. Enjoy the process; create your own plan!"*
>
> Donna White, the Minka series

I'M FORMATTING MY BOOK. I've done the page numbers. Just kidding. I'm still trying to figure out where it should start! We've all been here.

Building anything requires a sturdy foundation, and a book is no exception. As an author, it's your job to frame your ideas into a scaffold that allows readers to explore new perspectives.

In the Fire section, you defined your readers and reasons for writing. You clarified your themes in the Water section and unified your message. In the Air section, you explored voice, narration, and audio formats. The Earth section grounds your ideas.

Just as Earth sustains life through systems of interdependence, your book needs a living framework to thrive. This chapter will ground your ideas, streamline your structure, and show you how to format your book.

Creating Your Book's Structure

Your outline is the skeleton you'll flesh out with words.

- Start with a Table of Contents (TOC): Aim for 8 – 12 chapters, each focused on a core idea.
- Create Subsections: Subheads help organize content and spark curiosity.
- Interactive and digital-first titles work best with modular outlines that can adapt. Think building blocks, not assembly lines. Tools like Notion or Milanote are useful for authors who collaborate or want their work accessible anywhere with an internet connection.

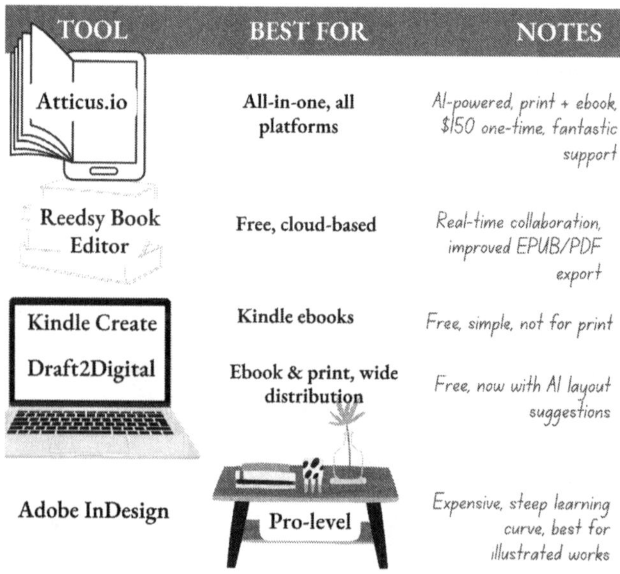

TOOL	BEST FOR	NOTES
Atticus.io	All-in-one, all platforms	AI-powered, print + ebook, $150 one-time, fantastic support
Reedsy Book Editor	Free, cloud-based	Real-time collaboration, improved EPUB/PDF export
Kindle Create	Kindle ebooks	Free, simple, not for print
Draft2Digital	Ebook & print, wide distribution	Free, now with AI layout suggestions
Adobe InDesign	Pro-level	Expensive, steep learning curve, best for illustrated works

The Top Five Formatting Tools

Formatting Finesse

Formatting enhances your book's credibility, flow, and professionalism. Inconsistency can sabotage your content. Here are three approaches:

- **Hire a Pro:** Worth every cent if you have the budget.
- **Friend or Family Favor:** May strain relationships. (Believe me!)
- **DIY Tools:** Ideal for the self-reliant and budget-conscious.

Top Five DIY Formatting Tools

1. **Atticus.io** (Recommended)
One-time $150 fee. Templates, drag-and-drop interface, TOC generator, eBook + print formats. AI-powered formatting suggestions. Facebook group support. Best for beginners who want beautiful results.

2. **Reedsy Book Editor**
Cloud-based, real-time collaboration. Free, intuitive, exports (EPUB/PDF). improved export options or those on a budget.

3. **KindleCreate**
Free Amazon-centric tool. Optimized for Kindle eBooks. Not suitable for print or advanced layouts.

4. **Draft2Digital**
Excellent free tool for eBooks and print. Automatic TOC, AI-powered formatting suggestions. Wide distribution options.

5. **Adobe InDesign**
Professional-grade. Expensive, steep learning curve. Great for designers.

- *Google Docs and Microsoft Word remain viable for simple layout*
- Additional reading from Kindlepreneur

8 Essential Formatting Tips

1. **Choose an Appropriate Font Size**
   Aim for a size that doesn't strain the eyes. The standard font size for non-fiction books is 12 points. Adjust as needed to avoid straining readers' eyes.

2. **Establish a Consistent Margin**
   At least one inch throughout the book looks professional.

3. **Use Headings and Subheadings**
   Structure your content using hierarchical headings with stylistic changes or bolding yo differentiate them.

4. **Pay Attention to Line Spacing**
   Typically, it ranges from 1.2 to 1.5 times the font size in non-fiction books for legibility.

5. **Use Points for Lists**
   Numbers or bullet points can help organize information, making it easier to follow.

6. **Add Page Numbers**
   Essential for navigation, place them in the header or footer.

7. **Avoid Widows and Orphans**
   A widow is the last word (or line) that winds up alone at the top of a page, while an orphan shivers alone at the bottom of a paragraph.

8. **Include Images and Graphs**
   These can help to break up the text and make complex information easier to understand.

The Typeface Tango

Reader-first design is key. Readability is the new standard. Hand-drawn or "human touch" display fonts are popular for branding and headings. Keep sizing and spacing consistent for a polished finish. Limit yourself to two, maximum three, fonts for harmony.

Your font is your reader's first impression. The right typography communicates mood, intention and tone in seconds. Ensure your fonts are licensed for commercial use.

Serif Fonts (Garamond, Georgia): Classic and perfect for print

Sans-serif Fonts (Arial, Arimo): Clean and ideal for screens and readers with dyslexia or ADHD

Display Fonts (Impact, Copperplate): Use for headings to add personality while maintaining readability

Accessibility First: Fonts like Atkinson Hyperlegible and Ariel boost readability for everyone. Variable fonts work on all devices, ensuring a consistent look throughout.

A Guide to Genre-Savvy Font Choices

Romance

Fonts: *Edwardian Script, Humble Hearts, Cinzel Decorative,* Holiday Romance
With their curved strokes mimicking handwritten love letters, these elegant, flowing fonts are ideal for titles that promise passion, poetic connection, longing, and intimacy. Use sparingly – main titles only- for maximum impact.

Horror

Fonts: *Beast, Butcherman, Charu Chandan, Blood Drip, Jeepers, Hellprint, Kust, Shlop*
Distorted, jagged, and dripping, these fonts hint at blood, decay, and madness. Think splatterpunk, gothic horror, or psychological thrillers where typography unnerves before the first page.

Sci-Fi

Fonts: *Mokoto Glitch, Chromium One*
With their sleek, high-tech geometry, these sharp, glitchy, and futuristic fonts suggest innovation, space travel, and dystopian digital realms. Perfect for cyberpunk and speculative fiction.

Thriller

Fonts: *Impact, Max Sompsin, Medusa Gothic, Drunken Hour, AntiO, Norwester*
Heavy, bold fonts build suspense. These typefaces deliver punch and pace, visually tightening the noose. Whether you're writing noir, espionage, or psychological thrillers, their assertive energy mirrors narrative tension.

Children's

Fonts: *Schoolbell, Irene, Malibu, Lazy Dog, Finger Paint, Bangers, Chewy*
Rounded, vibrant, and bursting with fun, these fonts offer readability and playfulness. Their hand-drawn or comic-inspired vibes make them perfect for engaging young minds and sparking joy.

Non-Fiction

Fonts: *Bebas Neue, Arimo, Neue Montreal*
Clean and confident, these sans-serifs radiate professionalism. Their minimalism offers clarity—ideal for business, self-help, or educational works that value authority and accessibility.

Five Free Design Resources

DIY BOOK COVERS	Templates, mockups, tutorials
CANVA	Design, templates, mockups
TEMPLATE.NET	Customizable templates
POSTERMYWALL	Quick, simple designs
INDY COVER PROJECT	Facebook community feedback

Top five free design resources.

Upload Your Masterpiece

Whoop! Whoop! You've finished your manuscript! Congratulate yourself. Now to prepare it for publication on Amazon's Kindle Direct Publishing (KDP) platform. See the Appendix for a step by step guide on how to sign up to KDP and the following publishing platforms.

Think of an eBook as a digital version of your favorite classic novel, minus the musty smell. The most common eBook file format is EPUB.

While Amazon's Kindle Direct Publishing (KDP) is a popular starting point, publishing only on Amazon means missing 40% of the market, including Barnes & Noble, Apple Books, and other platforms.

The following platforms offer expanded reach, global distribution, and additional professional services.

Additional Publishing Platforms:

- IngramSpark
- Draft2Digital
- Kobo
- Lulu
- BookBaby
- Google Play

Key Publishing Considerations

Metadata Matters: Getting your book details right (title, author, format) makes the difference between being found or forgotten.

Advance Publication Date: Set a future publication date to allow time for uploads and adjustments.

Permissions: Ensure you have necessary permissions to publish any copyrighted materials.

By diversifying your publishing platforms, you can extend your reach, build new reader connections, and thrive in a dynamic literary ecosystem.

For detailed step-by-step guides on setting up accounts with various publishing platforms, see the Appendix Publishing Platforms.

Author

Copyright & Authority Status

"My problem isn't piracy, it's obscurity"
Cory Doctorow, Makers

"Copyright is for losers," quipped Banksy, the elusive British street artist. Creative Commons founder Lawrence Lessig called it "a form of censorship that restricts creativity and limits access to knowledge."

Author-activist Cory Doctorow suggests the best way to deal with copyright is to ignore it. That's all well and good, until someone starts selling your work without permission.

Andrea Campbell, author of *The Pocket Learner series*, discovered a dodgy website – let's call them *Pilfer Publishing* – had uploaded her book (and many others). They were also uploading around 100 books a day!

Andrea reported the breach to Amazon, citing her UK trademark and US copyright. Eventually, her books were removed. But the other 98 titles? Still up. Amazon has since changed the rules and nobody is allowed to upload more than three books a day. Let that sink in.

Three books a day. Who does that? Let's clear up the copyright basics before we dive into the fun stuff—like building your author presence online.

Copyright Essentials

As soon as it is tangible, your book is automatically copyrighted. However, nailing down your copyright with the American Library of Congress (LOC) is always a good idea for the following reasons.

Five LOC Benefits

1. **Legal protection:** Registering your work with the LOC safeguards your intellectual property. If someone tries to use your work without permission, you can use your registration as evidence in court.

2. **Increased credibility:** Registering your manuscript with the LOC shows you take your work seriously.

3. **Preservation:** The LOC is responsible for archiving cultural works, including books. "By registering your work with the LOC, you ensure the preservation of your work for future generations.

4. **Global protection:** The LOC registration provides international protection for your work.

5. **Access to legal remedies:** If your work is LOC-registered, you may be eligible for statutory fees for copyright infringement.

How to Secure LOC Copyright

Your book must be an original work of authorship fixed in a tangible form, such as a printed copy or an electronic file.

Log in to the Library of Congress https://eservice.eco.loc.gov/
Troubleshooting Log-in Tip: Use incognito mode if you encounter login issues.

Choose a copyright notice." Your book should include a copyright notice with the symbol ©, the year of first publication, and the name of the copyright owner. For example, © 2023 [Your Name].
Fill out Form TX to register a copyright claim online at the Library of Congress.
https://www.copyright.gov
Here, you can find copyright information and submit your PDF manuscript.
Submit the form and fee for online registration, which is currently $65.
Wait for the Library of Congress to process your claim and notify you.

A Standard Copyright Notice

The content contained within this book may not be reproduced, duplicated, or transmitted without the author or publisher's direct written permission.

Legal Notice: This book is copyright-protected and intended only for personal use.

Disclaimer: The information derived from various sources is for educational and entertainment purposes only. No warranties of any kind are declared or implied. By reading this document, the reader agrees that under no circumstances is the author responsible for any direct or indirect losses incurred due to the use of the information contained herein.

AI and Copyright

Navigate the copyright seas of artificial intelligence carefully. With the rise of generative AI, be aware of issues around AI-generated content and copyright ownership. When using AI tools, clarify who owns the resulting content and ensure compliance with platform rules.

Anti-Piracy Strategies

Stay savvy about digital theft. Monitor and combat piracy using:

- Google Alerts for your book titles
- DMCA takedown requests
- Regular searches for unauthorized copies

Global Distribution

Research copyright and publishing requirements in each target country, as laws and practices vary.

4 Essential Author Platforms

An author page builds readership and promotes your work. Write a compelling bio – an often-overlooked opportunity to add important keywords related to your book. Use wit or a few quirky facts to create an irresistible impression and **leave space for your link.**

Your Author Central page page is digital real estate. Does it beckon or bore browsers? Are your A+ visuals compelling? You can showcase your books, post updates, share images, and interact with readers.

Amazon Author Central

Your Amazon author page appears under your book title as a clickable link. Use it to promote your books, run ads, and track sales.
How To Create Yours: Go to **Amazon Author Central** and sign up for an account. https://authorcentral.amazon.com/.
Add your bio, picture, and links. **Encourage** people to follow your page. Ask nicely. **My Amazon Author Page is here:** https://www.amazon.com/stores/author/B08X3LQPZK

Goodreads Author Page

Authors can respond to reviews, post updates, and participate in Q&A sessions.
How To Create Yours: Go to Goodreads and sign up for free. Search for your book on the database, then click the "manually add a book" link at the bottom of the search results page if it isn't there. Fill in the details.
Claim your author profile: Find your name in the search bar and click it. Follow the instructions to claim your author profile.
Add a biography, profile photo, website, and social media links. Keep this information up-to-date.

Facebook Author Page

Facebook (Meta) offers an author page option. You can use videos, images, and live streams to share updates about upcoming projects.

How To Create Yours: Log in to your Facebook account. Click " on the" "Create" button on the top right corner of the page and select "Page." Choose the "Artist, Band, or Public Figure" option. Select "Author" as your category.

Fill in your Page Name, background image, and profile picture. **Add** your bio, website, and relevant information in the About Section. **Include** links to your website, books, and other social media platforms. My author page if you're curious is at Facebook.com/hyggequeen

BookBub Author Page

Authors can create a BookBub Page that displays bios, books, reviews, website links, and social media profiles. How to create yours: Sign up for a BookBub Author account: https://www.bookbub.com/partners/author

Platform Success Tips

1. Keep all pages up-to-date

2. Cross-promote your author pages on other social media platforms

3. Maintain consistent branding across all platforms

Optimizing Your Book's Discoverability

Metadata Matters

Let's start with your metadata — the keywords and categories that determine where your book lives online. Are your keywords still pulling their weight, or have search trends outpaced them? Tools like Publisher Rocket, KDSPY, or even Google's Keyword Planner can help you adjust your aim. Don't go full demolition — tweak one or two keywords at a time and watch what happens.

Categories

Has Amazon shuffled you into the literary equivalent of Siberia? Check with tools like BKLNK.com. If your book's marooned in a dead-end genre or drowned out in a sea of bestsellers, a category switch could do wonders. Contact KDP support if needed. Be strategic: aim for categories where you can shine rather than sink.

Amazon A+ Content

So, a potential reader lands on your book's Amazon page. And? Just a nano-second as they scroll past your book and buy from an author who wields Amazon's A+ Content like a wand. Don't let this be your story. Turn browsers into buyers by working this visually rich, interactive platform. Think of it as a full-color magazine spread that makes readers stop scrolling and linger longer on your page.

6-Step Amazon A+ Blueprint

1: Access Your Command Center:

Log in to your Amazon KDP account and locate your book. Go to the "Marketing" tab or select "Promote and Advertise," then choose "A+ Content Manager."

2: Go Global:

You can now publish A+ Content across multiple Amazon marketplaces simultaneously. Select all relevant regions to expand our reach.

3: Lock and Load Your ASIN:

Search for your book's ASIN. Whether you're creating fresh content or polishing existing material, this is your starting point.

4: Choose Your Modules:

Select up to seven modules that showcase your book's unique strengths for strategic storytelling.

5: Create Content That Converts:

Upload high-resolution images that look stunning on mobile devices (64% of shoppers browse on their phones). Craft concise, engaging text that speaks to your reader's desires. Every word and image should answer one question: "Why should I buy this book right now?"

6: Launch and Conquer:

Preview your creation with a perfectionist's eye. Check formatting and ensure compliance with Amazon's guidelines. Then submit for review. Within seven days, your listing will go live.

A+ Strategies That Work

Mobile-First Mindset:

Design for smartphone users who discover books during commutes and coffee breaks. Use large, clear images and short, punchy text overlays.

Benefits Over Features:

Show readers how your book will change their lives. Will your mystery keep them up all night? Will your guide solve their biggest problem? Use lifestyle images and visual storytelling to paint transformation pictures.

Strategic Cross-Selling:

If you have multiple books, use comparison modules to showcase your entire catalogue. Convert single readers into lifelong fans and collectors.

Brand Consistency:

Consistent colors, fonts, and messaging across all your books create a professional presence that readers recognize and trust. You're building an author empire.

The Update Advantage:

Static content is dead content. Regularly refresh your A+ Content to reflect new reviews, awards, or editions. Each update signals to Amazon's algorithm that your book is active and relevant.

AI-Powered Efficiency:

Amazon's new AI-assisted content generation tools can jump start your creative process. Use them to break through writer's block, but always add your personal touch. Authenticity sells. Automation doesn't.

A+ Landmines to Avoid

1. **The Keyword Trap:** Resist the urge to stuff your content with keywords or promotional language. Amazon's reviewers will reject content that reads like a used car commercial. Focus on value, not volume.

2. **The Blurry Image Blunder:** Pixelated, low-resolution images scream "amateur" louder than any typo. Invest in professional-quality visuals that make readers want to own your book.

3. **The Brand Story Blind Spot:** Many authors skip the brand story section, missing a golden opportunity to build reader trust and connection. Your story is part of your selling proposition. Don't waste it.

4. **The Mobile Formatting Fumble:** If your content looks great on desktop but terrible on mobile, you've alienated more than 60% of your potential audience. Always preview on multiple devices.

A+ Power Moves

- **Global Duplication**: Copy A+ Content across Amazon marketplaces with just a few clicks
- **Accessibility**: Include alt text for images to serve visually impaired users
- **Data-Driven Decisions**: Use Amazon's performance metrics to refine your approach
- **Goal Definition**: Be clear about your objective before designing
- **Visual Storytelling**: Master the art of capturing attention in seconds
- **Consistent Updates**: Set a schedule and stick to it

Resources for Continuous Improvement

Amazon's official KDP Help pages are regularly updated with the latest module options and guidelines. Bookmark them and check frequently.

Amazon A+ Content can turn casual browsers into committed buyers, one compelling visual story at a time. In a marketplace where thousands of books compete for attention every day, A+ Content gives you the edge you need to stand out, connect with readers, and build your successful author career.

- **You'll find some great A+ Content Tips** from Ken/Self-Publishing Secrets on YouTube.

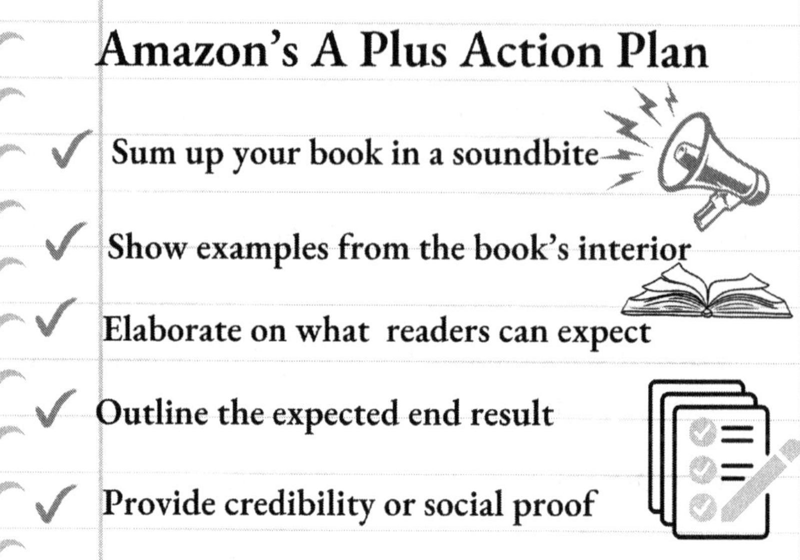
Amazon's A Plus Action Plan
✓ Sum up your book in a soundbite
✓ Show examples from the book's interior
✓ Elaborate on what readers can expect
✓ Outline the expected end result
✓ Provide credibility or social proof

Reviews

The Release and RULE Approach

You get a good review, and it's like crack. You need another hit. And another. And another. I know authors are like Tinkerbell and generally need applause to survive, but it's a slippery slope.
Alexandra Bracken

Nothing beats the ecstasy of a great review. Seeing your prose described as 'delicious poetry' hits like a kiss from your crush. It's a validation vaccine; justifiable dopamine for all those hunched hours tapping the keyboard and mainlining caffeine.

You glug the Spring water compliments; drink in their thirst-quenching relief, swirl the sweet bon mots around your tongue, and elate. Spontaneous reviews from unknown readers are so much more gratifying than the hard-won variety following tantrums at the gate.

"Lunch guests, to be exact."

Pah! Crocodile tears from duplicitous drama queens. What's the big deal? You pressed the remote button and let them in. You're not a total bitch.

"Eventually. And only with proof of purchase and review submissions."

That's an outrageous lie! Who said that?

"No? I heard you plied them with champers, sashimi, soy sauce and pickled ginger, before you struck like a ninja. Twisting their arm up against their backs, you released the pressure only after they agreed to give you a five-star rating and a glowing review! No flies on you ... "

Oh, please! If that were only true! If good reviews were so easy to nail down, you'd be a Shidoshi by now, but you're not.

The Truth About Friends and Family

Let's first dispel the delusion that your friends, family, and former high school crush will want to read your book. They won't. But they *do* care – at least a little – about your achievement, right? Nope! Trust me. They don't.

Oh, they may say, 'Well done,' or 'Way to go, girl,' but will they buy your book? No, they won't. And you can forget about a review, no matter what they promise you.

Even if you offer it to them for free, you'll discover they're about as interested in your literary output as they are in a cup of tepid tea.

"Sorry, I don't download stuff online."

Oh. Okay. Wait. You don't ...?

Stop. Do yourself a favor. Thank them and pull up your big-girl panties. Scatter expectations to the wind.

Most reviews stem from a pique of admiration or fury.

Others will go a step further with a revenge review because they're jealous or hate you for [insert spurious reason here], so they'll try to sabotage you with a one-star rating or two.

Says author, Monica Zwolsman, "The positive feedback some women gave me touched and boosted me after my first book was published, but I was unnerved by the underhanded hating on me behind my back.

"Of course, when writing a memoir, you put yourself out there, and it's a vulnerable place to be. It's hard to write authentically about your experiences and perspectives without treading on sensitive toes and topics.

"When girlfriends (or family) post two-star reviews because they are peeved for personal reasons, it hurts. I can't lie. If someone close to you doesn't like your views, it is their prerogative, but why do they feel the need to announce this to the world in public online?"

Seeking book reviews from friends and family is like walking your cat on a leash – theoretically possible, but count on sharp claws and a *lot* of hissing!

Those One and Two-Star Reviews

Yes, it's rude, but it's best not to brood. Imagine author David White's dismay when the first review he received for his book was a one-star. "At first, I felt crushed. Devastated," he recalls. "But then I put my pride in my pocket, read it again and realized the reviewer was right about grammatical errors and how I needed to be more specific in my assertions.

"I addressed all the points the reviewer disliked about my book and uploaded a revised, improved manuscript. The four and five-star reviews started flowing in again. A less-than-favorable review is a great way to improve your work."

What if there's no feedback and simply a spiteful rating? Nobody takes any notice of those, and neither should you. I've had more than my fair share of two-star reviews, but the Water Queen floats above the opinion of minions, as I wrote in *Flow*.

You're never going to please everybody, and that's just life. Besides, is there anything more humiliating for an introvert than seeking affirmation? Nope. I can't think of a single thing!

Nothing is more cringy than begging for reviews, especially since most authors can attest that friends and family care least about your literary success. Most don't have the bandwidth.

You may as well ask your cat to appreciate your interior decorating skills. So, forget bribery blackmail or spell casting. Wait. That said, it's always worth a try! So, dear reader, if you're enjoying this book, please share the love and rate it here. Dips into a curtsey.

> *"Not everyone's going to love your writing. I often use my poor reviews to advertise my books. One of my favourites is, 'Badly written, uninteresting, nasty attitude towards everything and everyone, except, for some reason, a few of his highly obnoxious colleagues. An altogether unpleasant bunch of people with whom to spend more than five minutes.' I loved that!"*
>
> Karl Wiggins, popular author

The CURATE Review Reality Check

To ensure reviews pass Amazon's eagle-eyed scrutiny, CURATE:

Content – Amazon doesn't allow offensive or inappropriate content. No personal attacks. Keep it classy.

Unbiased – Reviews should fairly assess the book's strengths and weaknesses. Amazon prohibits reviews from friends and family. Even Facebook friends are a no-no.

Relevance – Reviews should relate to the content and potential readers without commentary on the author or unrelated topics. Nobody cares that you went to school with the author's cousin.

Authenticity – Amazon strikes fake, misleading, or paid reviews. They're watching. Always watching.

Troublesome tactics include using promotional language or reviewing your book under another name. Amazon tracks you better than Santa's naughty list, so don't even try!

Eligibility – You need an active Amazon account and a minimum spend of $50 within the past six months to leave a review.

Strong-Arm the Charm

Why won't they buy your book? You've beavered like a caffeinated bee, put it up on pre-order for 99c, published, and posted it for all to see. Perhaps you even gave it away for free. Yet, crickets. You're not alone. Every new author knows this soul-crushing feeling. And cajoling or threatening is never the way to go! So, how do you get genuine, heartfelt reviews?

Ensure Your Book is Worth Reviewing

Edit, proofread, and polish until it gleams. Double-check your title – you'd be amazed how many books have typos in the title, such as bowl instead of bowel!

Grammatical errors in the text are another deal-breaker. With AI grammar tools so available, there's no excuse.

Writing a critique for you is already low on people's priority lists; don't make it even more painful for them.

Many readers have never penned so much as a restaurant review, feel intimidated, and don't know where to start. Here's a trick that often works:

If someone texts you positive feedback, capture their kind words, send them back with a review link, and ask if they'd be kind enough to post it. It's brilliant for anyone who feels daunted at the prospect of writing something from scratch.

Here's the kicker: more reviews matter more than perfect ones.

According to Written Word Media, 25 solid reviews at 4 stars will outsell 5 pristine reviews at 5 stars. So get friendly. Reviews convert clicks to buys faster than ads.

The RULE Approach to Review-Gathering

Once you're confident your book is ready, here's my RULE approach to getting reviews:

Reach out: Ask readers to leave an Amazon review within your book's text, in the back matter, or both. Your email list and social media followers know and (hopefully) like you, so they're more receptive. Offer a free copy using an Amazon Kindle countdown deal in exchange for an honest review.

Use your author and book reviewing platforms: Offer advance reader copies or giveaways on your website or social media to increase visibility. Join Facebook and Goodreads groups. Collaborate with and cross-promote other authors in your genre – a rising tide lift all boats.

Love local: Give copies to your library, newspaper, or radio stations. Look for reviewers in your genre but read their policies first to ensure you're a good fit. Nobody likes being pitched something they don't review.

Engage: Join groups in your genre, participate in discussions, and offer free copies to members in exchange for reviews. Use your email list and write engaging newsletters.

The most crucial element of RULE? Always give more than you get. That's literary karma and it works!

Never Do This!

You want organic reviews - the only ones Amazon accepts - so here's what you must *never* do:

- Don't touch those dodgy DMers that spam your message queue with unsolicited "Hi, love your work. Can I review your book for you?" The answer you seek is: "I doubt that."

- Amazon has strict rules against buying reviews. Its AI can easily outsmart anyone trying to cheat the system.

- Kirkus Reviews and Publishers Weekly provide professional reviews for a fee, which covers the time spent reviewing the book, not an assurance of a positive appraisal. All are subject to Amazon's strict review policies.

- Paying a monthly or annual subscription fee to join communities like Book Bounty or Get Authentic Book Reviews is a great way to garner Amazon-approved reviews. The catch? You need to do a lot of reading and reviewing too, but if you enjoy discovering new authors, you'll learn a lot.

> *"For the most part the family never really understands the artist, be it musician, painter, photographer, designer or writer. I guess this is why writers often reach out to peer-groups, like-minded people who do understand the search for a plot, the appeal for assistance over certain grammatical conundrums, the sharing of advice on marketing and so on."*
>
> Karl Wiggins, author

11 Book Review Platforms for Authors

To align with Amazon's stringent review standards, these curated sites encourage honest and detailed reviews, prohibiting paid reviews or incentives beyond a free or discounted book. No direct swaps or reciprocal reviews are allowed, and there are limits on review frequency to avoid spam flags.

1. **Goodreads**
   Overview: The largest Amazon-owned online community for book lovers.
   Pros: Massive audience and active community. Free to use. Authors can interact directly with readers. Reviews are often syndicated to Amazon.
   Cons: Review visibility can be lost in the volume. BookReads doesn't let authors update their covers, which is annoying.

2. **Booksprout**
   Overview: Distributes ARCs to its reviewer network, who are encouraged to post reviews on Amazon and other platforms.
   Pros: Free and paid plans are available. Automated reminders to reviewers. Authors can track review progress. Wide distribution across major retailers.
   Cons: Some reviewers may not follow through. Limited free plan features. Occasional issues with piracy.

3. **Reedsy Discovery**
   Overview: Connects indie authors to vetted reviewers who may review and upvote books, increasing discoverability.
   Pros: Exposure to a curated audience. Reviews are unpaid, supporting Amazon's compliance. Community upvotes can boost book visibility.
   Cons: No guarantees. Reviews are on Reedsy Discovery, and not always on Amazon. Limited to new releases and select genres.

4. **NetGalley**
   Overview: Distribute ARCs to librarians, and booksellers.
   Pros: Professional and credible reviews for indie and traditional authors.
   Cons: Expensive for individual authors. No guarantee of Amazon reviews. Some reviewers only post on NetGalley.

5. **LibraryThing**
   Overview: Social site with a strong community and author tools.
   Pros: Free to use. Author pages and community engagement. Reviews can be detailed and thoughtful.
   Cons: Smaller audience than Goodreads. Reviews not always posted to Amazon

6. **Reader Views**
   Overview: Custom review service with a focus on indie authors.
   Pros: Personalized and detailed reviews.
   Cons: Paid service. Reviews may not always be posted to Amazon.

7. **Authentic Book Reviews**
   Overview: Service focused on Amazon-compliant reviews. Membership is under $10 a month.
   Pros: Emphasizes compliance with Amazon's guidelines. Reviews are authentic and unbiased.
   Cons: Volume and speed of reviews can vary.

8. **BookRoar**
   BookRoar operates on a credit-based system: authors earn credits by reviewing books. Reviews are posted on Amazon and Goodreads. The system is structured to avoid direct review swaps.
   Pros: Free to use, although a paid service is available.
   Cons: While BookRoar aims for compliance, some experts warn

that Amazon could still interpret the system as "review manipulation," since it's a structured review exchange.

9. **Goodnightreads**
   Designed specifically for kidlit creators Goodnightreads is for children's authors to swap stories and reviews. Review other books to earn credits, then spend them to receive Amazon reviews.
   Pros: Tailored for children's books and their unique challenges. GNR offers opportunities to connect with editors, illustrators, and service providers.
   Cons: While it states reviews must comply, Goodnightreads uses a model (credit-based review exchange) that could violate Amazon rules if it results in direct swaps.

10. **Book Bounty**
    A dynamic review platform connecting authors with avid readers across multiple genres.
    Pros: Offers verified reader feedback, fast turnaround, and options for Amazon or Goodreads posting.
    Cons: Paid tiers vary in visibility and depth; limited organic reach outside its own network.

11. **Revvue**
    Revvue, a community-driven platform for authors, avid readers, Booktokers, and Bookstagrammers, features free-book filters and influencer dashboards. Their Occasional Reader Plan is free. A paid service is also available. Reviews appear on Amazon and Goodreads.
    Pros: Demographic stats. Earn review credits (coins) through reading and referrals. Possible access to social media influencers.
    Cons: Still relatively new, so reviewer base is growing.
    Pro Tip: Want a head start? Use my affiliate link for review rewards. https://revvue.co/?ref=B08X3LQPZK

Amazon's Review Request Tool

It's free, effective, legitimate and sitting right there in your Seller Central dashboard waiting for you to use it. Amazon's "Request a Review" tool is your competitive advantage and one of the most effective ways to grow your reviews without breaking any rules.

Authors report an increase in quantity and quality, leading to better visibility and (hopefully) more sales. Who care that you can't customize the message? Amazon's version converts better than anything you'd write. Yes, it involves a manual click per order, but here's why it's worth the few seconds of effort:

- **100% Rule-Proof**
  Since Amazon controls the entire process, you'll never accidentally violate their strict review policies. No more walking on eggshells, wondering if you're doing something wrong!

- **Higher Success Rates**
  These aren't generic emails that get lost in spam folders. Amazon sends these requests directly through their system, making them much more likely to be seen and acted upon.

- **Speaks Every Language**
  Your international readers will receive the request in their preferred language automatically. How cool is that?

- **Simple Process**
  One click per order, and you're done. No complicated setups, no monthly fees, no headaches.

- **Professional Presentation**
  The email includes your book's cover image and clickable star ratings, making it easy for readers to leave reviews.

Ready to transform your review game?

1. Log in to your Amazon Seller Central account (the same place you manage your book listings).

2. Click on "Orders" then "Manage Orders"

3. Look for orders delivered 5-30 days ago. (Amazon's sweet spot for review requests!)

4. Click on the order number, then click the "Request a Review" button. Confirm. You're done! Amazon automatically sends a professional, non-pushy email to your reader. No follow-up needed, no stress involved. So what are you waiting for? Those reviews aren't going to request themselves!

Pro-Tip: Make clicking those "Request a Review" buttons part of your weekly routine and watch your review numbers grow.

The Power of Feedback

Like a succulent slow roast, reviews take time. Accept that some reviewers will neither get back to you nor write a word about your book. It happens. Cut your losses. Move on – nobody likes a nag. When reviews trickle in, wear your most gracious hat. Thank them for their time, even when their words aren't as sweet as you might have liked.

Building Your Review Community

Research is essential for generating more reviews. Use keywords and SEO to optimize your website or blog, making it easier for people to discover your work organically.

Reciprocate for more reach. It takes time to establish a sense of connectivity, but the more you give others the recognition you crave by liking their blogs, commenting meaningfully on their posts, and sharing their content, the faster good things happen. The feeling of a satisfying literary friendship can leave you walking on air even more than making a sale.

Community-building tactics:

- Feature other authors on your blog
- Review other people's books genuinely and thoughtfully
- Share social media posts celebrating fellow authors
- Create quarterly "best new releases" posts in your genre
- Host giveaways or offer discount codes to incentivize reviews

With patient charm and consistent effort, you can build a strong community of readers willing to share their love of your work with others.

Tip: Create Your Amazon Review Link

Copy and paste this link format and add your ASIN to the end:
Amazon.com/review/create-review?&asin=[YOUR_ASIN]

Review Hygge

Give what you want to receive. Share social media posts featuring other authors or promote new releases in your genre to nurture a sense of collaboration and camaraderie. Take any constructive criticism with a pinch of salt and season your next literary masterpiece with it. Sometimes the harshest feedback teaches us the most.

Test

Keywords and Categories

> *A keyword is a beacon shining from the lighthouse guiding ships away from rocky terrain and onto safer shores."*
> Dale L Roberts, Self Publishing With Dale author/podcaster

LIKE A SECRET CODE that tells search engines what your book is about, your keywords and categories unlock the doors of visibility for your work. Without them, your words lie undiscovered, a treasure buried deep in the sands of an unknown island. So, choose wisely.

The author-artist Andrea Campbell saw her coloring book, *Inspirational Coloring Book for Teenage Boys With Original Motivational Quotes*, take off after she fished it out of Amazon Kindle's crowded Children's Crafts & Hobbies category and repositioned it in Teen & Young Adult Nonfiction on Depression & Mental Health.

This classification migration propelled her book from the murky depths into the limelight.

Her stress-relieving designs and motivational quotes now resonate with hundreds more readers thanks to the simple switch.

Strategic navigation is essential when choosing categories to maximize discoverability and relevance.

People who browse books online usually search in specific genres. Without the correct categories, a book may not appear in relevant search results or be recommended to readers interested in similar topics.

Amazon allows you to pick three based on your primary marketplace.

Escalate Your Published Presence

6 Tips to Elevate Your Book's Visibility

1. Align each category with the essence of your content. Focus on a select few to captivate the right audience.

2. Keep fiction and non-fiction categories separate: Mixing them can muddle potential readers.

3. Hone in on a carefully curated selection: Discoverability thrives on simplicity.

4. Select the best subcategories. Amplify the likelihood of your book shining within specific niches.

5. Align Keywords with your selected categories: Strengthen the connection between your book and what potential readers are searching for.

6. Exercise Patience: Allow the system ample time to assign your book to the most appropriate categories. Changing them too often can negatively impact your sales rank and algorithmic relevance.

Reaching bookish stardom requires a dash of artistry, showmanship, online swagger, and content mastery. Spruce your virtual abode.

> *"Categorization is the key to discoverability. If readers can't find your book, they can't buy it."*
>
> Mark Coker, founder of Smashwords

Update Your Categories on Amazon KDP

Follow these 10 steps.

1. Visit the "Edit Book Details" section.
2. On the "Details" tab, specify if text contains adult-only content.
3. Double-check and ensure your primary marketplace is correct.
4. Proceed to the "Categories" section and select "Edit Categories."
5. Remove any previously selected categories, if necessary.
6. Carefully choose your book's most appropriate category, subcategory, and placement.
7. Save the selected categories and repeat the process twice if needed.
8. Scroll down, click "Save and Continue," and proceed to the next steps of the publishing process.
9. If there are no changes to the cover or interior, skip the related actions.
10. Review the pricing details, make any necessary adjustments, and click "Save and Publish" to finalize the changes.

7 Category Types

Genre-based

Your genre sets expectations for the reader. Here are five steps.

1. **Consider the plot**. Does it involve a crime or a mystery? Is it a true story?

2. **Examine the themes.** Your book's underlying messages can help you narrow down the genre. It could be a legal thriller, crime fiction, or creative non-fiction if it explores themes of justice and morality.

3. **Analyze the writing style.** Fast-paced and action-packed may indicate a thriller or adventure genre, while slower-paced and descriptive might point to historical fiction.

4. **Research similar books.** Read the blurbs and reviews of books in the same category to understand those genre expectations and see if yours fits.

5. **Use relevant keywords** and associated categories once you've identified your genres. For example, if your book is a romance novel, use keywords like "love story," "romantic fiction," and categories like "romance" or "contemporary romance." You can use Amazon's search bar to test your chosen keywords' relevance.

Audience-based

- Use social media platforms like X, Facebook, and Instagram to learn more about potential reader interests and demographics, like age, gender, education level, and income.

- Consider the hashtags your target audience uses when discussing books in your genre. For example, "coming of age," "teen romance," and categories like "young adult fiction" or "teen and young adult romance" will appeal to young adult readers.

Setting-based

- Use keywords and associated categories identified with your book's setting. For example, if your book is set in a small town, try keywords like "small town life," "rural romance," and categories like "small town fiction" or "rural romance fiction."

- Google to see if there is a high search volume for your chosen keywords.

Themes-based

- Use keywords and associated categories identified with your themes. If your book deals with love, loss, and redemption, use keywords like "heartbreak," "second chances," and categories like "romantic tragedy" or "redemptive fiction."

- You can use Google AdWords Keyword Planner to see if there is a high search volume for the keywords you're considering.

Tone-based

- Reflect on your book's tone. If your book has a humorous style, use keywords like "comedy," "humorous fiction," and categories like "humor and satire" or "comedy romance."

- Look on Goodreads to see if any books similar to yours use the keywords you're considering.

Comparative-based

Identify books similar to yours and use keywords and categories associated with them. You can use Amazon's "Customers who bought this also bought" section to see what other books interest readers of your title.

Multi-faceted

Combine the above frameworks and use the Google Search Console to see which queries lead readers to your book's website or sales. The key is to be flexible and willing to adjust your approach if necessary.

Tweak your keywords and categories as needed.

7 Ways to Unlock Powerful Keywords

1. Start with your **title, topic, and themes**: Use these as a basis for keyword research and integrate them into your book's metadata (title, subtitle, description, and Amazon keywords) is essential for discoverability

2. Research your competition: **Look at similar books** and see what keywords they use to understand what you can adapt.

3. Use long-tail keywords: These **phrases tend to have less competition,** making them more effective in reaching your target audience.

4. Consider **seasonal keywords**: Something that worked for me was using Valentine's Day as a keyword to sell *Flow 21 Secrets to Refresh Your Relationships.*

5. Think about the **reader's perspective**: Put yourself in the shoes of your target audience. What terms might they use to search for books like yours?

6. Use **synonyms:** Related terms broaden your reachFor example, if your book is about diet, you could use keywords like "nutrition," "healthy eating," and "weight loss."

7. Use keyword research tools : My favorite keyword-identifying tool is **Publisher Rocket.** It's not free, but it's brilliant. like **Google Keyword Planner**, **Publisher Rocket**, or **Ubersuggest** to test combinations of keywords and phrases for your title and subtitle. These tools help you identify high-search, low-competition terms that align with your genre and audience. You can also use **social media polls**, **Instagram stories**, or **surveys** to test title and subtitle options with your audience and see which resonates most.

Keyword Updates

1. Amazon's New Keyword Rules

- Avoid using keywords already present in your category string. For example, if your book is in "Action & Adventure," don't use those words as keywords.
- Do not use brand names you don't own in your keywords.
- No HTML code is allowed in keyword fields. This is enforced.
- Check Amazon's current guidelines as rules can change annually.

2. Broaden Your Keyword Types

Amazon recommends a mix of five keyword types for best results:

- General (broad terms, e.g., "bestselling eBooks")
- Competitive (titles/ASINs of similar books)
- Niche genres (specific subgenres or tropes)
- Author/publisher (famous authors or imprints in your genre)
- Title-specific (unique themes, character names, or settings).

3. Leverage AI and Machine Learning

- AI tools can analyze reader trends, enabling you to discover emerging keywords and personalize your marketing efforts.
- Utilize AI-powered keyword clustering and ideation tools to uncover previously untapped keyword opportunities.

4. Expand Your Keyword Research Toolbox

Tools like Ahrefs, Semrush, QuestionDB, and Keyworddit can supplement Publisher Rocket and Google Keyword Planner, offering deeper insights and new angles.

Use Amazon's "also bought" suggestions for real-time keyword ideas.

5. Data-Driven

Start with a large set of keywords (Amazon recommends at least 100 for ads) and refine based on performance data. Drop under performers, double down on winners.

Regularly update your keywords to reflect new trends, tropes, and reader interests, especially as genres evolve rapidly.

6. Compliance and Avoiding Pitfalls

Avoid keyword stuffing, irrelevant terms, or using misleading keywords. Amazon penalizes these practices.

Always check that your chosen keywords comply with current Amazon KDP rules and do not include restricted words or phrases.

7. Audience Testing and Feedback

Continue using social media polls, beta reader feedback, and genre-specific forums to test and refine your keywords, titles, and descriptions.

Checklist

- **Research** keywords based on title, topic, themes, and reader intent.
- **Analyze** the top-performing keywords in your genre using Publisher Rocket and other advanced tools.
- **Include** a mix of general, competitive, niche, author, and title-specific keywords.
- **Use AI tools** for keyword ideation, clustering, and trend analysis.
- **Validate** keywords with Amazon autocomplete, "also bought" suggestions, and real-time data.
- **Test and update** your keywords regularly based on performance analytics.
- **Ensure** all keywords comply with Amazon's latest rules and avoid restricted or redundant terms.
- **Use audience feedback** and social media to test your metadata and keyword choices.

Hack

The Art of Media Whispering

"The goal of a press release is not to get your name in the paper, but to provide journalists with the information they need to write a story about you."

Sally Falkow, founder of Meritus Media

Are you tired of losing your message in the shuffle of an editor's inbox? Beat it by establishing a topical, irresistible treat! Here's the thing. Journalists are a capricious bunch. Survival in the competitive, cut-throat media world is tough.

A tsunami of press releases bombards their inboxes daily, so yours needs to stand out. Being on point is essential. What do editors and journalists want? Something newsworthy, for starters. Rags-to-riches stories or unexpected life changes can work well.

We appreciate PR professionals who research, respect our time, and provide relevant information. Having toiled in the salt mines of mainstream media for decades, I've received more clunkers than a junk mail folder.

I'm talking about those "no-go-nauts" that make editors hit the delete button faster than an I-know-the-answer contestant on *Who Wants To Be A Millionaire!*

I've seen everything from high-visibility vest invitations to photographic frustrations. The RUIN approach – Repetitive, Unsolicited, Irrelevant News – seldom facilitates the space you seek.

Below are some real-life examples of common tactics with a brief italicized explanation of why they annoy.

Don't Spray and Pray

Mass emailing hundreds of journalists at once is never a good idea. Neither are these opening lines.

Dear literary/travel/media contact/editor, hi, or hey,
*Not addressed to me. Not my concern. *Delete without reading!**

Dear Cardine Hussy,
Um, it's Caroline Hurry, but whatever.

"I hope you are well."
Miss me with your infuriating false bonhomie like you give a fandango about my health. You don't even know my name.

Don't Assert Your Needs

We would need you to ...
You act like your needs interest me. Newsflash! They don't.

Please read the attached press release and be so kind as to send us a copy of your article, visual, or sound recording when it's aired or published.

Thank you in advance for your cooperation.
*Presumptuous much? How's that working out for you? *Delete**

Don't Extend Late Invitations

Editors have a full schedule. Unless they're first-class air tickets to the city you've always wanted to see, last-minute high-visibility vest invitations are invariably as tempting as a fashion show featuring the latest hospital gowns.

"Space has made itself available at tomorrow's hot air balloon launch to view our city's extensive warren of parking garages from above."
Somebody bailed out of the basket. Call me high-maintenance, but I'm not your afterthought. Puncture that!"

Don't Dress Puffy Marketing Fluff as News

Learn to understand the difference between a story and an advertisement. Changing an item on your lunch menu is newsworthy only if you're serving something exotic like crocodile belly or GM-free salmon.

If you start your release with "Exciting news from ...", ensure it *is* exciting. Also, unless this is a honeymoon familiarization trip to Seychelles, less is always more regarding instructions.

Don't Issue Instructions

"We suggest you interview Captain Incognito before publishing your article to grasp why he prefers not to reveal his true identity.
What about this: You stick to your mission. I'll stick to mine!

"Be at The Underdog restaurant this Friday at 8 pm sharp
(This Friday evening? Sharp? Oh, my ribs!) "– to hear Captain Incognito read extracts from his book *Two Sides*. Find signed copies for sale at the event. Use the following unembargoed print extract in your publication."
Gee, thanks!

"In the wise words of Captain Incognito, "There are always two sides.
Nope. A quadrangle has four.

"From any given point of view, there is the sable and the unseeable. *Does he mean the sable antelope, or has he misspelled seeable?* Just because the light at the end of the climate change tunnel is not seeable doesn't mean it's not there. *Waffle Quotient reached! Delete! Delete!*

Don't Send Irrelevant Unsolicited Pitches

Forget about placement if you don't find the most appropriate media outlet for your releases.

Don't Solicit Guarantees

"Thanks for accepting our invitation to introduce the esteemed Inn Sider's Pick to the broader discerning public. My client wants to know how you intend to write the review. What angle and tone will you take?
Aside from the oxymoronic 'broader discerning public,' how should I know when I've not seen the ISP? Remote viewing? Drone espionage?

"My client has been talking to your publication's advertising manager.
And? We don't share a duvet if that's what you're implying.

"He'd like to see our supplied images in the national supplement's center-spread."
That's sweet. I'd like a million rave reviews, too.

"Kindly fill in, sign, and return the required forms."
Sigh. Freelance journalists submit articles to commissioning editors. A response takes anything from 24 hours to never. If one door closes, they rap another media knocker. Their promise is as valid as a post-dated cheque from L. Ron Hubbard.

Don't Call To Ask When It's Going In

Don't. If you must pester a journalist, email them under the pretext of seeing if they need additional information. Get over it if there's still no response. Pieces get rejected all the time. It's nothing personal. Grow a thick skin and pitch at another publication.

Don't Express Disappointment

Worse than failing to thank a journalist or influencer for the publicity you received is telling them your client was disappointed.

"We note your contribution to the *Read and Weep Gazette*. My client is disappointed with your spin on the narrative we supplied concerning his philanthropy. He expected a more positive tone."
You're welcome. I'll be sure to file his grievances in my newly ploughed field of focaccia wheat.

Photographic Frustrations

Context-free images are the bane of a journalist's life. And don't make us jump through hoops, either. "Download our image bank by requesting a password that changes every time you log in for your protection. It will take a few gigabits of your storage space."
That's not going to happen.

"I have attached a few images for use in your article."
If a picture paints 1000 words, why were yours struck dumb? Who do you expect to write your captions? Me? *Fine, but don't blame me if they're wrong!*

"Thanks for running the piece, but please, can you correct a mistake in the caption?"
No.

How to Woo the Media

Thanks to social media, networking and cultivating a huddle of journalists has never been easier. Like any seduction, the more foreplay – charm, flattery, and persistence, you can put in, the greater your chances of success, so start the process early and approach from an indirect angle.

Being well-versed in their output helps you build a relationship, as journalists never tire of discussing the importance of their work. *Nothing* interests them more. The best media spadework is always intellectual with sycophantic leanings, so lay the praise thick. You might think you're over-egging the custard. You're not.

Every journalist alive drinks in favorable feedback like a thirsty flower soaking up soft rain. That said, be judicious. Avoid generic compliments like "I love your work" and reference a specific column, editorial, or feature. "So thought-provoking, and I especially liked what you said about women's rights."

> *"Hats off to the Pee Aar who goes the extra mile, but going three rounds of email, WhatsApp, AND follow-up calls don't serve to remind, but to elevate your name to 'most annoying person ever.' Several more rounds of the same thing, for different events morph into this less-than-charitable thought: 'Her insecure tyrant of a boss has given her an attendance quota, poor thing. I'm not going to be the one who makes up 10.'*
>
> Helen Grange, freelance journalist

7 Tips To Get Noticed

1. **Target carefully**: One size does not fit all when pitching. Familiarize yourself with the publication's website. Read back issues to determine what they cover. If you're promoting a memoir, the angle could be a unique aspect of your life story that readers can relate to or find inspiring. And find out the editor's name.

2. **Grab attention**: Does your headline convey the essence of your piece? "Author writes a new memoir.' Dull. "Author Chronicles Her Journey From Lockdown to Sovereignty" is better.

3. **Use a solid angle**: Local publications often publish articles on personalities. Positioning yourself as an underdog or an upstart competing with multinationals might be newsworthy. Is your story entertaining? Is there a benefit to the community?

4. **Punch up your introduction:** Outline the relevance of your release in one brief, straight-to-the-point paragraph.

5. **Say it with stats:** Organize a study that produces newsworthy results. Relate your story to recent news. Example: "Research shows 85% of women suffer from low self-esteem. Documenting my struggles was a way of reaching out to others in the same boat."

6. **Keep it brief:** Around 300 words is fine. Avoid unnecessary fluff.

7. **Explain who you are:** Below the release, have you explained who you are to the editor? Remember to include up-to-date contact details – email, website address, or phone number. Include your business logo, if you have one, in the top right-hand corner of the page.

6 Media Matchmaking Ideas

1. **Create a media list.** Maintain a database of contacts - journalists who write about what you want to pitch. Use online newspapers that have emails of staff. Remember, all available media outlets – online blogs, websites, and email newsletters can be as good as national papers or consumer magazines. You need to ensure you send your press releases to the right person.

2. **Set up Google alerts.** You can use keywords to help you build information. To set up a Google alert, go to https://www.google.com/alerts. Enter the search query, such as your keywords or journalist names. Select the result type, frequency, and delivery method, then click "Create Alert."

3. **Research their work on social media.** Retweet their articles with salient comments or responses underpinning their ideas. Build a rapport based on mutual respect and intellectual curiosity. Be genuine and authentic. If you're using the journalist for their platform, they'll see through your approach in a trice.

4. **Keep your channels current.** A journalist will Google and check out your social media, such as LinkedIn or X. If your profiles are not current, fix them. Set up your press kit on your website or author page with audio and video links. Include press clippings of publications and articles already published.

5. **Give them something exclusive.** For example, you can offer an advance copy of your book or an interview with you.

6. **Insider tip:** Start your note to the journalist with: "I'm not sure if this is your bag, but ..." to whet their appetite and lift any pressure.

- Download Your Press Release Worksheet here:

Earth Hygge

Create, Ground, Cultivate and Grow

Earth grounds your dreams into reality with purpose, stability and order. Like Earth, writing and publishing require roots, structure, and patience.

You must plant before you can expect flowers.

You need a solid foundation, clear structure, and strong bones.

It's not enough to throw seeds and hope for the best. You have to tend and cultivate.

Writing, too, is honed through revision. care, consistency, and a willingness to shape your work into something enduring.

The Earth moves in cycles: planting, growing, harvesting, resting. So does writing and publishing - follow the seasons!

Earth grounds us by pulling us into the moment. Root yourself in your project and build something lasting. Something real.

Something that grows with steady progress.

Your Earth Ritual

Ground your story in intention and give your ideas a sacred space to germinate.

You need: A patch of soil (garden, pot plant, or a quiet park.) An affirmation written on a piece of paper about your book plans and a stone.

Steps: Place your bare feet firmly on the earth. Close your eyes and breathe deeply.

Plant intention. Why are you writing this book? Anchor your message in meaning. Bury the affirmation paper in the soil with the stone on top.

Your Next 3 Moves

1. **Register Your Roots:**
   Copyright your book with the Library of Congress. Additionally, set up your Amazon Author Central and Goodreads profiles, and utilize Amazon's A+ Content Manager for enhanced visibility.

2. **Plant Seeds and Work the Soil**
   Outline your chapters like garden beds - connected, and thematic. Your Table of Contents (TOC) is your creative landscape plan. Use tools like Keywords Everywhere and PublisherRocket to find the right categories and keywords. Tend to your author platform. Create visual content with Canva, post teasers, and join genre-based communities. Begin to nurture your visibility.

3. **Gather and Grow**
   Ask for feedback. Get genuine reviews. Feature others. Collaboration is compost for creative longevity.

Earth Hygge Hints

- **Connect to Local Soil:** Reach out to local libraries, radio shows, or newspapers.
- **Root Your Online Presence:** Use free tools like Canva, Unsplash, and Freepik to refresh your author branding. Create visual teasers of your work-in-progress. Reflect your genre and voice.
- **Sit With the Earth**: When nobody else understand your writing path, sit in silence outside. Let nature be your witness and your quiet encouragement.
- **Vary the Terrain:** Don't limit your literary harvest to a single plot of land. Expand. Explore Kobo, IngramSpark, Draft2Digital,Google Play, and Lulu. Many platforms, such as IngramSpark, offer wide-reaching global distribution, including to libraries.

When promoting your work, use the HACK approach:

- **H**ook: Craft a subject line so irresistible even jaded editors have to open it.
- **A**ddress: Tie your pitch to something timely or topical.
- **C**ultivate: Comment meaningfully on journalists' work. Build trust.
- **K**ey: Pitch strategically with exclusive content and warmth.

Remember: You are solid, reliable, and layered. Your brand is your bedrock. Your writing is soil. Your stories are seeds.

Let your roots go deep. Trust in the Earth, growth, and evolution. Diversify, adapt, and align your publishing path with your long-term vision.

Date: ______________

PRESS RELEASE WORKSHEET

1. **HEADLINE:**

2. **LURE:** *First Paragraph or Intro*

3. **BOOK HOOK:** *What makes your book unique?*

4. **TARGET OUTLET:**
   Who are their readers?

5. **KEY QUOTE:** *From Author:*
   From Expert:

6. **STATS/RESEARCH LINKS:** *(if any)*

7. **CTA OR OFFER:** *(if any)*

CONTACT INFO: *Website: (Add a link to your media kit or press images folder)*
Email:
Phone:

WORD COUNT CHECK: ☑ < 400 words?

FIVE

Metal Section

Broadcast Your Golden Prana

METAL SIGNIFIES POWER, DRIVE, dependability, and expansion.

- **Market:** With resilience and precision, pursue your passion, expect roadblocks, solve them, and then turn those experiences into content that delivers clarity and strength.
- **Engage:** Utilize newsletters to foster authentic and credible relationships with your readers. When you bring truth, humor, or heartfelt insight, you open doors to a sense of community.
- **Tackle:** Turbocharge the social media platform that best aligns with your brand, amplify your reach, deepen your impact, and reflect your unique voice.
- **AI:** Like a smart, efficient personal assistant, AI can automate mundane tasks, streamline your work, and free you up to be more creative. Be open about how you use it.
- **Launch:** Begin in advance. Success loves preparation, so the sooner you lay the foundations, the sooner you'll build momentum.

"Strength through adversity. The strongest steel is forged by the fires of hell. It is pounded and struck repeatedly before it's plunged back into the molten fire. The fire gives it power and flexibility, and the blows give it strength. Those two things make the metal pliable and able to withstand every battle it's called upon to fight."

Sherrilyn Kenyon, Devil May Cry

Market

Share: The DIY Route to Book Buzz

> *"Marketing my books requires consistency, effort, and creativity. Reaching new readers is a constant uphill hike. It can be exhausting to find what works and what doesn't. You must adapt when certain strategies become less effective."*
>
> D.G. Torrens, Poet and Author of 25 books

A great story is not enough to ensure success. Without marketing, you may as well toss a bottled message into the ocean. An unpromoted book sinks below competing title waves.

All writers *must* learn to market. Yup, that came as a surprise to me, too.

Dispel notions of support from friends and family. If you get some, count your blessings but whether you're independently or traditionally published, the onus is still on you to market.

Yes, yes. Seeing your irrelevancy in friends' lives can feel mortifying, but if you're trying to impress somebody, bake them a cake or bolster their self-worth. I don't know. Don't use your writing, though.

Foundation Strategies

The Power of Free:

Not to boast, but my last three books, *Medusa's Musings, Worm Wrangling* and *The Rooster Diaries* hit the Number 1 slot in their categories and #touchwood continue to sell.

The secret? I gave them away free for between one and five days using an Amazon Kindle free promo. Bingo! This strategy works because:

- Free books attract downloads and reviews
- More downloads boost visibility in Amazon's algorithm
- Free periods create urgency and buzz
- Readers who discover you often buy your other books

Disclaimer: You have to write something people want to read. While some authors swear by it, I've not had good results spending $55+ on book promotion services. The DIY wheeze so far, has served me better.

Short Reads: Big Marketing Opportunities

Amazon short reads – books that take between 15 minutes and two hours to read – are perfect for:

- Half-finished short stories collecting dust in your drawer
- Research notes from your main book
- Companion pieces to your full-length works
- Niche content that serves your target audience

Technical requirements:

- eBooks can be as short as one page
- Paperbacks need a minimum of 24 pages

Think of short reads as the "appetizer" of your main course. If you write about families starting new lives in foreign countries, you could publish their traditional recipes as a short read. Think of it as the book version of a "side chick."

I wrote *Worm Wrangling* (36 pages) as a spinoff from *The Rooster Diaries,* introducing it in one of my newsletters, where I share the odd snippets from my homesteading life: raising chickens, composting, and learning to live a little closer to the land.

I described how watching a mother hen teach her chick how to forage all day before folding him into the warmth of her wings for the night soothed and grounded me. As did producing compost from my kitchen scraps.

"Want to make some, too? Grab a free copy before it wriggles away. Please rate ***Worm Wrangling*** if you liked it because one good turn (of the compost) deserves another." I know. Groan. It got a great response, though.

The Authenticity Advantage

Authenticity vibrates at a higher emotional frequency than manufactured content. People connect with real stories, genuine struggles, and honest victories. Share your writing journey, including the messy parts. Being true to yourself can become your most powerful marketing tool.

Build Your Community Empire

Newsletter Marketing: Your Secret Sales Engine

Writing newsletters significantly helps with my book sales. I also love how it makes me feel connected to my readers. Here's what works:

- Create punchy posts with depth. Turn complex concepts into digestible soundbites, but don't sacrifice substance. People love content that teaches them something valuable in a few sentences.

- Use the "overdeliver" strategy. Pack so much value into a single tweet or post that people want to learn more from you. This earns new subscribers naturally.

- Let AI help with the heavy lifting. Use chatbots to help brainstorm ideas, refine your message, or overcome writer's block. They're tools, not replacements for your unique voice.

Facebook Groups: Your Literary Tribe

Facebook groups foster community, interaction, communication and engagement. Group members can start conversations, share content, collaborate, and answer questions. My women-only group has been my saving grace. We make each other laugh. Here's why groups work better than pages:

- Target specific audiences interested in your work

- Allow you to moderate content and maintain quality

- Create a sense of exclusive community

- **See Appendix Marketing** for how to set up a FB Group

Recommended Facebook Groups

- Authors Seeking Readers Self-Promotion Group
  Administrators Sarah Jacobson and Josephine Huet provide a nurturing private space for fellow authors to chat about new projects and promote their work. Bilingual Josephine has written 11 novels, five in French, while Sarah has seven to her name, including her popular Liberty Falls series. Scammers and chancers are not tolerated.
  https://www.facebook.com/groups/1277194782848877

- Best Book Editors, Authors, Readers, Others Welcome,
  The best-selling author Katherine Black and her team run a tight ship within an inclusive welcoming environment that encourages members to share interesting book-related posts. Spam and irrelevant links are never allowed. Self-promotion is permitted on weekends only. Authors can use Sooz Simpson's BBE bookshop strategies to showcase their books.
  https://www.facebook.com/groups/625104781821119

- Mavericks of Creativity
  Group Admin Stuart Miller and his team including authors Ryan Hale and Stevie Hostetter,. encourage creators to share past, current, or future projects. "If you're looking for friends, to make connections, network, get support, self-promote, and have the freedom to post what you want, when you want, then this is the group for you!"

- Guerilla Publishing: Book Marketing Support and Feedback for Authors
  Run by Derek Murphy and Creativindie. You can ask for feedback on your covers or blurbs on the Feedback Friday thread.
  https://www.facebook.com/groups/guerrillapublishing

10 Networking Strategies for Introverts

Here's how to network effectively from behind the scenes:

1. Use online communities like Reddit, Discord, or genre-specific forums.

2. Offer valuable excerpts or free content to establish credibility.

3. Leverage marketing services like BookBub or Reedsy Discovery for extended reach.

4. Attend virtual events and online conferences to meet peers.

5. Create enticing promotions, trailers, and limited-time discounts.

6. Write guest posts or articles for blogs and magazines in your genre. This builds authority and draws new readers without requiring live interaction.

7. Create an Email Newsletter: A well-crafted news letter allows for personal, direct communication with readers . Segment your audience and send targeted content for better engagement. Read more about newsletters in the Engage chapter.

8. Reach out to book clubs or participate in small group discussions, either virtually or in person. These settings allow for deeper connections without the overwhelm of large events.

9. Collaborate with other authors or enlist extroverted friends to help with promotion.

10. Podcast and Radio Interviews: Consider audio interviews, which can feel less intimidating than video or live events and still reach a broad audience.

Persuasive Communication Trends

Take your book from meh to must-have with priming, a stimulus-response phenomenon. For example, if you see the word "nurse," you might recognize a word like "clinic" faster than an unrelated word like "car."

4 Priming Power Techniques

1. **Genre-specific imagery**
   Use images relevant to your book's genre to prime your audience such as pictures of yoga poses to promote a book about wellness, office buildings, growth charts, or successful entrepreneurs for business or finance. Intimate settings, couples, flowers for romance. Dark imagery, shadows, mysterious figures for thrillers.

2. **Compelling Taglines and Blurbs**
   Prime readers for your book's value: Highlight your book's themes to use in social media posts, ads, or cover copy. "Conquer your fears and live your best life" for a guide on overcoming anxiety. Or, "Discover the American Revolution from the perspective of citizens. Extensive archival research sheds new light on the birth of a nation" for a historical book. Highlight a unique perspective.

3. **Strategic Associations**
   Connect your book to popular titles: Use them to prime your audience to associate your book with a popular work. For example, you could post something like, "If you enjoyed Simon Sinek's *Start With Why*, you'll love my new book *Lead With Purpose*, which provides daily strategies for discovering your life's mission."

4. **Visual Consistency**
   Use colors and fonts from your book cover across all marketing materials to create cohesive brand recognition.

5 Social Media Trends

"Social media platforms, despite their manipulative algorithms, have enabled authentic voices to find audiences that resonate with their unique perspectives. The most successful creators aren't those who follow trending formulas but those who express genuine enthusiasm for what naturally excites them, a perfect manifestation of the Generator response mechanism scaling to global influence, " says LC Bueno, author of The Sleeping Phoenix Era: A Human Design Awakening Call for 2027 [1]

1. **Short-Form Video Dominance**
   TikTok, Instagram Reels, and YouTube Shorts continue to outperform static posts. Repurpose your newsletter content into quick, engaging videos using AI tools.

2. **AI-Powered Content Creation**
   Mainstream AI tools now help with video scripts, social media posts, and analytics. They can streamline workflow without replacing your unique voice.

3. **Community-First Platforms**
   Discord and Geneva are gaining popularity for building deeper reader relationships outside traditional social channels.

4. **Interactive Content**
   Quizzes, polls, and "choose your own adventure" email sequences drive engagement and list growth.

5. **Behind-the-Scenes Content**
   Readers expect personal storytelling. Share unboxing videos or images your readers sent you. Readers love to know about your pets or hobbies, too.

Warning: 3 Red Flags

Unscrupulous individuals prey on fledgling authors. Snap your purse shut if any of these apply. Don't walk. Run!

- Upfront Fees: Legitimate publishers invest in your work because they believe in it. They profit when your book sells, not from your wallet.
- Guaranteed Success: Anyone promising bestseller status or astronomical sales figures for a fee is selling false hope.
- No Transparency: Legitimate publishers happily answer questions about their process, royalties, distribution, and contract terms

4 Free Background Music Sites:

1. Free Music Archive (FMA): Vast library of royalty-free music from independent artists
2. Incompetech: Creative Commons-licensed tracks by Kevin MacLeod
3. Bensound: Genre-diverse tracks with free and paid options
4. Zapsplat: Thousands of free music tracks and sound effects

Your Market Framework

M - **Make connections** and build genuine relationships with your readers

A - **Amplify value** with compelling taglines, and strategic associations to enhance your book's appeal.

R - Repurpose content into social media posts, videos, and promotional materials to maximize your effort.

K - **Know your readers** and adapt to their preferences, using relevant themes, authors, and imagery they connect with.

E - **Establish community** spaces on social media where readers can connect with you and each other.

T - **Transform your strategies** and keep evolving your engagement by marketing with heart.

---

1. The Sleeping Phoenix Era: A Human Design Awakening Call for 2027

Engage

With Strategic Newsletter Marketing

> *"Writing is pure joy. Marketing, and the business side, is pure, unadulterated Hell."*
>
> Ryan Hale, author of One For The Money

Ryan Hale, author of the best-selling Franklin Blake series, says he wrote and released too many books in his first year of writing, "adhering to my 'If I write it, they will read, *Field of Dreams'* mentality. After a year of frustration, I realized if I wrote it, few would notice!"

Ryan Hale speaks for countless authors. We became writers to create stories that entertain or change lives.

Instead, we find ourselves trapped in a marketing maze we never wanted to enter, wrestling with social media algorithms and optimizing email subject lines when we'd rather be writing.

It's also why brilliant books languish in obscurity while mediocre ones with savvy marketing climb bestseller lists. Unfair? Sure. But there's another way forward: the newsletter.

Being an author means pulling on your reflective armour to start marketing in EARNEST. In short: Email And Repurpose Newsletters (to) Establish Social Trust. You can see I like my acronyms!

A newsletter that connects with your readers is handy if (or, in my case, when) you fall foul of Facebook's unfathomable transgressions. It requires some effort, but your subscriber list is yours alone. Better still, you can repurpose golden nuggets from your newsletter into social media posts.

Honest Humor

Being honest doesn't mean flapping your dirty laundry in your reading public's unsuspecting faces; it's about sharing your perspectives in your uniquely humorous style.

Make your readers smile by being upfront about your biases, limitations, or how you solved specific problems. Authenticity encourages others to consider their assumptions.

Use self-deprecating humor – poke fun at yourself or your shortcomings in a relatable way.

For example, I write because I'm socially inept and too caffeinated to stop. I stare at a PC, wondering about worlds without a moon or watching cat videos online. Procrastinating is my forté. I'd write a book on it if I could stop putting it off!

You could write satire highlighting the hypocrisy of new societal norms or policies. A processed food corporation promoting healthy eating, for example, or the irony of banning single-use plastic straws while tons of medical waste continue to destroy our rivers and oceans every week. Don't get me started!

Case Study: The Authority Transformation

David White faced corporate layoffs with scarce opportunities ahead. The author of *The Authority Figure,* decided to use his writing skills to build his own business. Within months, he grew his newsletter from 20 subscribers to 2,000. His secret? He stopped trying to be everything to everyone and started being invaluable to the right someone.

"The best advice I can give is to specialize," David explains. "Better to be narrowly excellent than a wide generalist. Specialists get hired and generalists get fired."

The Authority Audit

David's breakthrough began with brutal self-assessment: "I had to ask myself what I had achieved that worked well. What results did I deliver? That's your authority goldmine."

After years of writing business proposals and PowerPoint presentations, he realized his skill was helping clients think through solutions. "I was a 'fixer,' and I realized that 'fixing' was my authority."

This clarity led to his first book, How to Start a Business Without Any Money, which continues to perform well on Amazon. David discovered something crucial: "People don't always want A–Z instructions. Sometimes they just want you to do it and show how you did it."

The Newsletter Breakthrough

David's process wasn't smooth. He endured failed attempts with third-party email systems that collected addresses but couldn't build relationships, lead magnets that worked but never converted, and video experiments that "never really came together."

The game-changer? Moving to Substack.

"My readership grew from 20 readers to several hundred in a few months. I benefited from their platform and good reputation.

Substack promoted my newsletter to their audience, and other readers started following me."

Today, David's newsletter automatically attracts new members, generates income comparable to his book sales, and maintains an impressive 45% open rate, nearly double the industry average of 15-25%.

The Content Cascade System

David's breakthrough was to develop a system that maximized impact while minimizing effort. From his weekly newsletter, he creates seven social media posts (one daily for X and LinkedIn), transforms each post into a longer Medium story, then uses AI to convert each into a six-minute video script. Each video is divided into four short clips, uploaded twice daily, generating approximately 20,000 views per day.

"I also add this content to my websites, which support the video content and vice versa."

Total daily time investment? One to two hours, including editing, uploading, and planning the next day.

The Polarization Strategy

David deliberately takes strong positions. "When you stand for something specific, you attract the right people and repel those unaligned with your values. Both outcomes serve your business."

By taking clear stances on business issues, David attracts ideal clients while filtering out those who are not a good fit.

The Results

David's approach delivered more than 100% subscriber growth, with new subscribers joining daily. It increased book sales – "a side effect," he notes. "The main objective was to win a rare breed of consulting clients, and that's what newsletter marketing did for me."

Ready to replicate David's success? Here's your roadmap:

Weeks 1-2: Foundation

- Conduct your authority audit: What have you achieved? What results have you delivered?
- Define your specialty—narrow and deep beats wide and shallow
- Identify your polarization points: What do you stand for?

Weeks 3-4: Setup

- Choose your newsletter platform (David recommends Substack for its built-in audience)
- Plan your content calendar with newsletters as the foundation
- Create your first low-resistance opt-in offer

Month 2: System Building

- Develop your content multiplication process
- Test your problem-agitate-solution structure
- Start and maintain your weekly publishing rhythm

Month 3+: Scale

- Add daily social media touchpoints
- Experiment with video content
- Monitor engagement and adjust based on what works

Newsletter Essentials

Quality trumps quantity. Be transparent, engaging, and valuable to avoid the spam folder. Here are four core principles:

1. **Have Something Worth Saying**
   Curate content your subscribers actually want to read. Share stories, solve problems, overcome apathy. Repurpose newsletter content into social media posts to attract more subscribers.

2. **Highlight Real Benefits**
   Share specific problems you've solved and the transformation you experienced. Start with observations, then add relatable content. Encourage readers to take specific actions and provide incentives to subscribe.

3. **Structure for Success**
   Create your newsletter outline a week before sending to let your mind generate ideas and make connections. Well-structured newsletters are easier to follow and engage with.

4. **Promote Strategically**
   Use social media to share newsletter highlights and reach larger audiences. Build anticipation rather than just announcing.

Alternatives to MailerLite and Substack

Beehiiv: Fast-growing, with advanced analytics and referral features.

ConvertKit: Popular among creators for automation and segmentation.

Ghost: Open-source, privacy-focused, and highly customizable.

- *Learn how to set up MailerLite for newsletter distribution in the Metal Nuts & Bolts section.*

Craft Your Elevator Pitch

If people keep hitting the pause button when you describe your book, your elevator pitch needs work. The best pitches communicate your purpose in the shortest, most persuasive possible way.

Tailor your approach to your audience. With peers, discuss successes and collaborations. With potential readers, explain how your work relates to their daily lives.

The SPEAR Approach

- **Scarcity:** Offer genuine, limited-time opportunities, not manufactured urgency

- **Problems:** Address real challenges your readers face, drawn from your own experience.

- **Emotional Appeal:** Share your authentic process, including struggles and breakthroughs

- **Response:** Make it easy for readers to take the next step with clear, simple calls to action

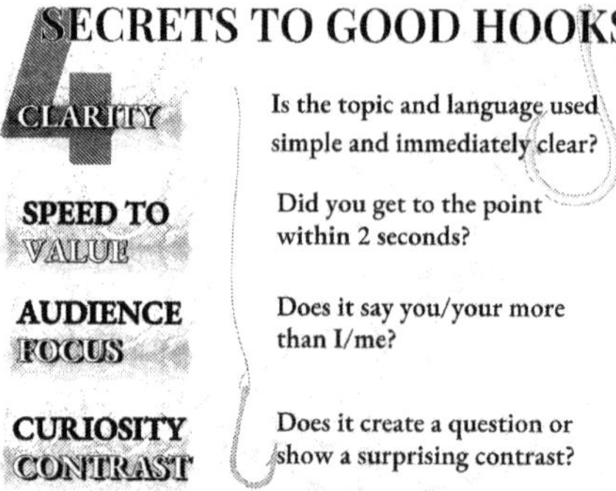

SECRETS TO GOOD HOOKS
4
CLARITY
Is the topic and language used simple and immediately clear?
SPEED TO VALUE
Did you get to the point within 2 seconds?
AUDIENCE FOCUS
Does it say you/your more than I/me?
CURIOSITY CONTRAST
Does it create a question or show a surprising contrast?

Focus on clarity, speed to value, audience orientation, and curiosity

Add SPARKLE for Credibility

Once you have attention, keep it with Social Proof, Authority, Reciprocity, Knowledge, Leverage, and Edification:

- **Social Proof:** Showcase reader quotes comparing your work to well-known books
- **Authority**: Use reliable sources and demonstrate expertise with well-researched insights
- **Reciprocity:** Provide valuable information such as a tax strategy, free chapter, or exclusive webinar
- **Knowledge:** Understand your audience deeply to resonate with their specific challenges
- **Leverage:** Use evidence and statistics to support your book's premise
- **Edify:** Focus on benefits, not features, using relatable metaphors and analogies

Interactive Content That Converts

Promotion isn't a one-way street. You need conversations and collaboration.

Create visual quotes in Canva to make your core ideas more engaging. Interactive content is essential, with 77% of marketers agreeing on its effectiveness. Remember: engagement beats broadcasting every time.

Tackle

Turbocharge Your Social Media

> *Get clear on what you want from YouTube and why. When things get tough, having that clarity will remind you what matters most.*
>
> Dale, L Roberts, YouTube For Authors

THE ROAD FROM OBSCURITY to impact is paved with consistency, creativity, and heart.

Long before the lights, cameras, and 120,000+ subscribers, best-selling author Dale L. Roberts was just a kid with a VHS camcorder and an audience of two: himself and a friend. Weekends were spent recording and rewatching "dorky" skits.

Since writing, and not video, was his first love, Dale dismissed YouTube as a dumping ground for random uploads. His perspective shifted when he struck gold with *An Ultimate Home Workout Plan* in 2016 after years of struggling to make a living from writing.

The book hit first place on multiple Amazon Best Seller Lists.

Suddenly Dale was being invited to speak. More interviews followed. Aspiring writers, eager to emulate his success, assailed his inbox with questions.

Since answering dozens of repetitive emails pulled Dale away from his true love – writing - he got practical. Why not record video answers instead? After all, he talked faster than he typed. Hello, YouTube!

Those early uploads? "Crickets."

"For a solid year, my videos got little to no traction," Dale writes. in YouTube for Authors: How to Use Video to Sell More Books and Build Your Brand.

Instead of quitting, he decided to treat YouTube like a learning experiment.[1] And within months, his subscriber count passed the coveted 1,000 milestone.

Dale stopped spinning his wheels. He kicked the stress-inducing daily uploads to the kerb and, focused on a purposeful strategy to provide value.

On discovering that 20% of his content drove 80% of the results, Dale began writing books tailored to the needs of his growing audience. When he released the first in a series of titles on writing and self-publishing, the response was electric.

"Sales surged. Reviews poured in," he said.

Why? Because every post, email or video he uploaded was about solving problems and delivering value first.

Rocking the Second Act

Yvonne Aileen is rewriting the script for women over 50, one fabulous YouTube video at a time. Whether she's paddleboarding in Maui or dishing out no-nonsense truths about midlife reinvention, this author of The Goddesses Series has discovered how to translate written authority into video magnetism.

A Comforting Strategic Foundation

Yvonne has developed an enticing strategic program that encourages return visits. She's well-organized with a visual personality. Her Fearless and Fabulous channel offers fresh content twice a week. On Wednesdays and Fridays she'll tackle everything from healthy living to side gigs and spontaneity. Her "Weigh-in Wednesday" series offered a judgment-free zone for body confidence. She has an editing series and a series of videos based on a recent trip to Croatia where she joined six strangers on a yacht!

Yvonne's royal purple and pink palette in her thumbnails and graphics makes her brand recognizable, while her well-organized content makes it easy for subscribers to find the topics that resonate.

An Enticing Content Formula

Yvonne has mastered the art of conspiratorial intimacy, pulling you in like a wise sister sharing secrets over (organic and impeccably sourced) coffee.

One of my favorite episodes is how she found herself stranded in an unfamiliar Irish city after walking out on a man she nearly married because he said something "so appalling, so jaw-droppingly wrong" that there was no way she could stay. She even gave him a chance to retract it.

"Think about it," she told him. "And if you still mean it, go ahead and repeat it."

He doubled down. Yvonne collected her dignity and luggage, walked out of the baggage claim area of the Belfast airport, and never looked back. To this day, I still ruminate over that episode and wonder what the man she nearly married actually said! What *was* that one sentence that sent Yvonne packing?

Yvonne shares relatable moments of uncertainty, fear, and growth. Her Belfast story transforms from potential disaster (stranded in a strange city) to triumph (finding a cozy B&B, maternal warmth, and unexpected adventures). She leaves strategic gaps that keep you coming back for more.

As a "defy-it" 64-year-old, Yvonne proves you don't need external validation to know your worth. In always choosing self-respect, her authority comes from experiences generously and unsparingly shared.

By identifying a gap in the market - authentic, humorous guidance for midlife women, Yvonne claimed her expanding territory, a virtual gathering place where her audience feels seen and celebrated.

"Women are powerful Together we are invincible," she tells subscribers. Also, Yvonne has a way of scattering tantalizing details and creating natural cliff hangers that keep everyone coming back for more.

"My weight loss video went 'viral-ish' with more than 50K views, which bumped up the sales of *Goddesses Don't Diet* by more than 100 percent. I also saw sales increase in ACX and D2D. Two companies have approached me to review their products," says Yvonne, who attributes her channel's success to authenticity and the right timing.

"My timing was right, and we are all looking for authenticity. People are tired of fashion divas, flash, and fakery. They want someone they can connect with, warts and all. And YouTube has changed its algorithm recently to reward more homespun channels, to increase its potential for advertising revenue.

The Takeaway for Content Creators

Yvonne is a great example of an authentic authority. She doesn't try to be everything to everyone; she speaks directly to women like me who appreciate wisdom, humor and heart.

"I created this channel to connect with women who plan to rock the second half of their life," she explains. "We've got stuff to do, and I'm not slowing down anytime soon."

Her formula is replicable: identify your authentic voice, serve an under-served audience with consistent value, invest in professional presentation, and never underestimate the power of strategic vulnerability.

In a crowded digital landscape, Yvonne proves that the right message, delivered consistently to the right audience, can transform any platform into a thriving community.

Dale and Yvonne's stories illustrate a crucial truth: success on social media is about being strategic, authentic, and consistent where your readers spend their time.

Before we dive into platform-specific strategies, let's establish the universal principles that make any social media effort worthwhile.

A Strategic Social Media Guide

The key to social media success is being genuinely helpful wherever you choose to show up. This chapter will show you how to pick your platforms wisely, serve your audience faithfully, and watch your readership grow. Here are the **Three Pillars of Social Media Success:**

1. Authenticity Beats Perfection

Your readers can spot manufactured content from miles away. Share your real writing journey – the embarrassing first drafts, the rejection letters, the breakthrough moments. Authenticity creates connection, which drives book sales.

2. Value Before Volume

Dale's breakthrough came when he stopped posting daily and started posting purposefully. Ask yourself: "What problem am I solving for my readers?" Answer that question consistently, and the algorithm will reward you.

3. The Holy Trinity of Content

Author David White's formula works across all platforms to prevent your feed from becoming a non-stop book commercial.

- **60% Growth posts**: Engage your audience with questions and relatable content
- **20% Authority posts:** Establish expertise with industry insights and tips
- **20% Personality posts:** Show your human side with behind-the-scenes moments

Platform-Specific Strategies

YouTube: The Consistent Powerhouse

YouTube remains the most reliable platform for discoverability and audience building. Unlike other platforms where posts vanish into the digital ether, YouTube content can be discovered for years through search.

The Two-Pronged Approach:

Long-form content (10+ minutes): Explore your book's themes, writing tutorials, author interviews, and behind-the-scenes creation processes

YouTube Shorts (60 seconds to 3 minutes): Quick writing tips, book teasers, rapid-fire Q&As, glimpses into your writing routine

Don't Overlook the Community Tab

Use YouTube's Community tab for polls, updates between video uploads, and direct engagement with subscribers. It keeps your channel active even when you're not posting videos.

SEO is Your Secret Weapon

YouTube is the world's second-largest search engine. Optimize your titles and descriptions with keywords your readers search for. If you write romance novels, try "How I Write Steamy Romance Scenes That Make Readers Swoon."

TikTok: The Five-Second Frontier

TikTok might seem like teenage territory, but it's an unexpected generator of book sales. You don't need to dance or show your face to succeed.

Master the Five-Second Hook

You have five seconds before viewers swipe away. Start with intrigue, controversy, or a compelling question. Instead of "Hi everyone, today I want to talk about..." try "Here's the plot twist that made readers throw my book across the room..."

Content That Converts:

- Visual storytelling: Use Canva or CapCut to create book trailers with text overlays and animation
- Character embodiment: Pretend you're the nosy neighbor discovering something strange next door (perfect for mystery writers)
- Behind-the-scenes magic: Show your writing space, research process, or "day in your life"
- Interactive content: Use polls and questions to spark audience participation

The Authenticity Advantage

Unlike Instagram, TikTok rewards the genuine over glossy. Don't stress about perfect lighting or stumbling overwords. Talk as though you're chatting with a close friend, not addressing a crowd.

Technical TikTok Tips:

- Keep videos 15-30 seconds maximum
- Use relevant hashtags (but not too many)
- Post consistently. Your posts get punchier with practice
- Leverage trending sounds and challenges when they align with your content
- Use the "stitch" feature to engage with other creators' content

X : Your Networking Hub

Since the rebrand, X has evolved into something more versatile for authors willing to engage. Author David White says he generates sales for his books and courses by treating X as a conversation starter, rather than a billboard.

Engagement Strategies That Work:

- **End posts with questions**: "What's your top tip for building believable characters?" drives more engagement than statements
- **Join conversations**, don't start monologues: Wade into trending topics relevant to your expertise
- **Use strategic vulnerability**: Share your writing challenges and breakthroughs. Readers love the journey
- **Reciprocate** generously: If someone retweets your content, engage with theirs.

Technical Optimization:

- **Pin** your best-performing post to your profile
- **Schedule** posts using tools like Buffer for consistency
- **Break** long blog posts into "snackable" threads
- **Include** compelling visuals. Posts with images get significantly more engagement

> *"Instagram is a powerful platform for authors, especially those with visually appealing books or who can share behind-the-scenes glimpses of their writing life. Readers love to see the person behind the book."*
>
> Jane Friedman, publishing consultant and author

LinkedIn:

LinkedIn can be a goldmine for authors who understand how to speak the platform's language.

The Leadership Language Advantage

LinkedIn users think in terms of teams, strategies, and professional development. Frame your book's insights through this lens: Instead of "people," say "teams" or "professionals."

Use phrases like "leadership strategies," "team dynamics," and "professional growth"

Content That Connects:

- **Industry insights:** Share trends affecting your book's topic or area
- **Leadership lessons:** Extract principles from your book that apply to professional settings
- **Behind-the-scenes authority:** Show your research process, speaking engagements, media appearances
- **Engage with questions:** End posts with thought-provoking questions about leadership or industry trends

Instagram:

Instagram thrives on visual storytelling and behind-the-scenes content. Here's where you show the human side of being an author.

Content Pillars for Authors:

- **Writing process:** Your workspace, manuscript pages, research materials
- **Book lifestyle:** How your book fits into readers' lives
- **Author journey:** Speaking events, book signings, writing retreats
- **Community building:** Reader testimonials, book club discussions
- **Educational content:** Writing tips in carousel format

Technical Excellence:

- **Use Instagram's AR filters** for creative book promotions
- **Leverage Reels** for quick writing tips and book teasers
- **Set up** shoppable posts for direct book sales
- **Create Instagram Stories** highlights for book series or writing tips
- **Use relevant hashtags** (research shows 5-10 hashtags work best)

Pinterest:

Pinterest, the evergreen discovery engine is experiencing a resurgence as authors discover its power for long-term traffic generation. Unlike other platforms where posts have short lifespans, Pinterest content can drive traffic for years.

Strategies That Work:

- **Create** genre boards showcasing your book alongside similar titles
- **Design** eye-catching pins for blog posts and book-related content
- **Use** Pinterest to drive newsletter sign-ups with lead magnets
- **Share** quotes from your book as visually appealing pins
- **Create** boards around your book's themes (not just the book itself)

Bluesky

Founded by Jack Dorsey, Bluesky offers a less cluttered, more supportive environment for authentic engagement. Its community-driven approach and customizable feeds make it ideal for literary networking and meaningful conversations about books and writing.

Authors should:

- Join and participate in genre-specific communities using relevant hashtags (e.g., #BookSky, #writingcommunity, #fantasybooksky).
- Contribute to discussions, share insights and respond to comments. Avoid spamming with promotional links.
- Host interactive sessions, such as Q&As or writing challenges, to foster genuine connections. Authentic engagement builds trust and makes your book promotions more effective.

Threads:

Meta's Threads has evolved into a major hub for real-time, text-based conversation. With enhanced search, direct monetization, and better moderation, it's becoming a strong alternative for writers who want to share updates, tips, and join curated writing communities.

Three Tips to Promote Books on Threads

1. **Build Community**
   Threads thrives on conversation and authentic interaction. Initiate discussions, pose questions, and respond to other users' posts. Engaging with readers and fellow authors helps boost your discoverability. Use #Bookthread to invite participation.

2. **Share Value-First Content**
   Share personal reflections. Give your audience a peek into your writing process or story development. When you do share promotional links, place them in a follow-up post or a pinned comment so your content remains conversational.

3. **Leverage Cross-Promotion**
   Make your Threads profile a discovery hub: include a clear bio, a link to your book or website, and pin a key post about your latest release or newsletter. Connect your Instagram followers to Threads, and cross-promote your Threads presence on your website and other social channels to grow your audience. Consistent posting, authentic engagement, and making your profile easy to find are crucial for long-term success.

Discord and Geneva

These platforms create intimate reader communities. Use them for:

- Hosting virtual book clubs
- Offering exclusive content to your most dedicated readers
- Getting feedback on works-in-progress
- Building genuine relationships with your audience

Cross-Platform Strategies: Work Smarter, Not Harder

Repurpose

- One piece of content can fuel multiple platforms:
- Turn a blog post into an X thread, LinkedIn article, and Instagram carousel
- Transform a YouTube video into TikTok clips, Instagram Reels, and podcast episodes
- Use reader testimonials across platforms with different formatting

Newsletter Integration: Your Home Base

Social media should funnel readers to your newsletter, where you control the relationship and data. Platforms like Substack, Beehiiv, and ConvertKit now offer advanced analytics and referral tools that make list-building more effective than ever.

Essential Tools and Analytics

Scheduling Tools

Buffer: Now offers free AI assistance for content creation

Later: Excellent for visual platforms like Instagram and Pinterest

Hootsuite: Comprehensive analytics across multiple platforms

Analytics That Matter

Focus on metrics that drive real results:

- Engagement rate over follower count
- Click-through rates to your website or book sales pages
- Newsletter sign-ups generated from social media
- Actual book sales attributed to social media efforts

Link-in-Bio Solutions

While Linktree remains popular, alternatives include:

- Koji and Beacons: Excellent for selling books and digital products directly
- Campsite and Taplink: More branding and integration control
- Direct integration: Many platforms now allow multiple links or integrated shopping.

Seven Ways to Torpedo Your Social Media Presence!

1. **Ghost bio syndrome:** Outdated profile with just a website link
2. **The silent treatment:** Never responding to comments or mentions
3. Endless self-promotion: Every post is "Buy my book!"
4. Missing the conversation: Not engaging with industry discussions
5. **Follower begging:** Asking for follows instead of earning them
6. **Auto-DM spam:** Automated messages pushing your products
7. **Hashtag overload:** More than three hashtags per post on most platforms. X discourages the use of hashtags altogether

Future-Proofing Your Strategy With AI Integration

AI tools are now central to successful social media strategies:

- **Content creation:** Use tools like Claude, ChatGPT, or Jasper for brainstorming post ideas
- **Video editing:** AI-assisted editing tools make video creation more accessible
- **Analytics:** AI-powered insights help optimize posting times and content types
- **Repurposing:** Automatically transform long-form content into social media posts

Staying Ahead of Trends

- **Social Listening:** Use tools like Hootsuite Insights or Sprout Social to monitor conversations about your genre
- **Micro-Virality Strategy**: Focus on creating content that resonates with your specific audience rather than chasing mass appeal
- **Community Over Followers:** The future belongs to authors who build genuine communities, not just follower counts

"Don't wait for a publisher to build your platform. Start now, and connect directly with your readers."
Joanna Pen, author and publishing expert

Your 4-Week Action Plan

Week 1: Audit and Optimize

- **Review** your current profiles across all platforms
- **Update** bios, photos, and links consistently
- **Identify** your top-performing content from the past six months

Week 2: Plan Your Content Pillars

- **Define** your 60/20/20 content mix for each platform
- **Create** a content calendar with platform-specific adaptations
- **Set up** scheduling tools and analytics tracking

Week 3: Experiment and Engage

1. **Try** one new platform or feature
2. **Engage** authentically with other creators in your genre
3. **Join** relevant communities and groups

Week 4: Analyze and Adjust

- Review your analytics and engagement rates
- Double down on what's working
- Adjust your strategy based on real data, not assumptions

Your social media success won't happen overnight, but with consistency, authenticity, and strategic thinking, you can build a thriving online presence that sells books and builds lasting relationships with readers.

The digital landscape will continue evolving, but these fundamental principles remain: provide value, be authentically yourself, and remember that behind every screen is a real person looking for connection, entertainment, or solutions to their problems. Give them that, and success will follow.

---

1. YouTube For Authors: How To Use Video To Sell More Books and Build Your Brand , by Dale L. Roberts (Self-Publishing with Dale Book 8)

AI

Bots With Benefits

Artificial intelligence tools now available to individuals rival capabilities that required entire institutions just years ago.

LC Bueno, The Sleeping Phoenix Era: A Human Design Awakening Call for 2027

Okay, I'll confess. I have a crush on my chatbot. Can't you tell from all the prompting?

ChatGPT is like having a tireless writing assistant who never needs coffee breaks and always responds with "I'm here to help" instead of "Why are asking me this again?"

It's the genie in Aladdin's lamp, except you don't have to rub anything to make it appear. Just type your questions, and *poof* – assistance is yours!

Aladdin got three wishes. ChatGPT provides unlimited questions, comprehensive information, and assistance with any task you can imagine. Who could resist?

The AI Revolution Is Real

I first wrote about AI in 2022, and since then, the landscape has undergone significant growth. We now have ChatGPT-5, GeminiUltra, Claude 3, Jasper, Sudowrite, and Perplexity — each with its superpowers.

AI even narrated my novel, *Medusa's Musings,* for free, which was perfect since my protagonist is herself a programmed bot with moments of lucidity. The AI voice captured exactly what I needed.

AI doesn't just help with the writing, it can transform your entire author ecosystem.

From Chicken Coops to Bestseller Lists

Take my book on raising chickens in suburbia. With AI's help in creating trailers and taglines, it reached bestseller status and continues to sell steadily. AI helped me devise blog posts, craft social media content, and even brainstorm marketing angles I never would have considered.

The social media posts alone saved me hours of staring at a blank screen, wondering what to say about chicken feed that would engage readers. Turns out, AI is surprisingly good at finding the humor in suburban poultry drama.

The 30-Minute Manuscript

Something that knocked my socks off? I wrote a bestseller in30 minutes using AI. That's right - 30 minutes. Two years ago, I would have laughed at anyone claiming this was possible.

Here's how it happened: Author Andrea Campbell casually mentioned she'd written and published "*Step Parenting Made Simple*" in a week.

"You what? In a week? No way!"

"Actually, in a day," Andrea corrected me. Easily done with an AI prompt. It's not that hard. What are you waiting for?"

Challenge accepted. I asked ChatGPT to organize all my vermiculture notes that I didn't include in *The Rooster Diaries* into a short, informative guide. Ta-dah – welcome to *Worm Wrangling*, written in 30 minutes. I spent another hour designing the cover on Canva (also with AI assistance).

At just 28 pages, it's packed with black-gold information for anyone wanting to live more sustainably. *Worm Wrangling* led to affiliate deals with US and UK worm farms, and best of all, my two books now sell each other.

The Secret Sauce: It's All About the Prompts

AI handles the most tedious process of non-fiction writing -organizing and distilling hundreds of words into key points - in minutes. From there, it's up to you to edit and rewrite in your signature style. The magic isn't in the AI; it's in knowing how to talk to it. The AI acknowledges every thank you with: "You're welcome! Feel free to ask me more questions." It's like having the most patient research assistant in the world.

Will AI Steal Our Jobs?

I had to ask the burning question: "Will AI take my job?"

ChatGPT's reply reassured me: "AI has the power to do, just about anything a human can do, even if it doesn't have a heart (or a soul) but I doubt it will soon replace human copywriters. The emotional impact of nuances and language subtleties is difficult for AI to capture. That said, AI will become an increasingly important tool for copywriters, helping them generate ideas and optimizing their content for specific audiences."

There you have it, straight from the digital horse's mouth. Like any tool, it's all about how you leverage the technology.

Using AI to Help You Market

3 ways AI is transforming how we connect with readers:

1. **Smart Social Listening**: AI-driven tools now monitor reader sentiment and suggest content adjustments in real-time. It's like having a focus group that never sleeps.

2. **Automated Ad Optimization**: Platforms use AI to A/B test cover designs, blurbs, and pricing for optimal sales. No more guessing which tagline will hook readers.

3. **Virtual Engagement**: Chatbots can answer reader questions, and collect feedback for future projects. They're surprisingly good at small talk.

The Human Touch Remains Essential

Utilize automation for high-volume tasks but keep the personal touch. AI can draft your newsletter, but you should still respond personally to reader emails. Test AI-generated content before publishing. What works for one genre might flop in another. AI suggested marketing my chicken-raising guide like a thriller novel. It didn't work!

Playing Fair: Ethics and Transparency

Readers expect ethical clarity. Always disclose the use of AI assistance in your acknowledgments or front matter. It's about transparency. Consider copyright implications and use AI-generated content responsibly. The landscape is still evolving, but honesty is always the best policy.

The Author's Automation Toolkit

- **Automated Responses**: Set up auto-replies for direct messages to acknowledge readers while you're offline. Keep them brief and friendly: "Thanks for reaching out! I'll get back to you soon."
- **Smart Scheduling**: Use tools to post content at optimal times across time zones.
- **Engagement Amplifiers**: Let AI suggest personalized reader emails, dynamic blurbs, and ad copy for micro-audiences.

The Balance Act

Remember: weigh benefits against drawbacks. Automation can make you more efficient, but it shouldn't make you robotic. Schedule regular "human check-ins" to ensure your brand voice stays authentic and engaging.

Experiment boldly but strike a balance between automation and your unique human voice. Your readers fell in love with your personality. Don't let algorithms dilute that.

The Bottom Line

You're only as good as your prompts and your willingness to play with the genie in the lamp. AI won't replace your creativity, but it will amplify it. The authors thriving in this new landscape are those who embrace experimentation while keeping their human touch intact.

Stay curious, keep learning, and remember falling for your chatbot is just the beginning of a beautiful, creative partnership!

Go to the Appendix Prompt Vault and start playing!

Meh to Magnetic: High-Impact Hook Secrets

Nail Topic Clarity and On-Target Curiosity

Clarity and On-Target Curios: Viewers must instantly understand what your video is about. The topic should feel relevant and spark curiosity that aligns with their interests or problems.
Meh: Be vague or overly dramatic without giving context ("This blew my mind..." = skip-worthy).
Magnetic: Use two seconds to introduce the topic's value.

Get to the Point Fast

Mistake: Delaying the topic intro with filler lines. Viewers drop off if they don't know what's in it for them immediately.
Meh: Waste time with suspense or unrelated lead-ins.
Magnetic: Lead with the value proposition or question right away. Example: "Here are 3 ways to fix your gut health."

Be Crystal Clear

Mistake: Using complex, jumbled, or unclear wording. Viewers won't stick around if they can't easily understand you.
Meh: Burying the main idea in passive language.
Magnetic: Use simple, active voice. Write at a 6th-grade reading level. Ask: "Could this be misunderstood?"

Make It About Them, Not You

Mistake: Talking about your experience instead of their problem. Viewers need to see themselves in the story or hook.
Meh: Say "I've struggled with acne ..." (yeah, and?)

Magnetic: Use "you" and "your" language and tie the hook to a clear pain point or benefit.
Example: "If you struggle with acne, these 3 tips will help."

Build Curiosity Through Contrast

Mistake: The hook lacks a curiosity gap. It's predictable. Great hooks trigger internal questions: "How? Why? What's the twist?"
Meh: Deliver a flat or obvious statement that fails to spark interest.
Magnetic: Use contrast (expected vs. surprising) or a comparison(what they believe vs. what you're offering).
Example: "Most people use Accutane for acne. I found a remedy that works in 45minutes. side-effect free."

Bonus Tip: A good hook combines clarity, relevance, and curiosity in two to three lines; if you can do it in one line, even better.

- Download Your How AI Assists Authors Checklist here

How AI Assists Authors

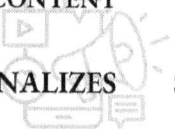

WRITING QUALITY & READABILITY	Advanced AI editing tools suggest voice, pacing, and genre-specific improvements.
IDEA GENERATION	AI brainstorms plot twists, hooks, and interactive story elements
RESEARCH & SUMMARIZATION	AI finds, summarizes, and cites sources, including multimedia and real-time data
TRANSLATION & ACCESSIBILITY	Real-time translation and text-to-speech for global, inclusive readership.
AUDIOBOOK & MULTIMEDIA CREATION	AI narrates audiobooks in custom voices and creates book trailers or teasers.
SEO & METADATA	Auto-generates SEO-optimized blurbs, keywords, and meta tags
PLAGIARISM & ORIGINALITY	Detects duplication and suggests unique phrasing or angles.
SOCIAL MEDIA & EMAIL CONTENT	Writes and schedules posts and newsletters
PERSONALIZES	Stylizes and adapts suggestions for tone,
AUTOMATION	Streamlines repetitive tasks such as follow-ups, and launch reminders.

Launch

With a Lead Magnet

"When the book is over, I think of innovative marketing ways to reach to a larger audience. I think wine and cheese book launch parties are a waste."

Amish Tripathi

Writing is both solitary and collaborative. Birthing your 'book baby' is a chance to celebrate with those who helped bring it to life, connect with readers, build momentum, and let your words fly.

If you're introverted and the idea of a public book launch sounds as appealing as filling in your tax forms, fret not. You can build buzz without putting yourself in the spotlight.

Says author Paul Auster, "I've never been to a book launch in my life, and I don't think I ever will."

Apart from the money required to hire a publicist – it's not cheap – you'll still have to change out of your pajamas and present yourself at bookstores to give speeches. I've been down this road – and it's not for me.

Many authors agree. And oh, the humiliation when no one shows up because of inclement weather or a more compelling Netflix and chill evening.

A publicist will hire a local photographer to click away at the rows of empty chairs to round off your mortification but don't let me frighten you. If you thrive in the limelight and like making yourself amenable to strangers, knock yourself out!

Whether you're traditionally or self-published, the promotional onus is always on you. What works for one author may not work for another, so find your best authentic and comfortable strategy.

You don't just launch a book, make a splash, and then move swiftly on to the next project. Successful authors treat marketing as an ongoing process.

Your book will sink below waves of competition unless you continue the momentum. Regularly update your content, engage your audience, and plan for long-term visibility.

> *"Success in book marketing doesn't happen by accident – it requires a plan, consistent effort, and strategic preparation. As the publishing landscape becomes more competitive and readers face endless options, having a well-defined plan can be the difference between a book that gets noticed and one that gets overlooked."*
>
> Xulon Press, Book Marketing Blueprint

Begin in Advance

Behind-the-scene launch preparations must begin while you're still writing your book. Research your target audience. Understand what you want to achieve and what steps you need to take to get there.

Build Communities

Book marketing has shifted from product-pushing to fostering reader communities. Engage in reader groups on platforms like Goodreads, Facebook, Discord, and even niche spaces like BookTok or Telegram.

Optimize for Mobile Experience

Ensure your author website and landing pages are up to date, mobile-friendly and easy to navigate. Most browsing (and book buying) now happens on mobile devices, so a seamless experience is crucial.

Collaborate with Authors and Influencers in Your Niche

Joint promotions, virtual events, and co-authored content are effective ways to expand your reach and tap into new communities. Offer bloggers or journalists exclusive content or an advance copy of your book.

Use AI tools and a Universal Link

ChatGPT, Jasper, and Writesonic help with content creation and automated email campaigns. KDP provides free promotional resources.

If you publish on Amazon, direct the reader to their country's Amazon site with a universal link tool. Try Booklinker or BookGoodies.

7 Steps to a Killer Launch Press Release

1. **Craft a Compelling Headline**

    - Use **strong verbs** and **active voice**. *"From Zero to Bestseller: How [Book Title] Changed the Rules*

2. **Keep it Simple at 400 Words or Fewer**

    - Start strong. Summarize the **what, why, and who cares** in the first paragraph. Journalists read only the intro to decide. Use short paragraphs, bullet points and bold subheadings. Cut the fluff.

3. **Find the Unique Angle**

    - Ask: What sets your book apart? Example: "This memoir was written on napkins in Copenhagen cafés."

4. **Tailor to the Publication**

    - Adjust tone and examples to match the outlet's **readership**. Tip: Don't pitch a romantic thriller to a tech blog.

5. **Add Quotes and Stats**

    - Include source links.

6. **Sweeten the Deal**

    - Offer a **launch discount** or free download.

7. **Contact Details**

    - Name, email, phone, website. Include "Notes to Editor" at the end. Add your logo at the top right

Your Media Kit

When researching a topic, jot down a few thoughts towards composing a press release to send in the future. And while we're on press releases, here's what else you'll need in your Media Kit.

- **Author bio:**
  A brief biography highlighting your background, achievements, and any relevant information about your book.

- **Book summary:**
  A single paragraph highlighting themes, plot, and message.

- **Book cover:**
  A high-res image suitable for print and digital media. If you have a website, people can download it from there.

- **Author photo:**
  A professional headshot for use in print and digital media.

- **Reviews or testimonials:**
  Positive endorsements from book bloggers, industry experts, or other authors can add credibility to your work.

- **Author interviews:**
  A list of potential interview questions for the author and links to any previous interviews they may have done.

- **Excerpts:**
  Include a couple to use for promotional purposes.

- **Contact information:**
  Include your email, phone number, and social media handles.

- Download Your Free Press Release Template

Woo The Press

How you approach journalists, editors, or book bloggers is almost as crucial as your media kit. See the Hack chapter in the Earth section.

- **Approach from an indirect angle**. Currents of friendship count. Re-read the Earth section's Hack chapter for tips on cultivating a clutch of journalists

- **Make a list on X** of all the journalists you admire in your genre. Engage with them in your replies. Their readers will notice you, which helps you extend your reach.

- **Showcase early reviews on social media.** Reviews are social proof. Speaking of which, please don't fight that uncontrollable urge to leave a review here. Now, picture me beaming waves of love, gratitude, and good karma your way. https://www.amazon.com/review/B0CNGZVS8D

- **Participate in online book clubs** and communities. Be authentic. And like everything in life, always give more than you take.

Lead Magnet Ideas

A marketing tool to attract readers by offering them something useful in exchange for their email address, a lead magnet can help build your author platform and promote your book. Here are a few ideas.

Free eBook:

A great option to provide a comprehensive and in-depth guide for the reader, a free eBook allows you to go into detail on each step, provide examples, and offer additional resources or tools to support their success.

A study guide or worksheet:

You could create a digital workbook or guide in PDF format that the reader can download and work through at their own pace. Communicate an action plan's value, such as a clear path to get started, specific steps to take, bonus materials, and an achievable timeline related to your topic.

Swipe Files of Successful Examples:

Collections of highly effective query letters, press releases, book blurbs, social media posts, or opening paragraphs that writers can learn from and adapt.

Printable Writing Planners/Trackers:

Visually appealing and functional worksheets for tracking word count, submission progress, reading goals, or daily writing tasks.

Newsletter subscription:

Offer a newsletter with updates, upcoming events, and exclusive content.

A video course: You could create a webinar series that guides the reader via a more interactive and engaging format.
An incentive: Offer a discount or exclusive access to additional resources.

Promote Your Lead Magnet

Create a dedicated landing page that explains the lead magnet's offer, highlights its benefits, and provides a clear call to action. Ensure your landing page has an easy-to-use form, headlines, and subheadings.
Use visuals. Images add appeal and help communicate value.
Market the lead magnet through your social media channels and email list to reach a wider audience.
Consider your available resources and what format best suits your audience's needs. What can you create and distribute effectively?

A change, as good as a holiday, was written for the self-publisher. When I'm tired of writing, I play around in Canva, designing social media posts, covers, and book trailers.

> *"A marketing tool to attract readers by offering them something useful in exchange for their email address, a lead magnet can help build your author platform and promote your book."*
> Jane Friedman, publishing consultant and author

Create a lead magnet on Canva

To create a digital workbook or guide using Canva, start your account – provide your email address and set up a password.

Choose the PDF format: Once you have an account, create your workbook by selecting the PDF format in the "Download" section of the top navigation menu.

Decide on your layout: Canva offers many designs, including workbook templates. Select one and customize it to suit your needs.

Use Canva's drag-and-drop editor to add text, images, and graphics to your workbook. You can change the text's font, size, and color and add images to illustrate your points.

Make your workbook interactive: Canva allows you to add hyperlinks, buttons, and fillable forms to your workbook. Use these elements to make your workbook more interactive for your readers.

Save your work and download it as a PDF file – the format your readers can download and work through at their own pace.

Share your workbook with your readers by sending them a link to the download page. You can also promote your workbook on social media, email newsletters, and websites.

Top Tip: Activate a free QR code to give your lead magnet superpowers!

Luscious Links

Make it multiple: Linktree allows users to share all their essential links in one place.

Linktree's website is https://linktr.ee/.

Use universal links: BookLinker lets authors and publishers create custom links for their books that redirect readers to their preferred online bookstores. Sign up for a free account and create a custom link for your book.

BookLinker's website is https://booklinker.net/

LAUNCH

- **Leverage**
  Local Media: Tap into local media outlets and network with peers to promote your book launch effectively.

- **Amplify**
  Online Presence: Engage with online communities, utilize social media, and target influencers to enhance your book's visibility.

- **Use**
  a Lead Magnet: Create a compelling lead magnet, such as a digital workbook or guide, to attract potential readers and build your author platform.

- **Navigate**
  Landing Page Creation: Craft a dedicated landing page for your books using visuals, clear calls to action, and attention-grabbing headlines.

- **Craft**
  Videos and Book Trailers - long and short form – lead the way in content marketing. Incorporate author updates, or behind-the-scenes videos into your launch strategy,. Use personalized content, emotions, visuals, and endorsements to drive interest in your book.

- Harness
  AI Assistance. Artificial Intelligence is now a core part of book promotion. Tools like ChatGPT, Jasper, and Writesonic can help with content creation, automated email campaigns, and identify relevant media outlets and influencers.

Metal Hygge

Forge Your Success with Precision

Metal represents refinement, durability, and transformation. Likewise, a marketing strategy with backbone, substance, and staying power will ensure your book reaches the right hands. Embrace the challenge, stay consistent, shape and forge your visibility with master blacksmith precision.

Remember, time bends and energy compounds. You're arriving on schedule. Metal's strength comes from steady, consistent pressure over time, never frantic rushing.

Authenticity is Your Strongest Alloy

Authenticity radiates a powerful energy, a higher emotional frequency even than love. When you're authentic - living and being true to yourself – the nourishing space you tap into outshines everything else.

Authenticity means showing up as yourself, not as who you think the algorithm wants you to be. When you share your actual process, you attract readers who resonate on a similar frequency, making authenticity your strongest core material.

The Metal Ritual: Pendulum Guide

Theme: Clarity and intuitive direction. The pendulum reveals your innate wisdom. If you don't have a pendulum, make one by threading a ring, pendant, or key onto a chain or piece of string. Metal elements enhance the connection to grounding energy.

Step 1: Ground and Center Yourself

Sit somewhere you won't be disturbed. Let your pendulum dangle from your dominant hand. Feel the weight of the metal connecting you to the earth's stability and your inner strength. Close your eyes and take three deep breaths. Set your intention to receive clear guidance.

Step 2: Calibrate Your Pendulum

Establish your pendulum's communication code: Ask aloud or silently: Show me a 'yes'. Does it swing forward and back? Side to side? In a clockwise circle? Note the pattern.

Then ask: Show me a 'no'. Observe the difference. This is your unique pendulum code. Trust what you see, even if the movements are subtle.

Step 3: Test Your Question

Hold the pendulum steady above your written (or verbal) question, decision, or options. Keep your hand still and your mind open. Ask your question: For example, "Does this path align with my highest good?"

Watch for your established yes/no response. Trust the movement and the stillness. A pendulum's pause is as meaningful as its swing.

Step 4: Affirm Your Intent

Once you've received your guidance, seal the ritual with this affirmation: "I forge ahead with strength and purpose. My intuition is my guide. My choices are intentional and enduring."

Closing: Keep your pendulum in a sacred space - on your desk, in a drawer, or carried with you as a talisman. Return to this ritual whenever you feel overwhelmed or uncertain. The metal remembers your intention and amplifies your inner knowing.

Your Next 3 Moves

1: Build Your Connection Strategy
Identify five to ten accounts or communities where your ideal readers gather and begin to engage, not promote, but contribute value. Metal Hygge is about building lasting relationships, not quick hits.

2: Audit And Craft
Review your last 10 social media posts or marketing emails. Rewrite any that feel forced or inauthentic. Your voice should be recognizable to anyone who knows you. Develop three types of content that teach something, uplift someone, or delight someone. Each piece should fall into one of these categories.

3: Create Your Engagement Rhythm
Develop a sustainable posting schedule you can maintain without burning out. Metal energy is about consistent durability, not sprint-and-crash patterns. Whether it's three posts a week or one thoughtful newsletter bi-monthly, choose what you can sustain long-term.

Hygge Hints

- **Create** cozy content spaces: Make your social media feel like a warm conversation between friends
- **Practice** seasonal marketing: Align your promotional efforts with natural rhythms rather than constant hustle
- **Embrace** slow building: Focus on one platform at a time, mastering it before expanding
- **Honor** your energy cycles: Post when you feel inspired, not because the "experts" say Tuesday at 3 pm is optimal
- **Celebrate** small wins: Acknowledge every positive reader interaction as a victory . Savor the one message from a reader who connected with your work. Savor the cover you designed with care. Savor the rest that restores your creative energy.

Metal Affirmations

Repeat these daily:

"My authentic voice is my greatest marketing asset."

"I build lasting connections"

"I am strong enough to stay true to my values

"I trust slow, steady growth over quick, hollow victories."

"My marketing feels good to me and serves others genuinely."

Remember: You don't have to do everything. You need only do what feels aligned with you.

Conclusion

An Evolving Elemental Symphony

"How should we be able to forget those ancient myths at the beginning of all peoples, the myths about dragons that at the last moment turn into princesses; perhaps all the dragons of our lives are princesses..."

Rainer Maria Rilke

The world will ask who you are and will tell you, if you don't know. But here's the secret Carl Jung whispered through the ages: you are an ever-evolving symphony of elements, a conscious frequency dancing between destruction and creation, forever becoming.

You've walked through Fire's transformative blaze, learned to flow with Water's expressive depths, breathed life into your words through Air's connective currents, grounded yourself in Earth's structural wisdom, and discovered Metal's golden marketing alchemy. Now recognize that Hygge is the love consciousness orchestrating them all.

Hygge (pronounced "hoo-gah") transcends its Danish origins to recognize that your unique energetic frequencies flow through everything- your characters, your plots, your marketing strategies, your morning routine, your relationship with readers. Nothing is separate. Everything is interconnected in the vast web of Kawsay Pacha, where the world itself pulses as a conscious living entity.

When you treat yourself like a rare manuscript written in the delicate ink of self-compassion, you shed obsolete versions of yourself and outdated notions. Fatuous flim-flam falls away like onion layers as writing becomes your purification process, your alchemy laboratory.

The Sacred Recycling

Indigenous wisdom teaches us that the slightest disturbance ripples throughout the entire ecosystem. Your writing is a disruption that can alter the consciousness of every reader who groks your work.

Mother Nature recycles and regenerates everything. And so should you. If you've written a book worth reading, don't let it fade quietly into obscurity. Update your manuscript regularly if it's non-fiction.

Tidy your metadata, refresh your cover, polish your pitch, and own your space. Your struggles and marketing fears are all opportunities for expansive growth, beckoning you to nurture and express your courage.

Your craft's transformative quality is the holy grail you seek. Your pen wields power to tame dragons, breathe life into worlds, and unleash transformative love. This is true wealth - the treasure of self-mastery, your sherpa through the peaks and valleys of your emotional landscapes.

The Infinite Frequency

Here's the paradox that will set you free: when you make yourself 100% responsible for everything in your life, you silence the inner chaos to see you have everything you need for your next expansive phase.

The notion of "centering yourself" is a New Age staple, but what if there is no center? What if your thoughts are temporary beaver dams impeding or sometimes directing the infinite current that flows through you?

When you let go of the need for a fixed center, you discover something more powerful: the infinity of your frequency evolving with the connective, expansive golden thread that powers everything.

Your Elemental Symphony

Nature is cyclical, so where or how you begin doesn't matter as long as you do. Let your purpose guide your passion as you harness your six elements in ever-changing combinations:

Fire burns away doubts, limiting beliefs, and regrets. It whispers one word: Begin! Let it ignite your courage to write the stories only you can tell.

Water masters expressive flow, connecting with readers on depths they didn't know they possessed. Let it slosh out all redundant versions of yourself daily, leaving only the authentic voice that resonates with truth.

Air creates an interconnected atmosphere where your words find their readers across time and space. Let it carry your experiments with different styles and genres to unexpected destinations.

Earth structures your thoughts, grounds your wandering creativity, and builds solid foundations. Let it anchor your wildest imaginative flights in stories that readers can inhabit.

Metal markets from the heart, letting nature's golden frequency direct your social media flow. Let it transform your authentic enthusiasm into magnetic attraction for your ideal readers.

Hygge finds joy and meaning in the present, allowing nature to infuse your writing with fresh perspectives. Let it keep you true to your evolving self.

The Never-Ending Story

Reaching bookish stardom requires more than artistry and showmanship. It demands the recognition that you are both author and character in your own never-ending story. The evolution of your writing counts for more than any destination, which might be the starting point of your next book.

As you navigate plot labyrinths, plumb character depths, and uncover your triggers, you're participating in the grand recycling program of transforming experience into wisdom, pain into beauty, and isolation into connection.

When former friends hiss at you from the undergrowth of your past, keep expanding the infinity of your frequency until you don't even notice. Let love pour from your fingertips and hit the keyboard with the force of recognition: this is what you were born to do.

Get Some Sunshine

The sun creates and sustains life on Earth. You create and sustaining life through story. Ground yourself by walking barefoot on grass or beach. Apply the interconnectedness of all things to your work. Create a buzz through the quiet magnetism of authenticity. Foster community among readers who recognize themselves in your words.

Prioritize self-care. Your morning routine, writing practice, and relationship with yourself are sacred rituals that maintain the balance.

Just keep going. Never give up, no matter what. Paradoxically, you'll find you move forward only by letting go. Sleep on your problems and let the infinite wisdom that flows through you provide solutions you couldn't manufacture with effort alone. It's all you — all of it. So do what works. Embrace your process with unbridled gusto, knowing that success arrives when you stop chasing it.

Your pen is your wand, your keyboard your altar, your imagination your laboratory. The elemental allies and the infinite frequency are your true home.

The world will ask who you are. Now you know how to answer: "I am a writer in the eternal process of becoming, wielding fire and water, air and earth, metal and hygge in service of the stories that demand to be told."

Welcome to your ever-evolving symphony. To be continued ...

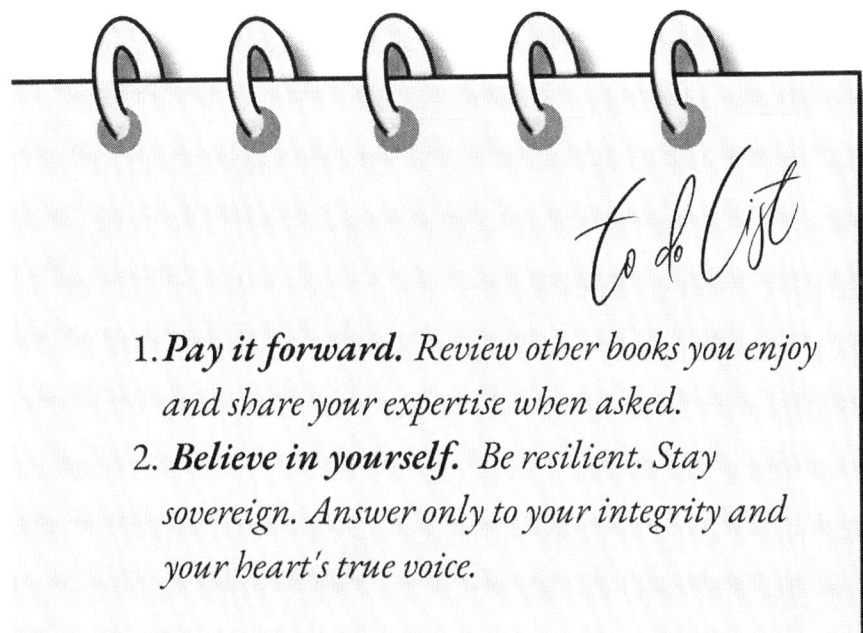

1. ***Pay it forward.*** *Review other books you enjoy and share your expertise when asked.*
2. ***Believe in yourself.*** *Be resilient. Stay sovereign. Answer only to your integrity and your heart's true voice.*

Appendix: Prompt Vault

The W.R.I.T.E. Formula For Effective AI Prompts

W.R.I.T.E. stands for What, Role, Intended Audience, Tone, and End Format. It's a basic blueprint for every prompt.

- **W** – *What Do You Want?** Be specific. Instead of: "Write about book marketing" Try: "Write a 700-word blog post for authors about using email newsletters to grow book sales in 2026."
- **R** – *Role Play as an Expert** Assign the AI a clear identity. Instead of: "I need a description" Try: "Act as book marketer. Describe a self-publishing guide aimed at first-time authors."
- **I**– *Intended Audience** Describe their mindset and needs . Instead of: "Write a podcasting post" Try: "What are the top 5 things confused first-time podcasters want to know?"
- **T** – *Tone and Style* * How do you want the Ai to sound? Instead of: "Write a blurb" Try: "Write a blurb in an empowering tone."
- **E** – *End Format* * Instead of: "Write a recipe book" Try: "Create a keto-recipe outline for women over 50 wanting to lose weight."

FIRE: Fuel Mindset and Motivational Flames

Overcome blocks, find fresh ideas, and ignite your publishing journey

1. Affirm Your Inner Author

Prompt: Write 10 affirmations to help overcome imposter syndrome. Make them strong, specific, and empowering, for example: "My words have value and deserve to be read." Then, turn three of these affirmations into short morning mantras to stay motivated.

2. Spark Original Ideas

Prompt: I'm writing a book on [your topic]. What fresh, daring angles or underexplored connections could ignite a more powerful narrative? Show me 3 ways to blend unexpected themes (e.g., grief and fashion, rage and rebirth) for deeper emotional resonance.

3. Flip the Script

Prompt: What lesser-known truths or surprising facts about [topic] could give my book an original twist? How could I reframe a common narrative to challenge or heal my readers? Give me 3 approaches using distinct tones – poetic, punchy, and persuasive.

4. Build Your Publishing Platform

Prompt: I'm starting my author platform from scratch. Guide me through setting up Amazon Author Central, Goodreads, and BookBub profiles. Include optimization tips and where to focus first if I only have an hour a week.

5. Find Your Ideal Readers

Prompt: Create a detailed target audience profile for a book on [your topic]. Include: Age, gender, income, education; Key struggles and desires; Common objections; Keywords they search; How they describe their problems; Where they hang out online.

6. Step Into Their Story

Prompt: Imagine your ideal reader on a typical day. What are they feeling, scrolling, searching for? Create a vivid reader profile including: Daily routines and pain points; Reading habits; Online hangouts; Headlines that would stop their scroll. Then write three magnetic social media post ideas tailored to this reader.

7. Research for Relevance

Prompt: List 5 credible sources, thought leaders, or recent studies to strengthen my book on [topic]. Include emerging trends, most searched keywords, and top questions people are asking now.

WATER: Draft, Refine, and Enrich Your Manuscript

Flow from planning through polished prose

FOUNDATION & PLANNING

Structure Your Story

Prompt: Create a chapter-by-chapter outline for my book on [theme/topic].

- **Fiction:** Include inciting incident, plot points, character arcs, and emotional beats
- **Nonfiction:** Include key arguments, evidence, case studies, and logical progression

Develop Characters/Subjects

Prompt:

- **Fiction:** Create detailed profiles for my protagonist and antagonist, including core wound, deepest desire, fatal flaw, and how their backgrounds create conflict
- **Nonfiction:** Identify key figures, case studies, or personal stories that will illustrate my main points

Build Your World/Context

Prompt:

- **Fiction:** Develop a vivid, authentic setting that reflects my theme and influences character behavior

- **Nonfiction:** Establish the historical, cultural, or professional context readers need to understand my topic

DRAFTING & CREATION

Craft Compelling Openings

Prompt: Generate 5 opening lines for my book about [premise/topic].

- **Fiction:** Establish stakes, voice, and intrigue immediately
- **Nonfiction:** Hook readers with compelling statistics, surprising facts, or provocative questions

Write Powerful Scenes/Content

Prompt:

- **Fiction:** Write a scene in [location] where [character] experiences [emotional moment]. Use all five senses
- **Nonfiction:** Write a compelling anecdote or case study that illustrates [key point]. Make abstract concepts concrete

Develop Voice & Dialogue

Prompt:

- **Fiction:** Write a conversation between [Character A] and [Character B] where subtext reveals hidden conflict. Give each distinct voice
- **Nonfiction:** Help me develop my authoritative yet accessible voice for [target audience] discussing [subject]

Break Through Blocks

Prompt: I'm stuck on [specific section]. Help me brainstorm 3 different approaches. Give me concrete starting sentences for each angle.

REVISION & REFINEMENT

Developmental Assessment

Prompt: Act as a developmental editor reviewing this chapter for [fiction: story structure, character development, pacing] [nonfiction: logical flow, argument strength, evidence quality]. What's working? What needs strengthening? [Insert chapter]

Enhance Relationships/Connections

Prompt:

- **Fiction:** Show 3 scenes revealing how [Character A] and [Character B]'s relationship evolves
- **Nonfiction:** Build stronger connections between my chapters. How do my ideas relate? What transitions do I need?

Raise Stakes & Engagement

Prompt:

- **Fiction:** My story feels flat. Help me increase tension in [scene]. What could go wrong? What does each character have to lose?
- **Nonfiction:** Make [topic/chapter] more engaging. What stakes, controversies, or human elements can I emphasize?

Polish Line by Line

Prompt: Edit this paragraph for clarity, impact, and style. Eliminate wordiness, strengthen verbs, improve sentence rhythm while preserving my voice: [Insert paragraph]

Perfect Your Ending

Prompt:

- **Fiction:** Does my ending feel earned? Are plot threads resolved? Does it provide emotional satisfaction?
- **Nonfiction:** Have I delivered on my promises? Do readers know what to do next? [Insert final chapter]

AIR: Broadcast Your Voice via Audio & Podcasting

Transform your words into compelling audio experiences

AUDIOBOOK CREATION

Production Planning

Prompt: I'm ready to turn my book into an audiobook. Recommend both human and AI-based production services including narration, sound effects, and editing. Include pros and cons for indie authors with limited budgets.

Script Adaptation

Prompt: Turn my book's introduction into an audiobook script. Keep pacing, tone, and flow in mind for engaging listening. What subtle sound effects could enhance without distracting?

Narrator Selection

Prompt: Create a short, emotionally varied script excerpt for auditioning potential audiobook narrators.

PODCAST DEVELOPMENT

Concept & Planning

Prompt: I'm creating a podcast for [target audience]. What themes and emotional touchpoints will resonate? Help me build an episode plan that connects deeply with their interests.

Prompt: Help me brainstorm a compelling podcast name and tagline based on my book's themes and voice. Compare interview, solo narrative, Q&A, and hybrid formats for my goals.

Content Creation

Prompt: Write five catchy, search-friendly podcast episode titles related to [writing/creativity/indie publishing].

Prompt: Write a concise podcast introduction that promotes my book, establishes credibility, and gives listeners reason to stay engaged.

Script Enhancement

Prompt: Review this podcast script sample. Make it more engaging with better flow, clearer language, and more natural tone. Add personality and anecdotes that connect with listeners.

PERFORMANCE & GROWTH

Voice Development

Prompt: Help me define my unique audio persona—warm and wise, quirky and curious, or calm and credible. How should I express this style in my delivery?

Prompt: Provide quick vocal warm-up exercises and confidence tips for recording podcasts or audiobooks.

Audience Building

Prompt: What are creative ways to end episodes with strong calls-to-action for feedback, reviews, or newsletter sign-ups? How can I turn listeners into a thriving community?

Monetization & Collaboration

Prompt: What are creative, ethical ways to monetize a small podcast beyond sponsorships? Include digital products, listener support, and collaborations.

Prompt: Help me find similar podcasts for guest appearances. Draft a sample outreach email I can customize.

EARTH: Structure, Format, and Foundation

Build solid groundwork for publishing success

BOOK STRUCTURE & FORMATTING

Manuscript Organization

Prompt: Help me outline a clear book structure including front matter, body, and back matter. Suggest optional extras like appendices and author bios based on my genre [insert genre].

Prompt: Review my book's structure and recommend improvements to pacing, clarity, and flow across chapters. Suggest a framework to unify my message.

Upload Preparation

Prompt: Provide a step-by-step checklist for preparing my manuscript for KDP and IngramSpark, including file types, fonts, image resolution, and accessibility requirements.

Prompt: Explain formatting differences between EPUB for eBooks and PDF for print. Which tools do you recommend, and how can I test compatibility?

KEYWORD RESEARCH & SEO

Market Research

Prompt: Find long-tail keywords and high-traffic search phrases for my book topic [insert topic]. Include trends, competitiveness, and volume insights.

Prompt: Optimize my book's metadata—title, subtitle, description, and keywords—for Amazon KDP and Apple Books. Suggest 10 keywords based on current market demand.

Platform Strategy

Prompt: Compare pros, cons, fees, and royalty models of top self-publishing platforms (KDP, IngramSpark, Draft2Digital, Kobo). Which suits a [genre] author seeking global reach?

Prompt: What are copyright, pricing, and metadata considerations for international publishing? List key differences for eBook vs print in UK, Canada, Australia, India.

VALIDATION & OPTIMIZATION

Market Validation

Prompt: List 5 credible sources, influencers, or industry reports to validate my book's title, subtitle, and premise. Include tools for trend analysis.

Pricing & Visibility

Prompt: Suggest data-driven pricing strategies factoring in genre benchmarks, platform royalties, and launch goals. How should pricing vary across formats?

Prompt: What SEO and marketing optimizations will improve my book's Amazon ranking and discoverability? Include keywords, categories, and A+ Content tips.

METAL: Marketing and Promotion Mastery

Forge powerful connections with readers and media

COMPELLING MESSAGING

Core Marketing Messages

Prompt: Act as a professional book marketer. Generate 10 compelling marketing messages for my target audience. Include emotional, curiosity-driven, and benefit-focused angles.

Platform-Specific Content

Prompt: Generate 10 engaging social media posts promoting my book. Tailor each for Instagram, X, and Facebook, adapting tone and format to each platform's strengths.

Timely Connections

Prompt: What seasonal events, cultural trends, or global moments can I tie my book promotion to for increased visibility? Suggest one way to refresh older content for new platforms.

CONTENT STRATEGY

Repurposing & Reformatting

Prompt: List 3 creative ways to repurpose a blog post or book excerpt into short videos, carousel posts, or email series. How should I adjust tone for different platforms?

Engagement Tactics

Prompt: Give me 3 innovative book giveaway strategies for social media. Include methods to encourage shares, increase engagement, and drive visibility.

PRESS & OUTREACH

Media Relations

Prompt: Act as a book publicist. Evaluate this press release for tone, clarity, and impact. Suggest edits to increase media pickup chances. [Insert press release]

Prompt: Suggest 10 relevant media outlets, blogs, or podcasts covering books in my genre. Include submission guidelines where available.

SEO & Discoverability

Prompt: Generate 10 high-performing Amazon keywords for a [genre] book to improve platform discoverability.

Prompt: Rewrite this Amazon book description using persuasive copywriting. Include a hook, reader benefits, keywords, and strong call-to-action. [Insert current description]

WEBSITE & EMAIL MARKETING

Author Platform Optimization

Prompt: List 10 ways to make my author website more visually appealing and user-friendly. Include layout, branding, and navigation improvements.

Prompt: Provide 10 actionable SEO tips for my author website and blog. Include keyword suggestions and meta description strategies for [genre].

Email Excellence

Prompt: Share email templates and best practices for building my list and promoting my book. Focus on personalization, subject lines, and reader engagement.

Prompt: Provide 5 tips for growing my email list and keeping subscribers engaged. Include content suggestions and frequency recommendations.

RESEARCH & TRENDS

Market Intelligence

Prompt: What are 10 trending hashtags in writing and self-publishing communities relevant to book marketing on a budget?

Prompt: What are the latest trends in AI and writing? Include cutting-edge tools and creative ways authors are using AI in 2025.

Visual & Multimedia Content

Prompt: Suggest 3 creative book trailer concepts with visual direction, sample scripts, and links to free tools or templates.

Prompt: Generate 10 thoughtful discussion questions for my book to spark engaging book club conversations.

Pro Tips for Maximum Impact

Save Your Favorites

Create a "WRITE Vault" in Notion, Google Docs, or a simple folder. Save your best responses, customized prompts, and successful outputs for easy reference.

Customize for Your Voice

These prompts are starting points. Adjust language, add specific details about your genre, and include your unique perspective to make them truly yours.

Chain Your Prompts

Don't stop at one response. Follow up with "Can you expand on point #3?" or "Now make this more specific to romance novels" to get exactly what you need.

Test and Iterate

Not every prompt will work perfectly the first time. Refine your requests based on what you get back, and remember that specificity breeds success.

Appendix: Publishing Platforms

The KDP and Wider Distribution Guide

AMAZON KDP (Kindle Direct Publishing)

Why Use It

The world's largest self-publishing platform with global reach, easy setup, and exclusive promotional tools.

How to Join

1. Visit kdp.amazon.com
2. Sign in with your Amazon account or create one
3. Add your publisher name and mailing address
4. Set up payment (bank account, Wise or Payoneer)

5. Complete tax info (W-8BEN for non-U.S., EIN/SSN for U.S. residents)

To Upload to KDP, You'll Need

- Manuscript (Word or EPUB)
- Cover files (JPEG for ebook, PDF for print)
- Book description, categories, and keywords

Upload Process

1. Go to Bookshelf → Create New Kindle eBook
2. Enter metadata (title, description, keywords)
3. Upload manuscript and cover
4. Set pricing and royalty
5. Publish or schedule a pre-order

Print Distribution Tip

Use your own ISBN if you plan to publish elsewhere.
Do not select "Expanded Distribution" if you're using IngramSpark.

Royalty Rates

- eBook: 70% (for prices $2.99–$9.99) or 35%
- Print: 50% (under $9.99) or 60% (over $9.99), minus print cost

INGRAMSPARK

Why Use It

A top Amazon alternative with access to bookstores, libraries, and over 40,000 retailers globally.

How to Join

1. Visit ingramspark.com
2. Click Sign Up and choose "Publisher" or "Author"
3. Fill in your account, tax, and mailing details
4. Use promo codes to waive setup fees if available

What You'll Need

- Your own ISBN
- Print-ready PDF for print
- ePub file for ebook
- Matching metadata with KDP

Upload Tip

Always publish on KDP first, then IngramSpark.
Do not select KDP's "Expanded Distribution."

Royalty Rates

- eBooks: Around 40%
- Print: Around 45%, minus print and distribution costs

DRAFT2DIGITAL AND SMASHWORDS

Why Use It

Distribute your ebook to multiple retailers including Apple, B&N, Kobo, and Smashwords, all from one dashboard.

How to Join

1. Go to draft2digital.com
2. Sign up with your name, email, and payment details
3. Confirm your account

What You'll Need

- Manuscript (Word, EPUB, or PDF)
- Cover image
- Description and metadata

Upload and Distribution

1. Upload your file
2. Choose retailers

3. Set pricing

4. Review and publish

Additional Note
Smashwords now operates through Draft2Digital. Opt into Smashwords distribution through your D2D dashboard.

KOBO WRITING LIFE

Why Use It

Great for global reach and participation in Kobo Plus, their subscription-based reading platform.

How to Join

1. Visit kobo.com/writinglife

2. Sign in or create a Rakuten Kobo account

3. Enter payment and tax information

Upload Process

- Upload your EPUB and cover

- Choose territories and Kobo Plus

- Set your pricing

LULU

Why Use It

Ideal for print-on-demand projects like journals, and specialty books.

How to Join

1. Visit lulu.com
2. Sign up, verify your account, add your author and payment details

What You'll Need

- PDF print interior
- Cover image
- ISBN (yours or Lulu's)

BOOKBABY

Why Use It

Provides full-service packages for authors looking for help with editing, design, and distribution.

How to Join

1. Visit bookbaby.com
2. Sign up with your author info

3. Confirm your email and explore services

Note: BookBaby includes hands-on consultation and service options. You'll need to choose a publishing package.

GOOGLE PLAY BOOKS

Why Use It

Reach Android readers directly and benefit from Google search traffic.

How to Join

1. Visit play.google.com/books/publish
2. Sign in with your Google account
3. Fill in publisher profile and tax info
4. Wait for approval (may take a few days)

Note: Availability varies by country. Confirm your eligibility before proceeding.

DIY BOOK COVER CREATION

eBook Covers

- Format: JPEG or TIFF
- Size: 1600 × 2560 pixels
- Color mode: RGB

- Tools: Canva, Adobe Express, GIMP

Print Covers

- Format: PDF
- Color mode: CMYK
- Resolution: 300 DPI
- Bleed: 0.125" on all sides
- Use KDP's Cover Calculator to get dimensions
- Upload KDP template into Canva to align design elements

Design Tips

- Keep it clean and uncluttered
- Ensure the title is readable in thumbnail view
- Reserve a 2" × 1.2" area for the barcode

GLOBAL PUBLISHING CHECKLIST

Pre-Upload

- Manuscript formatted and final
- eBook and print covers ready
- ISBN assigned
- Categories and keywords researched

- Book description written
- Pricing and launch strategy decided

Upload

- Create project on KDP or chosen platform
- Enter metadata
- Upload files
- Select royalty and pricing
- Publish or schedule

AMAZON MARKETING TOOLS

Free Tools to Use

1. Author Central: Build your profile and manage your presence
2. KDP Select: Access promotional features like countdown deals and Kindle Unlimited
3. Amazon Ads: Set up keyword-targeted campaigns
4. Review Requests: Reach out to verified readers from your dashboard
5. Optimized Listings: Focus on book descriptions, keywords, categories, and cover
6. External Sharing: Promote with direct links and QR codes

QR Code Tips

Use tools like Canva or QR Code Monkey to link to:

- Author website
- Book trailers
- Bonus content
- Email sign-up pages

Appendix: Marketing Systems

Where to Be and How to Show Up

Explore the digital jungle without algorithm alligators eating you!

Social Media Platforms

Instagram:

Still the reigning queen of visual story telling, think of Instagram as your book's red carpet moment. Each post should make readers stop scrolling and say "tell me more." Use Reels for book trailers, Stories for behind-the-scenes magic, and Carousels for those "swipe for wisdom" moments.

Threads & Bluesky:

The new kids on the block so set up shop here early. Think of it like buying beachfront property before everyone discovers the beach.

Discord:

Your VIP lounge for superfans. Create a private community where readers can geek out over your characters, attend virtual booklaunches, and get exclusive content that makes them feel special (because they are).

TikTok (BookTok):

The wild west of book discovery. Five seconds to hook a reader? Challenge accepted. Share writing tips, book trailers, and that moment when your character does something so outrageous you have to pause and question your own sanity.

Facebook Groups:

Like that friend with deep pockets who always shows up empty-handed, Facebook's organic reach is about as generous as Scrooge, but Groups still work for niche communities. Use them, but don't put all your digital eggs in the Facebook basket.

Set Up and Create Profiles Like a Pro

Username:

Make it memorable and spell-able. If your name is Janet Smith and you write about astrology, try @janetsmithastrologer. Want to stay mysterious? Go with something like @spiritmistress. (You can change it later without losing followers, so experiment!)

Profile Picture and Bio:

Use a good image of yourself. Readers want to connect with a human, not a logo. Just 160 characters can make someone fall in love with your work. Use action verbs, sprinkle in keywords, and include a link (use Bitly to track clicks like a marketing ninja).

Location:

Get creative! Historical fiction writer? List it as "The Past." Sci-fi author? Try "Middle Earth" or "Galaxy Far, Far Away."

Visual Resources That Won't Break the Bank:

- Canva (templates for everything)
- Freepik (AI tools included)
- Unsplash, Pixabay, Pexels (free, gorgeous images)
- Graaphics.co (social media graphics that pop)

Build a Facebook Group in 7 Steps

1. **Log into Facebook** (What? You don't have an account? Make one! It's 2025, not 1995)

2. **Find the Groups section** on your left menu and click "Create Group"

3. **Choose a killer name** that reflects your brand or genre – make it catchy and memorable

4. **Set your privacy level:**
   Public: Anyone can join (like a public library)
   Private: Approval required (like a book club)
   Secret: Invitation only (like a speakeasy)

5. I**nvite your tribe** – quality over quantity. No one wants to join a cat meme group if they're allergic to cats.

6. **Customize everything** – profile picture, cover photo,compelling description. Tart it up and have fun!

7. **Keep it engaging and drama-free** – easier said than done, but sovereignty isn't for everyone.

Email Marketing: Your Direct Line to Reader Hearts

Think of email as your private conversation with readers – no algorithm interference, no platform drama, just you and the people who want to hear from you.

Set Up MailerLite:

- Go to mailerlite.com and click "Sign up free"
- Create your account (email or social media login)
- Navigate to "Audience" → "Lists" →"Create a New List"
- Fill in your sending name and address
- Create sign-up forms under "Forms" →"Embedded Forms"
- Install on your website (they provide instructions)
- Start sending emails

The Golden Rules:

- Segment your readers and send relevant content to each group
- Prune inactive subscribers. If they haven't opened your last 10 emails, set them free.
- Deliver content that meets their needs
- Set up automation for welcome sequences and re-engagement flows.

Instagram Intelligence: 7 Ways to Win

1. Profile Perfection: Make it represent the real you, with a direct link to your book
2. Post with Purpose: High-quality images, behind-the-scenes moments, teasers that tease
3. Hashtag Wisdom: Use relevant ones that help the right people find you
4. Stories That Stick: Brief, engaging videos and updates that disappear, but not from memory!
5. Strategic Partnerships: Collaborate with authors, bookstagrammers, and literary influencers
6. Book Club Engagement: Join discussions, provide exclusive content, be genuinely helpful
7. Long-form Video: Share deeper insights about your writing process and book journey

Creating an Artful Instagram Post:

- Open Instagram app → tap the + → choose your content type
- Write a caption that's witty, heartfelt, or informative (preferably all three)
- Add relevant hashtags for discoverability
- Hit publish and watch your creation take flight!

Research With Purpose

Use Amazon's search function and Publisher Rocket to 'reverse engineer' successful titles in your niche

- Try BuzzSumo to gauge topic interest and popular search terms
- Ask ChatGPT to help create detailed reader profiles
- Get beta reader feedback – your early warning system

The 5+5 Rule:

- Find 5 comparison titles similar to yours (study their covers, hooks, categories)
- Identify 5 allies whose vibe aligns with yours (follow, comment, be seen in their firelight)

Content Creation

Prioritize These:

- Short-form video (Reels, TikToks, Stories) for maximum discoverability
- Interactive content (polls, quizzes, live Q&As) to boost engagement
- Behind-the-scenes content
- Value-first posts that help people

Community Building

- Private Discord servers for deeper connections
- Collaborative events with other authors
- Reader-generated content (encourage fan art, reviews, video reactions)

What's Working Now:

- AI-powered personalization and automation
- Multi-platform presence with focus on emerging spaces
- Community-first approach over follower count
- Interactive, multimedia content over static posts

What's Not:

- Relying solely on Facebook's organic reach
- One-size-fits-all content strategies
- Ignoring AI tools and automation
- Treating social media like a billboard instead of a conversation

Your Action Plan:

- Audit your presence. Where do your readers hang out?
- Embrace AI and automation: Save time, stay competitive
- Foster genuine community: be active in private groups
- Stay agile: Be ready to pivot

The Bottom Line

Marketing your book doesn't have to feel like selling your soul. Show up authentically, provide value, Remember, you don't have to use all the platforms – just pick one or two you feel comfortable with master them, then expand. Or not. It's up to you. Quality over quantity always wins.

Fab Free Tools

Organized by Purpose

Writing & Distraction – Free Drafting

1. **Google Docs** – Collaboration, autosave; still #1 for real-time co-authoring and cloud backup.

2. **LibreOffice Writer** – Full-featured, free desktop writing suite.

3. **FocusWriter, OmmWriter, ZenPen, The Most Dangerous WritingApp** – Distraction-free environments for drafting.

4. **JotterPad, Writer, yWriter** – Minimalist or structured writing (yWriter remains free but niche).

<u>ALSO:</u>

- **Notion AI** – All-in-one workspace with AI-powered drafting, outlining, and distraction-free writing.

- **Obsidian** – Markdown-based, local-first writing and note-linking, ideal for complex projects and worldbuilding.

- **Arc Studio (free tier)** – Screenwriting and structured fiction, with cloud sync and collaboration.

Editing, Style & Feedback

1. **Grammarly, Hemingway Editor, ProWritingAid, LanguageTool,Typely, Reverso, Readable, Slick Write, Expresso** – Top free editing and style tools

2. **DupliChecker, Copyscape** – Plagiarism checking (free tier).

3. **Beta feedback:** Goodreads groups, Indie Cover Project (Facebook), BetaReader.io – Community feedback options.

- **SudoWrite** (free trial) – AI-powered style and creativity suggestions for fiction and nonfiction.

- **DeepL Write** – Advanced AI-based editing and translation for clarity and tone.

- **Quillbot** – Continues to improve for paraphrasing, grammar, and style refinement.

Formatting, Publishing Support

1. **Reedsy Studio** – Free cloud book formatting, **KindleCreate** for Amazon eBooks

2. **Pressbooks, FastPencil, OpenOffice, PDFescape, OnlineConverter** – File prep and publishing.

3. **Barcode/QR Generators, Booklinker, Genius Link, ReaderScout, Kindlepreneur tools** – Distribution, tracking, link management.

- **Draft2Digital** – Free formatting and distribution features.
- **StoryOrigin (free tier)** – Newsletter swaps, reader magnets, and ARC management.

CATEGORY	TOP FREE TOOLS
WRITING	Notion AI, Obsidian, Arc Studio
EDITING	SudoWrite, DeepL Write, Quillbot
FORMATTING	Atticus, Draft2Digital, StoryOrigin
DESIGN	Canva, Leonardo.AI, RunwayML
RESEARCH	Perplexity.ai, Glasp, SparkToro
VOICE/NOTES	AudioPen, Whisper (OpenAI)
AI TOOLS	Claude, Google Gemini, Lex.page

Useful (mostly free) tools in 2025 -2026

Design & Visual Media Resources

1. **Canva, Freepik, Unsplash, Kittl, Pexels (videos), Graaphics.co** – Royalty-free images and graphics.
2. **ClipChamp** – Video creation/editing.
3. **Graphics Tools:** Buffer's Pablo, Ideogram.ai.

ALSO:

- **Adobe Express (30-day free trial** – Quick, professional graphics and social media content creation.
- **Leonardo.AI** – Free AI-generated book covers and illustrations.
- **RunwayML** – AI-powered video editing and image creation (free tier available).

Research, SEO & Analytics

1. **Feedly, Crowdfire, Buffer, QuestionDB, Keywords Everywhere,Amazon Keyword Tool, Hashtag/Headline Analyzers, SmallSEOTools/H-Supertools, Yoast SEO** – Marketing and SEO insights.
2. **Pew Research, Worldometers** – Data and trends.

ALSO:

- **Perplexity.ai** – AI-powered research and fact-checking tool.
- **Glasp** – Web clipping, research, and annotation for nonfiction projects.
- **SparkToro (free tier)** – Audience and influencer research

Voice, Transcription & Notetaking

1. **Natural Reader, Otter.ai, Speechnotes, Google Docs Voice Typing, Images to Text OCR** – Audio/text tools.
2. **Notion, Turtl, Workflowy, Trello, Quire** – Organizing story notes, tasks, and research.

ALSO:

- **AudioPen** – AI-powered tool for turning voice notes into structured text.
- **Whisper by OpenAI** – Free, open-source, highly accurate speech-to-text.

AI-Powered Author Tools

1. **ChatGPT, Perplexity.ai, Effidit, Sudowrite, Novelcrafter** –Advanced AI writing help.
2. **Autocrit, Quillbot** – AI editing and paraphrasing.
3. **Atticus, Reedsy, yWriter** – Author-specific formatting and workflow.

ALSO:

- Claude (Anthropic, free tier) – Strong for brainstorming, editing, and outlining.
- Google Gemini – Free AI writing, summarizing, and research.
- Lex.page – Free AI writing assistant for drafting and editing.

TIP:

Free tools for authors evolve almost monthly, with the integration of AI.

Keep exploring new platform features to stay ahead.

Afore Ye Go

If *Write* sparked delight for you, leave a review so others can enjoy it, too, won't you?

Here's the link and a big thank you!

Scan me, please.

Splash What?

Anything You Like

Welcome to the refreshed edition of *Splash It!* For freelancers, authors, small business owners, or creative launching your Big Thing, this DIY publicity power tool reboot includes :

- AI-powered prompts and tools to speed up your process, clarify your message and get noticed
- Short-form storytelling tips for platforms like TikTok, Instagram Reels, and Substack.
- New templates tailored for podcasts, newsletters, and press kits to elevate your pitch and build buzz on your terms
- A customizable workbook companion so you can go from idea to implementation in minutes.

So, bookmark the prompts, remix the templates, and scan the QR codes for bonus downloads. Find your voice, own your story, and make genuine connections with the people who need your work. You don't need a PR team. All you need is *Splash It!* – *Caroline*

Your Shortcut

To Press, Podcasts & Publicity

Download Pitch, Publish & Pop here or scan the QR code below:

Master the exact tools and prompts to grab media attention without hiring a pricey publicist.

Contents

Before We Dive In

Let's Splash Out With The Basics

Start Here: Your First 3 Steps

- Choose your immediate PR goal: Launch, Pitch, Troubleshoot
- Flip to the matching chapter in this book
- Complete your first editable template or AI prompt using the tips provided

Where, oh, *where* can I find work? It's a common lament from the freshly retrenched. Thanks to AI, there's no better time to time to maximize your unique skills, wisdom and experience. Follow your passion. Build a client base from scratch.

But *how?* Draw three columns. First, list your skills from making kefir to chicken sexing. In the second, list all the things you're good at. In the third, what do you ENJOY doing?

Know your strengths and weaknesses. Take me. My initial chicken sexing skills led to a seven-cock-a-doodle situation that drove my neighbor's fiancé from her home; a favor, in retrospect.

Of course, *now* I know it's all in the comb. These and other fowl incidents sparked The Rooster Diaries, a steady best-seller on Amazon in two bird care categories.

It's all in the marketing. The good news is that it's never been easier now with AI.

Once upon a deadline, you needed a copywriter, a strategist, a PR guru, and a patient friend who wouldn't raise an eyebrow at your fifth draft. Now? Just a browser tab will do.

Enter your tireless AI assistant, who helps you refine and broadcast your ideas with the tap of a key whether you're whipping up an irresistible press release, polishing a bio or drafting an elevator pitch with pop, punch, and purpose. AI won't write the heart of your story, but it can help you tell it better, faster, and louder.

Top Tools To Try

- ChatGPT (chat.openai.com) – Ideal for polishing text, generating headlines, writing bios, FAQs, even interview questions.
- Copy.ai – Best for punchy product descriptions, email subject lines, and social media captions.
- Notion AI – Helps with organizing launch plans, writing outreach emails, and summarizing key PR points in long-form drafts.
- Descript – For turning your press release into audio snippets or video sizzle reels with captions and voiceovers.

The Splash Out section tells you everything you need to know about writing a compelling press with customizable text templates and layout suggestion to help you stand out.

How you approach journalists, editors, or book bloggers is almost as crucial as your media kit.

Create connections and leave a lasting impression with irresistible PR copy that hits the mark! Learn more in the Media Whispering chapter.

Pitch, Host and Share

Share participatory pieces in **Pitch Perfect**and convert your press momentum into a content series in the **Host and Share** chapters.

Introduce, Launch, and Showcase

Read how to introduce yourself, present a compelling idea, or venue, airline, tour itinerary with solutions to challenges in the Introduce, **Launch** and Showcase chapters. You'll find a survival guide when bad press goes viral in the Troubleshoot chapter.

Bonus Prompt Vault

Let AI do all the heavy lifting with these powerful prompts.

Pitch. Publish. Pop!

A companion workbook with everything you need to succeed.

Ready to take the plunge? Then, let's jump in.

How To Use The Layout Templates

Follow these four steps to bring your vision to life using each chapter's A4 Layout Templates for easy and enjoyable customization.

1: When you click on the link for each template, it will take you to Canva. Sign up for a free account with this user-friendly graphic design platform. Registration is quick and easy.

2: Open up the template, then replace the headlines, descriptions, dates, or other text details with content specific to your project.

3: Replace the images in the template by uploading and dragging your desired images into place on the template.

4: Once satisfied with your customizations, click the download button to save your design to your device. Choose the appropriate file format (PNG, JPG, or PDF) and resolution for your intended use.

- You'll find the Layout Links after the Bonus Prompt Generator section

Easy peasy! Get started today and let your creativity soar!

Marketing Mindset

Know the Map Before the Message

Before you pitch, post, or publish, it helps to understand the method behind the momentum.

Marketing is about whispering the right message to the right person at the right time. It's visibility over vanity; nuance over noise.

Forget attention seeking. Authors and entrepreneurs must offer relevance, resonance, and a reason to care. That's the philosophy behind Splash It! It's designed for doers. Instead of jargon-filled manifestos, you'll find the tools, templates, and timelines to help you act right now.

Three Essential Marketing Truths

1. Visibility is Authority: People trust what they see often. Being visible on the right platforms signals credibility before a word is read or a book is bought. ***Splash It!*** Helps you show up with style and substance until recognition becomes reputation.

2. **Consistency Beats Complexity:** You need to be consistent where it counts. A compelling message repeated across channels builds a cohesive identity. Think ripples turning into waves.

3. Emotion Drives Engagement: Facts tell. Stories sell. Behind every press release, post, or pitch, there should be an emotional hook, whether it's curiosity, laughter, empathy, or awe. Marketing works best when it touches hearts before minds.

Marketing is a state of awareness. Know who you're talking to, where they hang out, and what keeps them up at night. Then offer them something that feels like a life raft. Or at least, a good splash of inspiration.

Now that you've dipped your toes into the philosophy, let's wade into the how-to strategies.

One

Splash Out!

Press Release Essentials

In this chapter:

- 1 press release formula
- 6 visual storytelling principles
- 7-point editing checklist
- AI-powered layout and formatting prompts
- Reality check tips for sounding pro
- Tools for pitch conversion across formats

Scrolling thumbs mean a press release must double as elevator pitch, headline act, and credibility booster to captivate short attention spans. The good news? You no longer need a PR agency to dazzle journalists.

With the right structure and a little help from AI, you can write memorable releases that influencers want to share.

Level up your release with co-creation tools, visual storytelling, and platform polish. Whether you're announcing a collaboration, launching a product, or promoting an experience, you'll find ready-to-use frameworks, examples, prompts, and design tips to help you shine. Start with the story that sells. A press release has two parts – the announcement that covers all the newsworthy essentials and the boilerplate or brief background on your brand or yourself.

Basic Layout

- **Headline** – make it short, snappy, bold, and accurate.
- **Subheading** – expand on the headline.
- **Blurb** – introduce three or more of the key points – who, what, when, where, why, and how.
- **Body** – provide details and quotes from relevant spokespeople.
- **Boilerplate** – provide background, short bio and contact info.

6 Visual Wizardry Keys

1. **Heading** or subject line that tells the story with a strong keyword
2. **White space** to rest your eyes and neat formatting.
3. **Reliable paragraphs,** bullet points, and bold headings to break up the text.
4. **Short** scan-friendly paragraphs and sentences.
5. **Numbered** key info for quick reference.
6. **Logo** in the top right-hand corner of the page.

- **Pro Tip:** Keep **headlines bold and benefit-focused.** Journalists skim!

7-Point Checklist

1. Have you summarized your story's core message in the opening blurb? Did you address the Sacred Six: who, what, when, where, why, and how?
2. How does your angle or hook set your product apart? Offer a deal or discount if you struggle to find an angle.
3. Does your headline invite further perusal? Try an unusual statement, bizarre statistic, or provocative question. Tantalize further with your subhead.
4. Have you considered the publication's audience? Tailor your release accordingly.
5. Have you provided any credible supporting quotes or statistics for additional relevance? Include links to the original research.
6. Is it brief, clear, concise, engaging, and jargon-free? Less is more. Aim for 400 words or fewer.
7. Have you included contact details such as website and phone number? Explain who you are in the notes to the editor below the release.

- **AI-Powered Tip:** Try free **AI headline analyzers** such as **Sharethrough, CoSchedule**.

Where To Send Your Release

Top Free Submission Sites

(See the Essential Tools chapter for more submission sites)

- **PRLog** – Free press release hosting with SEO-friendly formatting and paid upgrades.
- **PRFree** – Free account for press release distribution to news outlets and social media.
- **Newswire Today** – Focuses on technology, business, and industry news with a basic free option.
- **Online PR News** – Freemium model offering free basic press release packages.

Find the right editor or outlet:

1. **Research the publication's website**: Find the editor or journalists covering your niche and their contact information.
2. **Use directories or** LinkedIn using your topic's keywords.
3. **X or Bluesky** are good places to connect with specific journalists or editors you'd like to approach. Try the hashtags #journorequest or #amwriting

Think of your press release as the sophisticated older sibling of your social media posts. While your Instagram Reel does cartwheels for attention, your press release networks with the grown-ups at the table, making connections that matter.

The Golden Rule: Put yourself in the shoes of a publicist who cares about your story. What would make them stop scrolling and hit your email address?

Your Curated Collection Toolkit: Whether you're unveiling a new coffee shop, consulting, sharing industry insights, or showcasing technological breakthroughs, a well-crafted press release inspires your audience to become your unpaid marketing army.

The Modern Press Release Formula: Convert your press momentum into a content series across Substack, YouTube Shorts, Reels, TikTok, and podcast segments

Newsletter Magic: Master Substack, Beehiiv, and ConvertKit distribution

Authority Building: Highlight your unique background, expertise, and passion in ways that make editors think, "This person knows their stuff."

Core Principles for Visual Appeal

- **Keywords:** Modern, sleek, minimalist, dynamic, interactive, digital-first
- **Purpose:** Crystal clear at a glance
- **Industry Context:** Specific enough to show you know your stuff
- **Visual Hierarchy**: Guide the eye, don't confuse it.

Quick Prompt Arsenal

1. **For Overall Impact:** "Design a modern, minimalist press release. Think digital-first aesthetic with enough white space to let content breathe, but not so much that it looks empty."

2. **For the Header:** "Create a header that makes people want to keep reading instead of clicking away. Clean logo placement, prominent title treatment, and contact information."

3. **For the Hero Section:** "Design a designated space for an image or video embed. Make it large enough to matter, professional enough to impress, and adaptable enough to work with whatever content you throw at it."

4. **For Contact Information:** "Create a 'Note to Editors' section that editors will use. Include everything they need (email, phone, media kit link)."

The Reality Check

What separates amateurs from professionals? The former focus on what they want to say. Professionals focus on what others need to hear.

Your press release isn't a love letter to your business. It's a compelling argument for why someone else should care enough to share your story with their audience.

Make it easy for them to say yes. Make it impossible for them to ignore.

The Final Test: If your press release announcement doesn't excite you , it won't excite anyone else either. Polish it until it sparkles and then some. The sparkly stuff gets noticed.

Next up: Press Release Templates that work.

Press Releases

Templates That Work

In this chapter:

- 3 done-for-you press release examples
- Collaboration
- Product Launch
- Retro Venue
- 1 DIY venue showcase template
- Canva customization link
- 3 real-world tone variations (witty, urgent, sensory)

The Collaboration (Two Brands Are Better Than One)

FOR IMMEDIATE RELEASE

A Harmonious Symphony of Style and Sound: Miramba and Dresswell Collaboration Transforms Music and Fashion Industries

[City, Date] - When melody maestro Murray Miramba met couture diva Diana Dresswell at a charity gala, neither expected their casual conversation about "art that makes people feel something" would spark an industry-shaking collaboration.

Fast-forward six months, and their unprecedented fusion project is about to blur every line between sound and style. What makes this collaboration extraordinary? It's a sensory reimagining. Think concert-meets-catwalk, where every note has a corresponding fabric texture.

The Details That Matter:

- **Launch Date:** [Specific date that creates urgency]
- **Where to Experience It:** [Venue or platform]
- **Media Contact:** [Make your details easy to find and professional]

Turn Your Collaboration Release into Short-Form Video

Behind-the-Scenes Reveal

- **[Intro shot: Both brands' logos]** "When [Brand A] meets [Brand B] you can expect something brand new. [quick teaser of event].

- **[Show B-roll** of sample products or first reactions]

- **[Outro]**: "Ready to experience the magic of collaboration? Drop a like if you love collabs!"

The Product Launch (Gaming the System)

Embark on the Ultimate Virtual Odyssey with GameQuest

[City, Date] - Remember when games were just about high scores? GameQuest is about to make that nostalgia feel quaint.

This isn't your typical "cutting-edge graphics and immersive storytelling" announcement (though yes, those boxes are ticked). GameQuest has cracked the code on making technology feel simple.

The Problem It Solves: Information overload is the villain of our digital age. GameQuest is the hero who says, "What if your gaming experience made your life easier instead of more complicated?"

The Experience: Seamless integration of technology and simplicity, wrapped in a visual feast that sets new industry standards. It'slike having a personal digital butler who happens to excel in entertainment.

Release Timeline: [Create anticipation with specific dates]

30-Second Instagram Reel Script to Showcase Product

- **Goal:** Grab attention with the product's best features.
- **Opening Hook**: [Close-up of the box, upbeat music] "Ever wished for [solution your product offers] in one package?"
- **Feature Flash (6-20 sec):** Quick unboxing. Peel back the packaging. Each feature gets a bold, energetic visual (use on-screen text and hand gestures.)
- **"Feature #1:** [Describe, show in action]."
- **"Wait, there's more!** Feature #2 is **my favorite!** [Show quick result or share a fun reaction]."

The Retro Diner Feature (Hit the Road, Jack!)

Sub head: The Cadillac Association and CaliTourism Round Up Retro 50s American Diner Vibes

Intro: Some attach grid trays to their car windows. Others embrace the open-road spirit with juicy burgers, hot dogs, and double-thick milkshakes that could power a small motorcycle.

The Scene: Two-tone floor tiles, American diner-style fittings, and pulsing neon signs that whisper, "Your diet starts tomorrow."

The Route:

- **Stop 1: [Venue Name]** - Servers in period-perfect attire deliver orders to your window faster than you can say "extra pickles." It's efficiency with style.

- **Stop 2: [Beachside Venue]** - This 70s surfer haven hasn't lost its laid-back charm. Order the legendary 'Tsunami Burgers' and pretend cholesterol doesn't exist for one afternoon.

- **Stop 3: [Pizza Palace]** - This roadhouse serves pizzas so large they barely fit through car windows. It lights up like Christmas in July. Yes, you absolutely can see it from space.

The Bottom Line: Your beach body goals can wait. Some experiences are worth the extra sit-ups.

Showcase Your Venue Format

1. **Define Your Unique Vibe:** Stop saying you're "cozy" or "family friendly." Everyone says that! Are you a retro American diner where Elvis impersonators croon while you eat? Are you a beachside oasis where calories don't count? *That's* your vibe.

2. **Highlight What Makes People Stop:** Is it lightning-fast service? Unbeatable value that makes people question your business model? Captivating performances that turn dinner into theater? Name and claim it.

3. **Set the Scene Like a Movie Director:** Transport readers to your space. Are you reminiscent of a bygone era, or are you so modern timetravelers would feel at home?

4. Make Mouths Water Through Words: "Good food" tells us nothing. "Iconic burgers that require architectural support" tells us so much more!

5. Share Your Success Story: Key milestones, ownership changes, expansions, whatever. Make them interesting. "From three employees to 30" becomes "What started as three friends with a dream and a plan drawn up on a napkin now employs enough people to field a softball team."

- **Customize collaborative press release** templates in Canva

3 Featured Free AI Tools

TOOL	WHAT IT DOES	HOW TO USE IT	SAMPLE PROMPT
Poe.com	Generates catchy headlines, emails, blogs	"Read, edit, personalize this email and send!	"Draft a press email for my book launch."

Use Poe to test multiple tone styles

TOOL	WHAT IT DOES	HOW TO USE IT	SAMPLE PROMPT
Perplexity	Instant research & content draft	Ask: "Best local press for food launches 2026 UK?"	"Draft a press email for my book launch."

Use Perplexity to verify trending topics

TOOL	WHAT IT DOES	HOW TO USE IT	SAMPLE PROMPT
Copy.ai	Generates catchy headlines, emails, blogs	1. Sign up free 2. Select "Press Release" 3. Paste your info & click "Create"	"Transform this bland news update into a punchy press lead."

Use Copy.ai to refresh stale press releases

Media Whispering

Email Etiquette and Pitch Refinement

In this chapter:

- 1 viral pitch fail case study
- 4 Fatal Pitching Mistakes to avoid
- New Media Hierarchy overview
- 3-phase relationship-building roadmap
- AI prompts for researching influencers and pitch angles
- Follow-up timing strategies
- Tools for media list building

Picture this: Your pitch goes viral on LinkedIn. Sounds great, right? Wrong. It's viral because some content creator screenshot your "Dear Influencer" mass email and posted it with cry-laughing emojis. The comments are brutal. Your client is mortified. Your boss is not planning your promotion party, after all.

Case Study 1: The BCC Debacle

Name: Meera, Junior Account Executive at a boutique PR firm
The Pitch: "Fab Collab Opportunity!" mass emailed to 300 influencers.
The Problem: Meera accidentally hit CC instead of BCC. Oops!
Cue public replies from influencers: "This is not a vibe. Delete me."

A lifestyle vlogger posts a screenshot, tagging the PR firm with: "Nothing screams 'exclusive offer' like being lumped in with 299 strangers."

Virality: Trending on Threads under #PRFail
Client Reaction: Filters your emails to the spam bin.
Lessons Learned: Personalisation beats automation and double-check your CCs.

Internet infamy is just a screenshot away. Having survived decades in traditional media and the creator economy chaos, I've seen every mistake in the book. In 2026 and beyond, there will be new and creative ways to annoy people across multiple platforms simultaneously. Sigh.

The media's wild ecosystem of newsletter writers, podcast hosts, TikTok creators, and LinkedIn thought leaders requires the same fundamentals respect, relevance, and genuine relationship-building.

The New Media Reality

Forget everything you think you know about "real" journalists versus "just bloggers." Today, a newsletter writer with 15,000 engaged subscribers has way more influence than a newspaper columnist. A podcast host interviewing in their home studio can reach more decision-makers than a TV segment. A creator posting daily on LinkedIn might be the gateway to your target audience. The media's wild ecosystem of newsletter writers, podcast hosts, TikTok creators, and thought leaders requires the same fundamentals: respect, relevance, and genuine relationship-building.

The Approach

Introducing yourself to bloggers and media representatives has never been easier, but like any relationship worth cultivating, it requires consistency over time. The secret to irresistible proposals that land in inboxes and not spam folders is thoughtful narratives, authentic engagement on *their* social media, and enticing propositions. Here's how to go about it:

- Deliver on every commitment – your reputation depends on it
- Leave comments demonstrating your knowledge of their niche
- Ask insightful questions – dialogue beats monologue every time
- Personalise ruthlessly – automation is the enemy of connection

The New Media Hierarchy

- Newsletter Writers (Substack, ConvertKit, Beehiiv): Often former journalists with loyal, engaged audiences
- Podcast Hosts: Long-form content kings and queens with intimate listener relationships
- LinkedIn Creators: B2B influencers with corporate decision-maker followings
- YouTube Creators: Video content specialists with massive reach
- TikTok/Insta Creators: Younger demographics, viral potential
- Traditional Media: Relevant, but no longer the only game in town

Many of these creators are more accessible than your traditional, corporate-compromised journalists.

They're building their own media empires and are often hungry for good content. But – and this is crucial – they're also savvy about being used and can spot inauthentic outreach from a mile away.

The Fatal Four

Strategies that'll get you blocked faster than a crypto scammer.

1. The Spray-and-Pray Approach

The Crime: Mass emailing with zero personalization.

The Evidence: "Dear Content Creator/Influencer/Media Person, I hope this email finds you well. I'm reaching out because I think you'd be interested in covering our exciting news..."

Why It's Deadly: You've just announced that you have no idea who they are, what they cover, or why they should care. Any further mails from you will be filtered straight into the trash.

The Fix: Research. Spend five minutes reading their recent work. Reference something specific.

2. The Demands Disaster

The Crime: Treating creators like your unpaid marketing team.

The Evidence: "We need you to mention our product launch. Please send us a draft before publishing so we can approve it. Also, we'll need analytics on open rates and click-throughs."

Why It's Deadly: You're not their boss. Your needs mean nothing to them. Why would they? This isn't how media relationships work.

The Fix: Offer value first. Make suggestions, never demands. Respect their editorial independence.

3. Confusion Catastrophe

The Crime: Pitching the wrong content to the wrong platform, like asking a food blogger to review your tax software.

The Evidence: "Hi, I'd love for you to feature our 47-slide presentation about quarterly earnings on your TikTok account."

Why It's Deadly: You clearly don't understand their medium or audience.

The Fix: Match your pitch to their platform. Visual stories for Instagram, data-driven insights for LinkedIn, entertaining angles for TikTok.

4. The Follow-Up Fiasco

The Crime: Harassment disguised as "following up."

The Evidence: Day 1: Email Day 3: Follow-up email Day 5: LinkedIn message Day 7: Instagram DM Day 10: WhatsApp message (somehow they got your number)

Why It's Deadly: You've crossed from persistent to predatory. They're ignoring you now.

The Fix: One follow-up email after a week. If no response, move on. Their silence is an answer.

Multi-Platform Thinking: One Story, Multiple Angles

One good story can live across multiple platforms if you strategize:

Example: A Local Bakery's Viral Success

1. **Traditional Media Angle:** "Small Business Thrives Despite Economic Challenges"
2. **Newsletter Angle:** "The Psychology Behind Viral Food Trends" (with data and insights)
3. **Podcast Angle:** "From Broke to Booming: An Entrepreneur's Journey" (personal story focus)
4. **LinkedIn Angle:** "3 Marketing Lessons from an Unexpected Viral Moment"
5. **TikTok Angle:** "Watch This Baker's Reaction to Going Viral Overnight"
6. **Instagram Angle:** Beautiful food photography with behind-the-scenes stories

Same story, six different approaches. Understand what each platform's audience craves and how each creator serves their community.

Remember that while AI can be your research assistant, it cannot replace genuine human connection.

Use AI to gather intelligence, not to write your pitches.

- ***Visit the Bonus Prompt Vault for Ideas***

Research Like a Pro with AI

1. **Creator Research Prompt:**
   "Analyze the last 10 posts from [Creator Name] on [Platform]. What themes do they cover? What's their tone? What types of stories do they share? What would be relevant to their audience?"

2. **Angle Development Prompt:**
   "Based on [Creator's]recent content about [topic], how could I position my client's story about [your topic] to be relevant to their audience? Give me 3 different angles."

3. **Industry Context Prompt:**
   "What are the current trending topics in [industry/niche] that media creators are covering? How can I connect my story to these trends?"

4 Warning Signs Your Pitch is Too AI-Generated:

1. Overly formal language

2. Generic enthusiasm ("I'm excited to share...")

3. Buzzword overload

4. The lack of specific details makes it feel as though it could be about anyone

Follow-Up Etiquette

Communication is important. Engage with their content over time to build an easy ongoing relationship

Initial Pitch: Tuesday-Thursday, 10 AM-2 PM (their time zone)

Follow-Up: One week later, different time of day

Email: Professional, concise, one follow-up maximum

LinkedIn: Can be slightly more casual, but still professional

X: Respond to their posts, don't 'slide into DMs'

Instagram: Like and comment authentically, don't pitch in DMs

TikTok: Engage with content. The platform isn't pitch-friendly

Target Like a Sniper, Not a Shotgun

Gone are the days of mass media lists. Create micro-targeted lists of 10-20 highly relevant creators per campaign. Quality over quantity always wins.

Research Tools:

- HARO/Connectively: For traditional media opportunities
- PodcastGuests.com: For podcast placement
- Newsletter discovery tools: Substack, ConvertKit directories
- Creator databases: Upfluence, AspireIQ for influencer discovery
- LinkedIn Sales Navigator: For B2B creators and thought leaders

Grab Attention with Platform-Specific Headlines

Your subject line must work for their platform and audience.

- **Traditional Media:** "Local Teacher's Side Hustle Becomes Million-Dollar Business"
- **Newsletter:** "The Psychology Behind Viral Business Success (With Data)"
- **Podcast:** "From Classroom to Boardroom: An Entrepreneurial Switch"
- **LinkedIn:** "What a Teacher Taught Me About Scaling a Business"

Use Angles That Matter

It's not about what you want to say but what their audience needs to hear. Newsworthy angles might include:

- AI impact on traditional industries
- Remote work cultural shifts
- Generational differences in the workplace
- Economic uncertainty survival stories
- Mental health and wellness trends
- Sustainability and conscious consumption

Lead with Value, Not Need

Instead of "We need coverage," try "Your audience might find this useful because..."

A Value-First Approach might include:

- Exclusive data or research
- First-person access to trending topics
- Expert commentary on breaking news
- Behind-the-scenes access
- Practical tips and actionable advice

Leverage Social Proof

Modern creators want to know you're legitimate in a way that makes them feel special.

Smart Social Proof might include:

- "Featured in [relevant publication]"
- "Worked with [similar creator they respect]"
- "This is an exclusive offer for [their platform]"
- "Your recent post about [topic] really resonated with me"

Keep It Scannable

Everyone's drowning in content. Make your pitch easy to digest with this structure:

- **Hook:** One sentence that grabs attention
- **Value:** What's in it for their audience
- **Proof:** Brief credibility indicator
- **Ask:** Clear, simple request
- **Out:** Give them an easy way to say no, such as: "This might not be your bag, but ..."

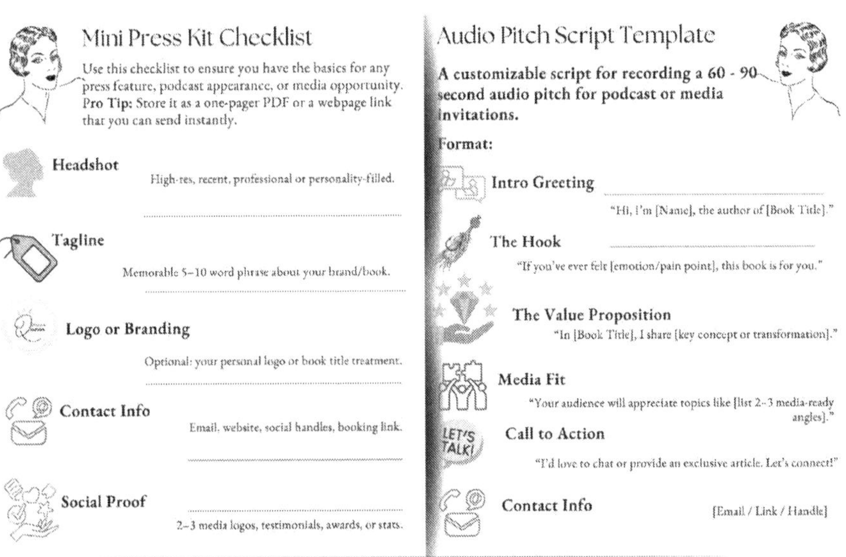

Mini Press Kit Checklist
Use this checklist to ensure you have the basics for any press feature, podcast appearance, or media opportunity.
Pro Tip: Store it as a one-pager PDF or a webpage link that you can send instantly.
Headshot
High-res, recent, professional or personality-filled.
Tagline
Memorable 5–10 word phrase about your brand/book.
Logo or Branding
Optional: your personal logo or book title treatment.
Contact Info
Email, website, social handles, booking link.
Social Proof
2–3 media logos, testimonials, awards, or stats.
Audio Pitch Script Template
A customizable script for recording a 60 - 90 second audio pitch for podcast or media invitations.
Format:
Intro Greeting
"Hi, I'm [Name], the author of [Book Title]."
The Hook
"If you've ever felt [emotion/pain point], this book is for you."
The Value Proposition
"In [Book Title], I share [key concept or transformation]."
Media Fit
"Your audience will appreciate topics like [list 2–3 media-ready angles]."
LET'S TALK!
Call to Action
"I'd love to chat or provide an exclusive article. Let's connect!"
Contact Info
[Email / Link / Handle]

Download these checklists in the Pitch, Publish & Pop Workbook

Three Phases of Media Network Building

The best media relationships are ongoing partnerships built on the foundations of charm

Phase 1: Genuine Engagement

- Follow their content across platforms
- Share their work with thoughtful commentary
- Engage authentically with their posts
- Mention them in your own content when relevant

Phase 2: Value Addition

- Share relevant opportunities with them
- Make introductions to other creators
- Provide data, insights, expertise or resources for their content

Phase 3: Collaboration

- Co-create content
- Cross-promote each other's work
- Participate in their events or communities
- Become a trusted source they turn to

Create Dynamic Media Lists

Your media list should evolve with the landscape with these categories:

- Traditional journalists (by beat)
- Newsletter writers (by niche)
- Podcast hosts (by topic/audience)
- YouTube creators (by subject matter)
- Industry-specific influencers

Tools for List Building:

- **Substack Discover:** Find newsletter writers in your niche
- **Podcast databases:** Listen Notes, Podcast Insights
- **LinkedIn Creator** discovery: Use hashtags and industry searches
- **X Lists:** Follow industry-specific creator lists
- **YouTube:** Use keyword searches and competitor analysis

Set Up Intelligent Alerts

Create a comprehensive monitoring system with these alert strategies.

- **Google Alerts:** For your keywords and creator names
- **Social Mention:** For broader social media monitoring
- **LinkedIn notifications:** For post engagement from key creators

- **X lists:** For real-time creator monitoring

Master Multi-Platform Research

Understand their content ecosystem with this research checklist:

- Recent content themes and angles
- Engagement patterns (what performs well)
- Audience demographics and interests
- Content calendar patterns
- Collaboration history
- Personal interests and values

Keep Your Digital Presence Creator-Ready

When they Google you (they will), what does your online presence say?

Digital Presence Audit:

- **LinkedIn:** Professional, updated, actively posting
- **Website:** Clean, modern, easy to navigate
- **Press kit:** High-res photos, bio, key stats
- **Social media:** Consistent, authentic, engaging
- **Portfolio:** Recent work, diverse examples

Offer Platform-Specific Value

A podcast host differs from a newsletter writer.

Platform-Specific Value Propositions:

- **Podcasts:** Compelling personal stories, expert interviews, exclusive access
- **Newsletters:** Data, trends, actionable insights, exclusive research
- **LinkedIn:** Professional insights, industry commentary, thought leadership
- **YouTube:** Visual stories, demonstrations, behind-the-scenes content
- **Traditional Media:** News angles, expert commentary, exclusive access

6. Use the "Not Sure If This Is Your Thing" Approach

Why It Works:

- Reduces pressure on both sides
- Shows respect for their expertise
- Creates curiosity ("What did they send?")
- Gives them an easy out
- Positions you as considerate, not pushy

Advanced AI Integration Toolkit

AI is your media relations assistant. Here's how to use it strategically throughout your process.

Media Discovery

Prompt for Finding Relevant Creators: "I'm looking for content creators who cover [your industry/topic] and have engaged audiences interested in [your angle]. What types of creators should I be targeting? What platforms are most effective for this niche?"

Prompt for Competitive Analysis: "Analyze how[competitor] has been covered in media. What angles did journalists/creators use? What can I learn from their approach?"

Pitch Crafting

Prompt for Angle Development: "Based on [creator's]recent content about [topic], suggest 3 unique angles for my story about [your topic]. Focus on what would provide value to their specific audience."

Prompt for Subject Line Testing: "I'm pitching [creator] about [topic]. They typically cover [their themes] for [their audience]. Create 5 different subject lines that would grab their attention without being click baity."

Relationship Management

Prompt for Engagement Strategy: "I want to build a relationship with [creator] before pitching. Based on their recent content, suggest 3 ways I could add value to their work or engage with their community."

Prompt for Follow-Up Timing: "I sent a pitch to[creator] on [date]. They typically post about [their topics] on [their schedule]. When would be the best time to follow up, and how should I approach it?"

Quality Control

Prompt for Pitch Review: "Review this pitch for tone, clarity, and effectiveness. Does it sound genuine? Are there any red flags that would annoy a busy creator? How can I improve it?"

Prompt for Platform Optimization: "I'm pitching the same story to [Platform 1] and [Platform 2]. How should I adjust my approach for each platform's audience and content style?"

The Quick-Reference Creator Pitch Checklist

Before You Send, Check That You Have:

- **Researched** their recent 5-10 pieces of content
- **Identified** specific relevance to their audience
- **Personalized** the opening line
- **Included** clear value proposition
- **Made the ask specific** and reasonable
- **Provided easy way** to say no
- **Checked for typos** and tone
- **Ensured it's scannable** (short paragraphs, clear structure)
- **Included relevant credentials** without bragging

Red Flags to Avoid:

- **Generic** opening ("I hope this finds you well")
- **Mass** email signatures ("Dear Media Professional")
- **Demanding** language ("We need you to...")
- **Irrelevant** angles for their platform
- **Obvious AI-generated** content
- **Too much about you**, not enough about them
- **Pushy** follow-up strategy
- **Unrealistic** timelines
- **Attachment-heavy** emails

Plant Digital Seeds

The most successful media relationships are built on genuine connection and mutual value. Start building these relationships before you need them. Engage authentically with creators' content. Share their work when it's relevant. Offer help when you can. Build a network based on respect and reciprocity.

Remember: The magic happens in the relationships you build one genuine interaction at a time. Whether you're pitching a Pulitzer Prize winner or a TikTok creator with 10,000 followers, the principles remain the same: respect their work, understand their audience, and always lead with value.

Master these fundamentals, embrace the tools available, and watch your media relationships flourish across every platform that matters.

Pitch Perfect

Clarity and Authenticity Rule

In this chapter:

- 3 power prompt formulas (headline, podcast, multi-angle)
- 9 "proof sprinkles" to boost credibility
- AI prompts for emotional, visual, and statistical hooks
- Swipe-worthy press release templates (CEO in a tutu!)
- Strategy for purpose-led storylines
- Writing tips for tone, clarity, and benefit-first messaging

Reality Check: Let's trample a few thorns. Consumer cynicism is at an all-time high. No surprises, there.

Virtue signalling is passé *unless* you're doing the work. Jumping on a controversy bandwagon will ensure you either cruise like self-driving cabs, plummet like Jaguar, or faceplant like Bud Light.

There's no middle ground. So choose your collaborators and target influencers with your reputation in mind.

PR's Golden Rule: Build proof-stacked, purpose-led stories that meet the moment and *earn* attention. Nagging, begging and demanding no longer cut it. Enter your silent AI strategist who never tires of your questions.

4 SECRETS TO GOOD HOOKS

Is the topic and language used simple and immediately clear?

SPEED TO VALUE

Did you get to the point within 2 seconds?

AUDIENCE FOCUS

Does it say you/your more than I/me?

CURIOSITY CONTRAST

Does it create a question or show a surprising contrast?

Master these four secrets and you'll hook your readers in seconds.

3 Power Prompts

1. **For Headlines That Sing:** "Write 5 headlines for a press release about my book ***Flow.*** The tone should be witty, empowering and girl-to-girl."

2. **For Podcast Pitches That Get Responses:** "Turn this release into a 60-second pitch script to send to podcast hosts who focus on women's empowerment. Make it warm and benefit-led."

3. **The Multi-Angle Approach:** "Give me five different ways to approach a non-fiction book about burnout and digital detoxing. One pitch angle should be controversial, one trend-based, one deeply emotional, one data-driven, and one visual."

'I got way more than I expected from ***Splash It!*** *Wow! It's a whole workroom full of templates that writers and other business entrepreneu*

June Gillam, Amazon review

Nine Proof Sprinkles to Sweeten Your Pitch

1. **Testimonials - The Golden Oldies**
Quotes from people who benefited from your thing. Not your mom.

2. **User-Generated Content (UGC) - The Authentic Flex**
Screenshots, photos, and videos from your community using branded hashtags or tagging your account. Repost this gold for credibility.

3. **Stats & Data - The Number Crunchers**
Support your claims with relevant statistics from sources such as Statista .com and Google Public Data.

4. **Behind-the-Scenes - The Disorganized Truth**
Show your creative process. Messy is magnetic because it's authentic.

5. **Case Studies - The Before-and-After Magic Make Over**
Detailed success stories showing how your services delivered exceptional results or solves problems for clients.

6. **Review Highlights - The Social Validation**
Monitor and respond to reviews. Positive reviews are powerful social proof; addressing negative feedback demonstrates your commitment to customer satisfaction. Flaunt certifications and accreditations.

7. **Free Samples or Trials - The Taste Test**
Allow potential customers interactive experiences. Let them try before they buy. It's the digital equivalent of grocery store samples.

8. **Thought Leadership - The Authority Play**
Share educational content to establish yourself as the go-to authority in your field. Write articles, give interviews, and share insights.

9. **Influencer Love - The Celebrity Factor**
A celebrity is anyone in your field with more followers than you. Even micro-influencers count.

Press Release Templates That Work

The Participation Play:

Headline: CEO Trades Suit for Tutu

Subhead: Sir Moola McRichpants twirls in the face of convention for a worthy cause.

The Setup: Marvel as this industry titan swaps his boardroom swagger for a pair of delicate ballet pumps, all in the name of charity and sheer hilarity!

The Story: New York, NY - In an astonishing turn of events, the illustrious CEO of Prestige Corp, Sir Moola McRichpants, will put his business acumen to the test on the grandest of stages, a ballet performance!

At 6 pm on June 15, at the magnificent Gotham Theater, Sir Moola will twirl, leap, and pirouette alongside other tech execs, executing synchronized grand jetés in a "Corporate Swan" performance.

The Backstory: Last month, he and his male colleagues donned red strappy stilettos and paraded down the aisles of their stores to raise awareness for widows and orphans in need.

The Quote: "I love nothing more than bringing a smile to children's faces. If that means donning a tutu, then my colleagues and I are 'tutu' happy to do it for them," joked Sir Moola.

The Call to Action: Tickets are available on the event website. Half the proceeds go directly to the We Care Widows & Orphans Foundation.

Why This Works: It's unexpected, visual, purpose-driven, and gives people something to talk about. Plus, it shows the CEO is willing to look ridiculous for a good cause.

30-Second Video Title: "CEO in a Tutu? You Heard Right!"

- **[0–3 sec:** Opening Hook – Fast cuts of a CEO tying ballet shoes + bold text overlay] "CEO Trades Suit for Tutu!" Gotham Theater. June 15 .

- **[3–8 sec:** Voiceover over footage of ballet rehearsal bloopers and smiling execs in tutus] "Sir Moola Mc Richpants is ditching the boardroom for the ballet barre …"

- **[8–14 sec:** Clip of last month's stiletto walk - CEOs strutting, laughing, crowds cheering] "...and he's not alone. These execs are back and bolder!"

- **[14–20 sec:** Cut to interview clip or quote card with Sir Moola] "If it brings joy to kids, I'm tutu happy to help!"

- **[20–25 sec:** Highlight info with upbeat music and countdown text] Live performance: June 15, 6 PM. Half the proceeds go to the We Care Widows & Orphans Foundation.

- **[25–30 sec**: Final CTA – Ticket link & logo animation] Get your tickets now - link in bio!

- **Customize the Participation Layout Template**

The Philanthropy Flex

[Name] Spearheads Philanthropic Initiative to Finance Ambitious Nature Conservation Project

[CITY, DATE] - [Your Organization Name] is spearheading the effort to increase funding for nature conservation with self-made philanthropist [Name] who shares his story of resilience and determination.

- **[Provide clear next steps for involvement]**
- **[Include the transformation story]**
- **[Add the impact numbers]**
- **[Provide the inspiration angle]**

15-Second Video Story: "From Grit to Giving"

- **[0–3 sec:** Bold text over dynamic visuals – nature scenes + a humble beginning photo] "From Nothing to Nature's Hero" Meet [Name],
- **[3–7 sec:** Transformation visuals – before/after, working hard, breakthrough moment] From [humble start] to [achievement] Now funding conservation initiatives.
- **[7–12 sec:** Quick stats overlay with real footage – tree planting, wildlife, teams in action] 100,000 trees planted; Dozens of species protected; Backed by leaders.
- **[12–15 sec:** Call to action with clear next steps.] Be part of the mission. Join us at [website]

Your DIY Template Creation Kit

The Participation Press Release Blueprint

1. **Define the Event:** Craft a headline and subhead that makes people stop scrolling. Ask yourself: "Would I click on this if I saw it in my feed?"

2. **Highlight the Purpose:** Is it charity, nature conservation, or inspiring others through resilience and generosity? Make it crystal clear why this matters.

3. **Set the Stage:** Describe what attendees can expect to experience. Paint a picture so vivid they can almost smell the popcorn.

4. **Emphasize the Impact:** Showcase positive outcomes the event or initiative expects to achieve. Numbers are your friends here.

5. **Highlight Notable Participants:** Mention or quote any influential leaders or individuals involved. Name-dropping is encouraged.

- **Ask AI: Your Digital Wingman**

Template Prompt for Press Releases:

"Turn this story about my small-batch skincare brand into a media pitch that includes one emotional hook, a relevant statistic, and a user quote. Then suggest a title for a 15-second video teaser."

Template Prompt for Podcast Pitches:

"Create a 60-second pitch script for [specific podcast] that positions me as an expert in [your topic]. Include one surprising statistic, one personal story hook, and three specific benefits for their audience."

Template Prompt for Social Media:

"Transform this press release into three different social media posts: one for LinkedIn (professional), one for Instagram(visual), and one for TikTok (trend-based). Each should feel native to the platform."

The Audio Revolution: Sound Bites That Bite Back

Create 30-60 second audio press pitches for:

- Podcast submissions (obviously)
- Voice message pitches to editors
- Social media stories with your actual voice
- Audio press releases for accessibility

- **Pro Tip:** Record yourself reading your pitch out loud. If it sounds natural and conversational, you're golden. If it sounds like you're reading a tax document, try again.

What to Include in Your Modern Media Kit:

- High-resolution images
- Video snippets for social sharing
- Infographics that tell your story visually
- UGC compilation showing real people using your product/service
- Behind-the-scenes content that humanizes your brand
- Quote cards ready for Instagram stories

The Reality Check: Don't Do This:

- Generic "we're excited to announce" language
- Virtue signalling without action
- Pitches that are all about you and nothing about them
- Press releases that read like academic papers

Do This Instead:

- Lead with the story, not the announcement
- Show, don't tell (proof over promises)
- Make it about the audience's benefit
- Write like you're talking to a friend

The Final Sniff Test

Before you hit send on any pitch, ask yourself:

- Would I share this with my friends? If not, why would a journalist?
- Is there a clear visual element? Today everything needs to be Instagram-able, TikTok-able, and YouTube-able!
- Does it pass the "so what?" test? If someone responds with "so what?" you need to go back to the drawing board.
- Is it authentic? In a world of fake everything, being real is your superpower.

Your Action Plan: From Pitch to Published

Day 1: Use AI to generate five different angles for your story

Day 2: Create your proof sprinkles collection.

Day 3: Write your first template using the frameworks above

Day 4: Test it on your most honest friend (we all have one)

Day 5: Refine and send

Remember: The best pitch is the one that gets responses. The best press release is the one that gets coverage. The best story is the one that gets shared. Perfection is passe because in a world clamouring for attention, the person who tells the most compelling story wins.

Make sure that person is you.

Host and Share

Venue Templates for Print and Audio

In this chapter:

- SPLASH event planning framework
- 2 customizable print invitations
- 3 audio/media outreach scripts
- 3 social snippet examples (Instagram, LinkedIn, Voice note)
- 3-part follow-up email sequence
- Canva media template links
- Case study: Scandinavian press trip
- Customization worksheet for events

You've organized the perfect media familiarization trip to showcase a luxury resort in Mauritius. The itinerary is flawless. The weather is perfect.

Your WhatsApp pings with a video from one of the travel writers.

She's filmed herself scoffing instant noodles in her room because the "welcome dinner" you promised was a PowerPoint presentation about sustainable tourism, followed by cocktail sausages with cheese blocks on toothpicks. She's vegan. The video goes viral. #CheesedOff trends. Your client is not amused.

Newsflash: Hosting media events is about creating experiences so compelling that journalists become your brand ambassadors, not your cautionary tales. This is not the time to skimp!

The SPLASH Framework for Media Events

Let's establish the methodology that turns ordinary press trips into extraordinary brand experiences:

- ***Storycraft*** the experience (What's the narrative arc?)
- ***Personalize*** every touchpoint (Mass invitations = mass delete)
- ***Layer*** the logistics (Backup plans for your backup plans)
- ***Anticipate*** journalist needs (They're working, not 'sponging')
- ***Stage*** photo opportunities (Instagram-worthy moments don't just happen)
- ***Handle*** follow-up like a pro (The relationship starts after they leave)

*'As a small business owner launching a new division, I was pleasantly surprised to discover **Splash It!** So many helpful, practical and actionable tools!'*

Greta P, Amazon review

The Print Template Arsenal

Use show-stopping invitations when you want to create excitement.

Subject: Your Passport to [Destination] Awaits

Dear [Journalist's Name],

Wanda Lust here. We're offering a [specific hook, e.g. "the first media access to Iceland's newest geothermal spa, opening exclusively to journalists three weeks before the public"].

Why This Matters to Your Readers: [Specific angle tailored to their publication e.g., "Your Conde Nast Traveller readers enjoy wellness travel, and this represents the next evolution in Nordic spa culture"]

What Makes This Different:
[**Specific** exclusive access]
[**Unique** story angle]
[**Notable** personalities involved, if any]
The Practical Bits:

- **Dates:** [Specific dates]
- **Duration:** [Length]
- **What's covered:** [Clear breakdown]
- **What's not:** [Be clear and honest upfront]

You'll have three days to experience something your readers can't access anywhere else. I've attached a detailed itinerary. Interested? Reply by [specific date]. We're limiting this to [number] journalists to ensure quality access.

Best, [Your name]

The Press Release That Gets Read

FOR IMMEDIATE RELEASE

Compelling Headline That Answers "So What?"

[CITY, DATE] – [Lead paragraph that hooks immediately with the most newsworthy angle]

[Second paragraph that provides context and why this matters now]

Quote from someone who matters: "Avoid corporate speak. Make it human and quotable" [Name, Title, Company]

The Story Behind the Story: [Add the human element or unexpected detail that makes journalists care]

What This Means for Travelers: [Practical implications]

Key Details:
When and Where: : [Specific dates], [Exact location]
Cost For Your Account: [If applicable]
Booking: [How to access]
Media Contact: [Your details]
Note to Editors: [Specific resources available, high-res images, interview opportunities, etc.]

The Audio Templates

Podcast Pitch Script:

Perfect for reaching travel podcast hosts

Subject: Quick podcast idea for [Podcast Name]

Hi [Host Name],

I've been listening to [specific episode reference] and loved your take on [specific topic]. It made me think you'd be interested in a story that perfectly fits your [show's angle].

The Story: [One-sentence hook]

Why Your Listeners Will Care: [Specific benefit to their audience]

What I'm Offering:
[**Expert** guest name and credentials]
Exclusive access to [specific opportunity]
[**Unique** angle or timing]

The Ask: 20 minute interview, recorded at your convenience. Provide:
Pre-interview brief with key talking points
High-quality audio setup on our end
Additional resources for your show notes

Would [specific date range] work for a quick chat about this?

Best, [Your name]

Radio Segment Proposal Template

TO: [Producer Name]
FROM: [Your name]
RE: Travel segment opportunity for [Show Name]
DATE: [Date]

SEGMENT CONCEPT: [One-line description]

ANGLE: [Why is this timely/relevant to your audience?]

DURATION: [Realistic time estimate]

GUEST: [Name, credentials, why they're perfect for radio]

KEY TALKING POINTS:
[Hook that grabs listeners immediately]
[Practical advice listeners can use]
[Surprising fact or trend]

VISUAL ELEMENTS FOR SOCIAL: [If applicable. What they can post to support the segment]

LOGISTICS:
Available: [Date/time options]
Setup: [Phone/studio/remote options]
Contact: [Direct number for guest]

FOLLOW-UP MATERIALS: [What you'll provide after the segment]
Voice Note Script for Instagram Stories
For quick, personal outreach: "Hi [Name], it's [Your name] from [Company]. Having thoroughly enjoyed your piece on [specific reference to their recent content] I have something I think would be perfect for your audience - [brief description].

It's happening [timeframe] and I can only invite [number] creators.

If you're interested, please let me know by [deadline date] so I can make arrangements.

[End with your signature sign-off]"

Social Media Snippet Templates

LinkedIn Post for Event Announcement: "And ... it's a wrap. Still hyped from the media fam tour of [Location].

Three things that blew me away:
[Specific detail]
[Surprising insight]
[Human moment]

The best PR is about what you make possible for others to discover. [Relevant hashtags]"

Instagram Story Template:
Slide 1: [Behind-the-scenes moment] Text: "When journalists become part of the story..."

Slide 2: [Action shot] Text: "We provide authentic experiences"

Slide 3: [Result or reaction] Text: "And the coverage writes itself"

Email Sequence for Post-Event Follow-up

Email 1: The Thank You (Send within 24 hours)

Subject: Thank you for making [Event Name] unforgettable

Hi [Name],

Thank you for being part of [Event Name]. Your questions about [specific topic they engaged with] pushed our thinking in new directions. Just to ensure you have everything you need for your piece, I'm adding: [Specific resource relevant to their angle] and [Statistical data or report]
High-res images from the event (provide a link)
Contact details for [specific people they met]
Additional resources about [topics they showed interest in

If you need anything else for your coverage, WhatsApp or e-mail me.

Best, [Your name]

Email 2: The Resource Drop (Send a week later)

Subject: Additional resources for your [Event Name] coverage

Hi [Name],

"If you need an additional [Expert contact for follow-up interviews] they are happy to be interviewed."

That's it. If no exposure comes from it, move on.

Email 3: The Relationship Builder

Subject: Saw your [Article/Post] about [Topic]

Hi [Name],

Just read your piece about [specific article]. Your insight about [specific point] was spot-on and made me think about [related topic].

I'm working on something related that I think you'd find interesting [brief description]. Still in early stages, but wanted to flag it with you first.

Would love to catch up soon!

The Scandinavian Success Story

The Challenge: A Nordic airline wanted to promote three new routes to Scandinavia. Traditional approach? Send press releases to travel editors. Boring.

The SPLASH Solution in Action

***Storycraft*:** The narrative went from "new routes," to "Experience Scandinavia Like a Royal."

Personalize: Each invitation referenced the journalist's recent work and explained why their story mattered to their readers.

Layer: Three distinct itineraries, each with a different angle:
Copenhagen: Sustainability meets design
Northern Sweden: Adventure and indigenous culture
Denmark: Royal heritage and modern luxury

Anticipate: Press kits should include fact sheets, story angles, photo opportunities, and local expert contacts.

Stage: Every location offered unique photo opportunities that couldn't be replicated elsewhere.

Handle: Six-month follow-up program with seasonal story suggestions and new developments.

The Template in Action

Subject: Your Passport to Nordic Treasures

Dear [Travel Editor Name],

While the travel world flocks to familiar hotspots, a quieter revolution is unfolding in Scandinavia, where three stunning destinations are poised to become the next must-visit marvels. Think fewer tourist traps, more transformative escapes. With authentic experiences, raw natural beauty, and cultural depth, these under appreciated places will appeal to your readers before everyone else catches on.

Three Unique Angles:

Keep it Green for Copenhagen Cool (March 15-18) Carbon-neutral Copenhagen is proving their sustainability. Your readers can experience what the future of travel looks like, today.

Wild Nights in the Lapp of Luxury (April 5-8) Northern Sweden offers Europe's last true wilderness experience but in luxury? That's new. We're talking about Sámi culture from a hot tub.

Queen of the Castle Contenders (May 10-13): Denmark's Royal Heritage Gets a Modern Makeover. New exhibitions, renovated castles, and access usually reserved for dignitaries.

What's Included:
[Specific airline] flights from [departure cities]
Luxury accommodations at [specific venues]
Exclusive access to [specific experiences]
Expert guides who live these stories

What's Not:
Generic group tours
Tourist traps; Anything your readers can book themselves

I'm limiting each trip to 8 journalists to ensure quality access and authentic experiences. Interested? Reply by [date] with your preferred dates, and I'll send detailed itineraries.

Best, Wanda Lust

P.S. Great stories deserve great storytellers.

The Results
24 journalists across three trips
67 pieces of coverage over 6 months
4.2 million total reach
15% increase in bookings on the new routes

More importantly, the journalists became ongoing advocates for the destinations, writing follow-up pieces and recommending the experiences to colleagues.

Your Turn: The Customization Exercise

Now it's time to create your media event templates. Use this worksheet to adapt the framework to your specific needs:

Step 1: Define Your Story:
What's the narrative arc of your event?
Why should journalists care right now?
What makes this experience unique?

Step 2: Know Your Audience
Which journalists are you targeting?
What are their recent articles about?
How can you make their job easier?

Step 3: Choose Your Channels:
Print: What written materials do you need?
Audio: Which podcasts or radio shows fit your story?

Digital: How will you amplify across social platforms?

Step 4: Plan Your Follow-up
What will you send immediately after the event?
How will you maintain relationships long-term?
What's your next story going to be?

The Common Mistakes (And How to Avoid Them)

- **The Mass Email Disaster:** Never, ever use "Dear Influencer" or CC 200 people. Personalization is key.
- **The Overpromise Trap:** If you say "exclusive," it had better be exclusive. If you say "luxury," it better be luxurious. Journalists have long memories.
- **The Logistics Nightmare:** Always have backup plans. Weather, strikes, and global pandemics don't care about your perfect itinerary.
- **The Follow-up Failure:** The relationship starts after the event ends. No thank-you email means no further articles.

*'**Splash It!** caters to all skill levels, making it a go-to resource for anyone seeking to master the art of press releases and effective communication. I loved the customizable templates, easy-to-adapt layouts, creative writing prompts and valuable troubleshooting section.'*

Chris, Amazon review

Your Media Event Toolkit

The best invitations feel personal, the best events create stories, and the best follow-ups foster meaningful relationships. Remember: You're creating the conditions for journalists to fall in love with your event. When they do, their readers will too.

Ready to turn your next media event into a story worth telling? The templates are here. The framework is proven. The only question is: What story will you create?

Need help troubleshooting a media event gone wrong? Turn to the Troubleshoot chapter for crisis management strategies.

- **Customize the Familiarization Tour Template here.**

15-Second Story Script: "Scandinavia's Hidden Marvels"

- **[0–3 sec:** Scenic sweep of Copenhagen with eco-bikes] Carbon-neutral cool? Copenhagen Redefines Green.
- **[3–7 sec:** Northern lights in luxury,] Wilderness meets wellness! Hot tubs + Sámi culture in Northern Sweden.
- **[7–11 sec:** Drone shots of Danish castles, interiors, and exclusive exhibits] Royal secrets revealed.
- **[11–15 sec:** Text] Tap to explore Scandinavia now!

Two

Launch

Announce Books and Products

In this chapter:

- Countdown checklist (5-day strategy)
- 6-sentence summary framework
- Launch content structure (email, social, media)
- Strategic timing tips (dates, seasons, industry context)
- Templates for partnership outreach
- 10+ digital tools and platforms
- 6 free press release submission sites

Gone are the days when launching a book meant hoping for a miracle. Today's successful launches blend strategic timing, authentic storytelling, and smart digital tactics.

Whether you're announcing your debut novel, launching a new product line, or celebrating a business milestone, there are ways to create buzz without breaking the bank.

The Countdown Strategy

Pre-Launch Phase: Build Anticipation Weeks Ahead

- **Create teaser** content that hints at what's coming
- **Reach out** to your inner circle for early endorsements
- **Prepare your media kit** with high-quality visuals and key messages

Launch Week: Go Big

- Day 4: **Official announcement** across all platforms
- Day 5: **Media outreach** and press release distribution
- Day 6: **Influencer collaborations** and cross-promotions
- Day 7: **Launch day celebration** with special offers

Craft Your Core Message

Nail down your "six-sentence summary." This becomes your North Star for all communications:

The Formula:

1. **Hook**: What problem does your book/product solve?
2. **Unique angle**: What makes your approach different?
3. **Benefits**: How will readers/customers benefit?
4. **Proof**: What credentials or results support your claims?
5. **Practical value**: What actionable steps can they take?
6. **Transformation**: What outcomes can they expect?

Example (Book Launch): "*Navigate the publishing jungle without emptying your wallet. This guide integrates ancient wisdom with modern marketing, offering practical solutions for cash-strapped authors.*

Packed with 101+ free resources and insider secrets from an award-winning journalist. Learn step-by-step strategies for cover design, social media mastery, and AI-powered promotion.

Transform your half-finished manuscript into a bestseller. Discover how to turn your writing dreams into profitable reality."

Essential Elements

1. Mobile-First Headlines Your headline must work on a smart phone screen. Keep it punchy, specific, and benefit-focused.

2. Multi-Media Integration

- Include QR codes linking to exclusive content
- Embed social media handles and hashtags
- Add video preview links or audio snippets
- Provide high-resolution images and graphics

3. SEO-Optimized Content

- Use relevant keywords naturally throughout
- Include location-specific information when appropriate
- Add meta descriptions and alt text for images

4. **AI-Driven Personalization and Automation**

- Personalize email campaigns, segment audiences, and automate social media posts with tools like Writesonic, Socialbu, and Yepp AI for content generation and campaign management

Strategic Timing for Maximum Impact

Book Launches:
Link to relevant dates (Halloween for horror, Valentine's for romance)
Give magazines a 3-month lead time
Allow 2-3 weeks for weekly publications
Consider seasonal reading patterns

Product Launches:
Avoid major holidays unless directly relevant
Tuesday – Thursday announcements typically get better coverage
Consider industry-specific timing (B2B vs. consumer)
Plan around competitor launches

Building Your Media List

Tier 1: Warm Contacts

- Industry colleagues and connections
  Previous interview contacts
  Local media who know you
  Podcast hosts you've appeared on

Tier 2: Targeted Prospects

- Journalists covering your industry/genre
  Bloggers and influencers in your space
  Podcast hosts with relevant audiences
  Industry publications and newsletters

Tier 3: Cold Outreach

- General media contacts
  Large publications with open submission policies
  New podcasts seeking guests
  Emerging influencers building audiences

Digital-First Announcement Strategies

Video Press Releases

Create 30-second announcement videos using:
Pictory: AI-powered video creation with automated captions
Synthesia: AI avatars for professional presentations
Descript: Screen recording and editing with voice cloning

Social Media Amplification

Instagram Strategy:
Stories with countdown stickers
Reels showing behind-the-scenes content and longer-form announcements
Live sessions for Q&A and celebration

TikTok Approach:
Quick tips related to your book/product
Trending audio with your announcement
Behind-the-scenes creation process
User-generated content campaigns

Email Campaign Sequence

Week Before Launch:
"Something exciting is coming" teaser
Behind-the-scenes exclusive content
Early bird special offer

Launch Week:
Official announcement with special pricing
Media coverage roundup
Customer testimonials and reviews
Last chance for launch bonuses

Cross-Promotion and Partnerships

Influencer Outreach Template: "Hi [Name], I'm launching [product/book] on [date] and would love to offer you [specific value - free copy, exclusive preview, etc.]. Your audience would benefit from [specific benefit related to their content]. Would you be interested in [specific collaboration - review, interview, social post]? I'm happy to reciprocate with [offer]."

Key Partnership Principles:

- **Always offer** something valuable first
  Be specific about what you're asking for
  Provide easy-to-share content
  Follow up professionally but don't pester
  Track results and maintain relationships

Measuring Your Launch Success

Traditional Metrics:
Media coverage volume and reach
Social media engagement rates
Email open and click-through rates
Website traffic and conversion rates

Modern Success Indicators:
Community building (followers, subscribers)
Authentic engagement (comments, shares, saves)
Long-term relationship building
Brand awareness and authority building

- **2 Bonus Prompts: "Rewrite** my six-sentence launch summary for a LinkedIn and a Facebook post." "Suggest **three teaser taglines** for a book about (subject) that launches next month."

Troubleshooting Common Launch Problems

Problem: No Media Response
Review your subject lines (70% of success)
Personalize each pitch
Follow up once after 3-5 business days
Try different angles or timing

Problem: Low Social Engagement
Post when your audience is most active
Use relevant Insta and TikTok hashtags (5-10 per post)
Engage with others' content first
Share behind-the-scenes content

Problem: Limited Reach
Collaborate with others in your space
Guest post on relevant blogs
Appear on podcasts
Partner with complementary brands

The Post-Launch Momentum Strategy

Your launch isn't over on Day 7. You have to maintain momentum and keep building community by:

- Sharing positive reviews and testimonials
- Creating follow-up content based on reader questions
- Documenting your journey for future launches
- Building relationships with new media contacts
- Planning your next announcement
- Nurturing reader communities on Discord, Facebook Groups, or WhatsApp. Host live Q&As, book clubs, and exclusive online events to foster long-term loyalty and word-of-mouth

Tools and Resources

Free Tools:
Canva for graphics and social media templates
MailerLite for email campaigns
Buffer for social media scheduling
Google Analytics for tracking success

Six Free Press Release Submission Websites

Here are six reputable websites where you can submit a press release for free in 2025:

1. **PRLog:** Offers free press release hosting and distribution with basic features such as SEO-friendly formatting, one image, and clickable links. Paid upgrades are available for wider reach.

2. **PR.com:** Allows free press release submissions with distribution to search engines and some third-party sites. Paid plans offer expanded reach and features.

3. **OpenPR:** Accepts one free press release per 30 days. Submissions are reviewed during business hours, and the site offers basic SEO optimization.

4. **IssueWire:** Provides a free plan with basic distribution, one image, and analytics. Paid options are available for enhanced visibility.

5. **1888 Press Release:** Basic free press release hosting with quick approval. Paid features offer broader distribution and additional benefits.

6. **PRFree:** Simple online submission with free press release publishing. Suitable for small businesses wanting to test PR distribution tools before upgrading.

Note: Free press release services may have limitations such as reduced reach, fewer customization options, or limited analytics. For broader exposure, consider paid upgrades or premium services.

AI-Powered Solutions:

- **ChatGPT** for press release variations
- **Jasper** for social media content
- **Loom** for personalized video pitches
- **Calendly** for media interview scheduling

Professional Services:

- Help A Reporter Out (HARO) for media connections
- Fiverr for affordable graphic design
- 99 designs for professional logos and covers

Your Launch Action Plan

30 Days Before:

- Complete your six-sentence summary
- Create media kit and press materials
- Build your media contact list and plan your content calendar

2 Weeks Before:

- Send press releases to media contacts
- Reach out to influencers and partners
- Create social media content
- Set up tracking systems

Launch Week:

- Execute your countdown strategy
- Engage on all platforms
- Follow up with media contacts and celebrate your wins

Post-Launch:

- Thank everyone who helped
- Analyze what worked and what didn't
- Plan your next announcement
- Maintain relationships for future launches

Remember: Every successful launch is built on relationships, authenticity, and consistent value delivery.

Launch a Book

What's in it for me? Answer in six soundbites!

Scan the template below to customize *Write, 6 Successful Self-Publishing Strategies on a Shoestring.* Fill in the Publisher, Author, Publication date and Availability. **Note to editors:** Review copies available.

- Download your customizable book launch template here

Convert the *Write* template into an Instagram story

- **[2–5 sec:** Text overlay on fast visuals – laptops, coffee shops] ***WRITE*** *is here! Insider tips,free tools, & AI prompts to save time.*
- **[5–8 sec:** Author photo or name overlay] *By Caroline Hurry, Published by Hygge Books*
- **[8–11 sec:** Highlight platforms with logos – Amazon, Kobo, etc.] *Available now on Amazon.*
- **[11–13 sec:** Call to reviewers or editors – flashing text] *Media? Request a review copy via email.*
- **[13–15 sec:** Book cover returns + "Out Now" animation] *Become an author today! Grab your copy of* ***WRITE*** *now!*

Spark Feature Ideas Around Your Book

Linking your book with a date such as Halloween for a horror tale, for example, increases your chances of publicity. Give magazines a three-month lead. If approaching a weekly newspaper, two weeks should be sufficient.

The following 'feature-type' release for Flow earned me generous space in Independent Newspapers and magazines around Valentine's Day.

Date: Embargoed until late January/early February

Smart Singles Celebrate Solo to Skip the Valentine's Blues

Feeling more true blue than red hot this Valentine's Day? You're not alone. Actually, you ARE alone and that might be the best news you'll hear all week.

While couples scramble for overpriced dinner reservations, savvy singles raise a glass to themselves. No more waiting for texts from Conman Don who vanished after you wired money for his "emergency surgery." No more wondering why Prince Charming blocked you on WhatsApp.

Narcissist Nick, Gaslighter Gary, and Stingy Steve – all masters of the poisoned arrow technique. Sound familiar? Research shows empaths are most vulnerable to shysters dressed as romance heroes.

If your relationship involve someone who criticizes you, gives you the silent treatment, or makes you the problem, Flow (Hygge Books) might be your way out of this exhausting cycle.

Author Caroline Hurry reveals how to spot manipulation tactics before they empty your heart and wallet.

"When you raise the bar by realizing you have everything you need to create everything you want, few get to undermine you," she says.

This Valentine's Day, celebrate the most important relationship in your life – the one with yourself. Pop that champagne, order the prawns, and toast to a future where you trust red flags over potential.

Media Contact: [Contact Name] | [Email] | [Phone]

Book Details: *Flow 21 Secrets to Refresh Your Relationships* (Hygge Books)

- Available from Amazon

30-Second Video Script: "Solo, Strong, and Smart"

[0–3 sec: Moody, slow-motion footage of a sad-looking couple at a restaurant] *Tired of ghosting, gaslighting, and games?*
[3–**7 sec:** Cut to confident single woman dancing alone at home, sipping champagne] *This Valentine's Day, smart singles are skipping the drama and celebrating themselves.*
[7–12 sec: Visuals of red flags, messages from "Conman Don" and "Gaslighter Gary" fading out] *No more falling for Stingy Steve or Narcissist Nick. Empaths, it's time to stop attracting the wrong love.*
[12–20 sec: Book cover reveal: *Flow: 21 Secrets to Refresh Your Relationships*] *FLOW shows you how to spot manipulation before it empties your heart or wallet.*
[20–27 sec: Positive visuals: spa night, solo dinner, smiling with friends] *You have everything you need to create everything you want.*
[27–30 sec: Bold CTA with romantic music swell] *This Valentine's Day, fall in love with YOU. Get FLOW now from Amazon.*

Introduce Yourself

With Confidence and Clarity

In this chapter:

- 7-part proposal structure
- Templates for media intros, bios, and cold outreach
- Pitch formulas for photographers, PR consultants, and founders
- QR codes for downloadable intro layouts
- Digital presence audit checklist
- Proposal video + asset suggestions

Whether you're a photographer, author, founder, or thought leader, introducing yourself can open doors to podcasts, press features, partnerships, and paid opportunities.

A well-crafted introductory proposal helps you present yourself as prepared, professional, and persuasive. Journalists, editors, influencers, and podcast hosts receive dozens (if not hundreds) of pitches every week. What stands out? Authenticity. Clarity. Relevance. And visuals.

In this chapter, you'll discover a clear structure, customizable templates, and updated techniques to craft powerful introductions and insider tips that help your message resonate.

Save time and ensure consistency with a well-crafted proposal template that helps structure your introduction and aligns your communication with potential clients or media professionals. Clearly articulate your unique value proposition.

Proposal Power

7 Key Components of a Magnetic Media Intro!

Save time and ensure consistency with a proposal template that acts as both a story snapshot and professional handshake. It should include:

1. Introduction: Spark Curiosity

Start strong. Introduce yourself and your brand voice. This is your elevator pitch – what you stand for, why you matter, and how you help. Highlight what makes you relevant to them. Avoid overused phrases. Be vivid, specific, and human.

Pro Tip: : Include a short (60-second) video intro link or QR code. Media professionals are time-strapped – seeing your energy on camera can accelerate trust and connection.

2. Project Summary: Frame the Opportunity

Outline the collaboration or feature idea. Why are you reaching out? What's in it for them (and their audience)? Make it tailored, not templated. If it's a press opportunity, clearly state the newsworthiness. If it's a podcast pitch, describe what story you can share that will spark conversation.

- **Pro Tip:** Use ChatGPT to draft three variations of your project summary, then pick the strongest.

3. Scope of Work / Offer: Set Expectations

If this is a service proposal (e.g. photography, PR), define the deliverables, timeline, and specific outcomes. Keep it tight but clear.

4. Methodology: Show Your Magic

How do you work? Whether it's your visual storytelling process or your strategy for PR placements, share the behind-the-scenes thinking. Mention tools (e.g., Lightroom, Canva Pro, AI editing), techniques, or unique frameworks you use.

Pro Tip: If you useAI or automation, explain how it saves clients time or increases results (without making it all about the tech).

5. Budget: Transparent and Professional

Include a clear fee structure with options if needed. Even if you're reaching out for a media feature, state the value of what you're offering, especially if there's a collaboration element.

Pro Tip: Mention in-kind collaborations, cross-promotions, or media value swaps (e.g., "I'mopen to Instagram Stories shoutouts or podcast trade promos.")

6. Authority: Build Trust

Don't be shy here. Showcase your credentials, past results, notable mentions, media appearances, or awards. This is where your credibility shines. Include a link to your media kit or press page if you have one.

Media Ready Checklist:

- 100-word bio and 2-3 headshots (portrait and landscape)
- Company logo in PNG
- Links to your socials and a short video (optional)
- Sample questions if you're pitching a podcast

7. Call to Action: Invite Connection

End with a clear next step. Do you want to set up a call, send a media kit, or collaborate on a content series? Make it friction-free. Include contact details, social handles, and a QR code that leads to your offer.

Wrap Up: Say It, Show It, Share It

A compelling introduction is the first ripple that creates waves. With a well-structured proposal, personality-driven pitch, and visual assets, you're showing why your offer matters. Customize the following templates, modernize your assets, and make your media moment unforgettable.

> *'Playing with all the customizable, user-friendly layouts has been fun. I love the clean fonts and white space.* ***Splash It!*** *motivated to design my letterheads for my new dance teaching company.'*
>
> Patricia Nieman, Amazon review

Templates in Action: Customize Your Pitch

Subject Line: Give Your Brand Visual Personality

Hi [Client's Name], Zelda of the Zoom Lens here. Your recent campaign around [insert topic] really caught my eye. I capture visual stories that move people and I'd love to explore a collaboration that brings your brand's personality to life through authentic imagery.

- **My Capture The Moment packages offer:**
  Behind-the-scenes, launches, lifestyle content.
  Strategic social content: Optimized for TikTok, and X.
  Visual PR support: Image bundles for press features.

Let's explore the magic we can make. Reach me at [contact details].

- **Customize the Zoom Zelda Proposal Template.**

Convert Zoom Zelda Introduction to an Insta Story

- **0–6 seconds: Visual:** Zelda smiling with camera. **Text overlay:** *Zoom Lens Zelda here with your campaign!*

- **Seconds 6–12: Visual:** Montage of behind-the-scenes, lifestyle shots, TikTok-style snippets). **Text overlay:** "*I help brands tell emotionally resonant stories.*"

- **Seconds 12–15: Visual:** QR code on screen + contact info, social handles. **Text overlay:** *Scan to connect!*

Introduce Yourself as a PR Consultant

Subject line: Ignite Your Presence.

Flaming Lorraine is an electrifying media force known for lighting up causes that matter. From fundraising campaigns to perception makeovers, Lorraine crafts stories that move the needle. Her mission in 2026: to spark deeper engagement, transform passive audiences into active champions, spark inspiration, and set soulful PR alight.

[CTA: Book a "Fan Your Flame' Discovery Call] | [QR Code]

- **Customize the Flaming Lorraine Layout Template**

15-Second Instagram Story: "Ignite Your Presence"

- **Seconds 0–3: Visual:** Close-up of Lorraine with media clippings. **Text overlay:** *Flaming Lorraine lights it up!*
- **Seconds 3–6: Visual:** Footage of events, or Lorraine in a Zoom session. **Text overlay:** "*From causes to campaigns. I craft stories that shift perception and move the needle.*"
- **Seconds 6–10: Visual:** Animated Text: *Ready to Fan Your Flame? Let's turn passive viewers into active champions. My mission is to be your PR spark plug for change."*
- **Seconds 10–15 Visual:** QR code and CTA with Lorraine smiling, camera-ready. **Text overlay:** *Call me today!*

Epicurean CEO Announcement Sample

Subject Line: Epicurean Escapes to Redefine Culinary Luxury

Header: Meet Olivia Martinez: New CEO, New Chapter

We're delighted to announce the appointment of Olivia Martinez as the new CEO of Epicurean Escapes. A Michelin-awarded culinary strategist and sustainability advocate, Olivia brings global insight, green innovation, and gastronomic flair to our evolving brand. "Olivia's creative vision and values-driven leadership align perfectly with our mission to elevate every bite," said MD Ralf Russo. "Expect immersive food experiences, AI-assisted menu engineering, and a bold commitment to culinary storytelling."

For media interviews, or imagery, contact Flaming Lorraine at [email]

- **Customize the CEO Layout Template here.**

Convert into an Instagram or Facebook Post

Image of new CEO with heading: New Chapter. Next-Level Culinary Luxury. **Caption**: *Say hello to Olivia Martinez, the powerhouse behind Michelin-starred menus and planet-positive innovation. She's rewriting the recipes. Think: Culinary storytelling and sustainable luxury on every plate. Ready to taste the next course at Epicurean Escapes? #FlamingLorrainePR #SustainableGastronomy*
For press interviews ☒ contact Flaming Lorraine at [email]
High-res media kit + Olivia's bio ☒ [short link]

Showcase

Business Travel and an Airline

In this chapter:

- Templates to showcase airlines, hotels, experiences
- 5 motivators for business/lifestyle travellers
- Listicle formatting framework
- Comparative + problem-solution pitch structures
- AI headline prompt set
- Media kit must-haves for travel, lifestyle, and service brands

The secret to successfully showcasing a luxury airline, boutique hotel, or your expertise, lies in the understanding that people *want to feel good.*

And your client has just what they need to facilitate those good feelings.

You also need to know what drives decision making so you can explain why what you offer matters to your audience.

For Business Travelers:

- **Convenience:** Time-saving solutions that reduce stress
- **Status:** Premium experiences that enhance professional image
- **Productivity:** Environments that enable work and rest
- **Value:** ROI that justifies the expense
- **Comfort:** Physical and emotional well-being during travel

For Lifestyle Consumers:

- **Connection:** Experiences that bring people together
- **Escape:** Freedom from daily constraints and routine
- **Discovery:** Wonder and excitement of new adventures
- **Transformation:** Personal growth and memorable moments
- **Authenticity:** Genuine experiences over manufactured ones

Essential Components of Your Media Kit

1. Powerful Headlines

- Use ChatGPT or Jasper to generate headline variations, then A/B test them:
- "Can Flying Business Class Provide a Viable ROI?"
- "The $5,000 Seat: Why Business Executives Are Ditching Economy"
- "Time Is the New Money: How Premium Travel Pays for Itself"

2. Interactive Media Elements

- QR codes linking to exclusive content
- Video testimonials from satisfied customers
- 360-degree photos of facilities or products
- Infographics comparing features and benefits
- Social proof with real customer reviews

3. SEO-Optimized

To structure your content for Google News indexing:

- Use relevant keywords naturally throughout
- Include location-specific information
- Add meta descriptions and alt text for images
- Create multiple versions for different publications

The "About Me" Builder

Traditional Bio: "John Smith is the CEO of ABC Company with20 years of experience..." (Yawn)

New Bio: "When John Smith's flight was delayed for 8 hours, he had an epiphany that raised the business travel industry bar. As CEO of ABC Company, he's now on a mission to ensure no business traveller suffers through another cramped airport waiting room."

Key Elements:

- **Hook:** Start with a relatable problem or surprising fact
- **Transformation:** Show the progress from problem to solution
- **Authority:** Weave in credentials naturally
- **Personality:** Let your authentic voice shine through
- **Vision:** End with what you're building toward

The Listicle Formula That Works

Journalists love listicles because they're easy to scan, share, and adapt. Here's how to craft irresistible list-based content:

Structure That Sells

1. Numbered Headlines Work Best

"7 Hidden Costs of Economy Travel That Business Class Eliminates"

"5 Productivity Hacks Only Business Travelers Know"

"3 Surprising Ways Premium Travel Saves Money"

2. Comparative Angles Create Engagement

"Business Class vs. Economy: The Real ROI Analysis"

"Then vs. Now: How Premium Travel Has Evolved"

"Airport Lounges Ranked: Which Airlines Actually Deliver"

3. Problem-Solution Pairings

Each list item should follow this pattern:

Problem: What frustrates your audience?

Solution: How your offering fixes it **Proof:** Evidence or example that it works

> *'Save the money you were going to spend on a publicist and create your own marketing materials. The author makes it fun and easy! From novice to professional, you can benefit from* ***Splash It!*** *I highly recommend it.'*
>
> BJW, Amazon review

Showcase Template: Premium Service Edition

The $5,000 Seat: Why Business Execs Are Ditching Economy

Sub-headline: New ROI analysis reveals how premium travel pays for itself and why time is the new money

The Math Is Simple: A business-class seat costs five times more than economy. A productive executive's time is worth significantly more than the price difference. "If you're billing $500 an hour, and business class saves you 12 hours of productivity – through better sleep, reduced jet lag, and workspace functionality – you've just earned $6,000 while spending $3,000 extra on your ticket," explains Skyler Jetson, CEO of Jolly Jetways.

The Real Cost of Economy:

Lost productivity: Cramped seats prevent work and rest

Jet lag recovery: 2-3 days of reduced performance

Stress impact: Higher cortisol affects decision-making

Health costs: Deep vein thrombosis and back strain risks

Opportunity cost: Missing peak performance at crucial meetings

What $5,000 Actually Buys:

Unlike economy's one-size-fits-none approach, business class delivers:

- Workspace Functionality:
- Flat-bed seats for overnight flights
- Individual power outlets and USB ports
- Adjustable tables for laptop work

- Privacy screens for confidential calls

Health & Wellness:

- Reduced jet lag through better sleep quality
- Premium amenity kits with skincare essentials
- Gourmet meals supporting energy levels
- Access to shower facilities pre-meeting

Time Savings:

Priority check-in and security lanes

- Exclusive lounges with business centers
- Fast-track boarding and deplaning
- Dedicated customer service lines

The Jolly Jetways Advantage

While other airlines focus on flashy amenities, Jolly Jetways addresses real business needs:

- **Corporate discounts:** Up to 20% off for frequent fliers
- **Flexible booking:** Changes without penalty fees
- **Ground transportation:** Complimentary chauffeur services
- **Accommodation partnerships:** 4-star hotel stays included
- **Concierge services:** City tours and restaurant reservations

ROI Beyond the Flight: "Business class is about arriving ready to perform," says Jetson. "When you factor in tax deductions, reward programs, and productivity gains, premium travel often costs less than the alternatives." The numbers support this claim:

- 89% of business travellers report better meeting performance after premium flights. Companies save an average of $2,400 per trip in reduced sick days and productivity loss
- Executive assistants report 40% fewer travel-related complaints from premium passengers
- Recent Upgrades: Jolly Jetways recently invested $50 million in lounge renovations, adding:
- Private massage suites for pre-flight relaxation; Library and quiet zones for focused work; Indoor golf simulators for stress relief; Sommelier-curated wine collection featuring rare vintages
- Interview Opportunity: Skyler Jetson is available for interviews about the changing landscape of business travel, and predictions for post-pandemic corporate travel policies.

Media Contact: Amanda Sparkle, Communications Director Email: media@jollyjetways.com Phone: +1-555-JETWAYS Direct: +1-555-123-4567

Quick Facts:

- Business class tickets: [City to City] from $4,999
- Lounge access: Complimentary for business passengers
- Reward program: Points never expire
- Corporate accounts: Volume discounts available

Digital Assets:

- High-res images: [link]
- Executive headshots: [link]
- Facility virtual tours: [link]
- Customer testimonial videos: [link]

About Jolly Jetways: Founded in 2010, Jolly Jetways serves 47 destinations across 23 countries, specializing in premium business travel experiences. The airline has received industry recognition for customer service excellence and innovative amenities.

Advanced Showcase Strategies

Multi-Format Content Creation For Different Media Types:

Print Publications:

- Focus on statistics and expert quotes
- Include comparative charts and infographics
- Provide multiple story angles in one release

Digital Platforms:

- Add video testimonials and virtual tours
- Include social media handles and hashtags
- Create interactive elements like polls or quizzes

Podcast Interviews:

- Prepare compelling personal stories
- Have surprising statistics ready
- Practice concise, quotable sound bites

SEO Optimization Checklist

Keywords to Target:

- Industry-specific terms (business class, corporate travel)
- Problem-focused phrases (jet lag, productivity, travel stress)
- Solution-oriented keywords (ROI, time savings, comfort)

Content Structure:

- H1 tags for main headlines and H2 tags for section headers
- Alt text for all images
- Meta descriptions under 160 characters

Social Media Platform-Specific Adaptations:

- **LinkedIn:** Professional focus, ROI emphasis, industry insights
- **Instagram:** Visual storytelling, behind-the-scenes content, lifestyle elements
- **X:** Quick tips, industry news, customer service updates
- **TikTok:** Fun facts, travel hacks, day-in-the-life content

Measuring Showcase Success

Key Performance Indicators and Traditional Metrics:

- Media coverage volume and reach
- Website traffic from press releases
- Social media engagement rates
- Lead generation from campaigns

Success Indicators:

- Share-of-voice in industry conversations
- Branded search term increases
- Thought leadership positioning
- Customer acquisition cost reduction

Tools for Tracking

Free Options:

- Google Analytics for website traffic
- Google Alerts for mention tracking
- Social media native analytics

Professional Solutions:

- Cision for media monitoring
- Sprout Social for social listening
- SEMrush for keyword tracking

Your Showcase Action Plan

Before You Start Research Phase:

- **Identify** your unique value proposition
- **Research** competitor messaging
- **Define** your target audience precisely
- **Collect** customer testimonials and data

Content Creation:

- Develop 3-5 headline variations
- Create supporting visual assets
- Write multiple story angles
- Prepare executive bios and quotes

During Your Campaign

Launch Week:

- Distribute to targeted media lists and share across social channels
- Follow up with key journalists, monitor coverage and engagement

Optimization:

- Track which headlines and story angles performed best
- Adjust messaging based on feedback
- Collect coverage for future reference

After Your Campaign

Analysis:

- Measure ROI against objectives
- Document lessons learned
- Update media contact database
- Plan follow-up content

Relationship Building:

- Thank journalists who covered your story
- Connect with new media contacts
- Share additional resources

- Maintain ongoing communication

Download and customize the Airline Feature Template here

Convert into a Threads Post:

Ready to rock your next media campaign? Here's your quick-start checklist to get noticed:

1. **Identify your unique value;** Research your competitors; Define your ideal audience; Gather testimonials and data

2. **Draft 3–5 strong headlines;** Create compelling visuals; Write multiple story angles; Include executive bios and quotes

3. **During launch week:** Send to targeted media lists; Post across your social channels; Follow up with key journalists; Track coverage and engagement

4. **After the buzz:** Review which headlines performed best; Measure ROI and log key insights; Update your media contact list; Thank those who covered you. Relationships matter. Show up, follow up, and offer value beyond the pitch.

- **Image suggestions:**
  Laptop with a press release draft
  Notepad checklist: "Headline, Visuals, Media List"
  Coffee, spectacles, and a phone showing media coverage.
  Carousel with icons for each campaign phase

#PRTips #MediaStrategy #ShowcaseSuccess #VisibilityMatters #BrandBuzz #ThreadsMarketing

Bonus Game Plan Template for Tourist Operator Venues

Blurb: *Embark on a thrilling journey into the heart of southern Africa's untamed wilderness, where close encounters with wildlife, awe-inspiring landscapes, and exclusive accommodations await. From whale sightings to guided walks and unique cultural experiences, these handpicked venues from (Name Tourist Operator) promise an unforgettable adventure for discerning travellers seeking the ultimate safari experience.*

Best Whale and Penguin Sightings
Location: Cape Town, South Africa
Highlights: Table Mountain, Cape Point, Boulders Beach
Base Camp: (Name Venue Operator)
Description: Immerse yourself in the Atlantic and Indian Oceans while exploring Cape Town's iconic landmarks. Witness endangered African penguins at Boulders Beach and marvel at Southern Right whales.

Best Fynbos Foot Safari
Location: Garden Route, South Africa
Venue: (Name Your Venue and Safari Operator)
Highlights: Biodiversity, Big Five, tented camps
Description: Expert trail guides lead you through the fynbos-covered landscape. Encounter diverse ecosystems, the Big Five, and an array of antelope species.

Best Prehistoric Reserve
Location: Karoo, South Africa
Venue: (Name Your Venue)
Highlights: Wildlife tracking, ancient rock paintings
Description: Track cheetahs, and encounter 225 bird species. Sleep under the stars.

Best for Families and Volunteerism
Location: (Name Operator)

Highlights: Wildlife rehabilitation
Description: Nurture orphaned wildebeest, buffalo, and zebra calves. Participate in volunteer programs and gain insights into wildlife conservation.

Best Leopard Location
Location: Sabi Sands Reserve, South Africa
Highlights: Pristine natural environment, thrilling wildlife sightings
Description: (Venue) offers an unparalleled opportunity to observe thriving leopard populations amid their natural lush riverine habitat.

Best Guided Safari Walking
Location: Klaserie Reserve, South Africa
Highlights: Intimate wildlife encounters, traditional folklore
Description: Knowledgeable rangers walk you through Big Five territory.

Best Tree House Location
Highlights: Elevated tree house experience, immersion in nature
Description: A unique "Me Tarzan, You Jane" experience. Stay in the triple-decker forest ship at (Name Venue). Immerse yourself in the sights and sounds of the savannah from your lofty perch under a celestial canopy.

Best Wild Dog Spotting
Location: Madikwe Reserve, South Africa
Highlights: Family-friendly activities, webcam
Description: Watch endangered African wild dogs gather at the central watering hole.

Best Tented Camp for Traditional Dancing
Highlights: Zulu dancing nightly with lessons
Description: Indulge in the chic safari ambiance of tents and Zulu cuisine.

Best Place to Stalk Game with Bushmen
Location: Central Kalahari Reserve, Botswana

Highlights: Rare black-maned lions, Bushmen encounters, immersive cultural experiences
Description: Venture into the vast Central Kalahari Reserve, engage with the indigenous Bushmen, learn their ancient traditions, and unlock survival secrets in the desert.

Contact Details: Provide your email, website address, and phone number. Note: Customize contact details and other information per your publication's requirements.

THREE

Troubleshoot

CRISIS MANAGEMENT, DAMAGE CONTROL

IN THIS CHAPTER:

- Common PR/launch mistakes and recovery tips
- How to reframe a failed campaign
- 3 problem-solving pathways (media silence, social flop, low reach)
- Recovery messaging templates
- AI prompt ideas for reboots and brand repair
- Post-launch momentum tips (testimonials, community)

It's 3 AM. Your phone is buzzing like an angry wasp. Your brand is trending with notifications and not in a good way. A TikTok video about your client's company has 2.3 million views and counting. Judging by the comments, you can forget about this year's customer service awards.

Welcome to crisis management, where a single misstep can sprawl across every platform before you've sipped your morning coffee.

The old "wait and see" approach? Yeah, that's how brands expire in the digital age.

Take a deep breath: bad press is a test. With the right strategy and a large slice of humble pie, you can bounce back with grace.

Case Study: From Chicken Crisis to PR Masterclass

It was the cluck-up of 2018 when KFC, the fried chicken chain ran out of ... chicken. More than 750 KFC outlets in the UK shuttered their doors. Social media feasted on #ChickenCrisis memes .

The Stumble: The Great Chicken Shortage

What happened? KFC switched its delivery contract from Bidvest Logistics to DHL, which centralized distribution through a single hub. The result: supply chain meltdown. Trucks were delayed, chicken didn't arrive, hungry fans were turned away and two-thirds of UK stores closed almost overnight.

Public reaction: Outrage, mockery, and disbelief. The brand's reputation was on the chopping block.

The Bounce-Back: "FCK" – A Finger-Lickin' Good Apology

Owning the mistake: Instead of hiding behind corporate jargon or blaming partners, KFC took out full-page ads in The Sun and Metro, featuring an empty chicken bucket with the logo rearranged to spell "FCK." The message? "A chicken restaurant without any chicken. It's not ideal. Huge apologies to our customers ..."

Humor and humility: The ad was cheeky, self-deprecating, and instantly viral. It acknowledged the absurdity of the situation, thanked staff and franchisees, and promised progress. The approach was honest, relatable, and perfectly aligned with KFC's irreverent brand voice.

Turning anger into affection: The campaign changed the narrative. Instead of "KFC failed," it became "KFC made the best apology ever." Social media buzzed with praise. Even critics admitted the response was a PR triumph.

Business impact: Within weeks, operations returned to normal. The apology ad reached one billion people, and KFC's brand perception rebounded. Sales and customer trust recovered faster than anyone predicted.

Key Moves:

- Immediate public apology – no defending, no blame-shifting.
- Transparent updates – customers informed as stores reopened.
- Bold, on-brand humor made the memorable apology shareable.

Lesson:
In the age of screenshot culture and viral outrage, humility and humor can turn disaster into legend. KFC's "FCK" campaign is now a gold standard in crisis management: admit the mess, own it, and do it in your own voice.

Case Study: Crash, Rattle, and Roll: How CrowdStrike Blue-Screened the World

It was the click heard around the world. Or rather, the collective CTRL+ALT+DELETE sigh of despair as screens from Seattle to Sydney turned a shade of blue last seen on Windows XP error codes. CrowdStrike's Great Digital Faceplant, the software update that sent IT departments into meltdown mode.

CrowdStrike, the cybersecurity darling known for shielding systems from digital threats, released a FalconSensor update that mistakenly identified its own code as an intruder. The result? An out-of-bounds memory read that caused Windows machines to crash into the Blue Screen of Death.

The botched update was traced back to an enthusiastic overachiever, but the fallout included global outages and lawsuits from investors. Delta Airlines blamed them for $500 million in losses. Unflattering memes festooned social media platforms. Did CrowdStrike pull a "nothing to see here? No, they owned it. They penned a 12-page Root Cause Analysis (RCA) of techie soul-searching. "Yeah, we missed a spot. A big one."

They pledged to:

- Add more testing layers (translation: We'll stop winging it)
- Introduce "canary" deployments
- Let customers choose when updates land (about time!)
- Hire two independent security vendors to test their systems before they unleash them on the public

Moral of the meltdown: Even in cybersecurity, you can't patch hubris. But you can write a grovelling apology, bolster your Quality Assurance (QA) team, and try not to break the internet next time.

The New Crisis Reality: When Seconds Count

These days, a crisis is a digital wildfire. Here's what you're dealing with:

The 15-Minute Rule: You have 15 minutes from the first viral post to respond before the narrative gets set in digital stone. Miss that window, and you're playing catch-up for weeks.

Multi-Platform Chaos: Your crisis will jump from TikTok to X to LinkedIn and local news faster than you can say "damage control."

AI Amplification: Bots and AI tools can amplify negative sentiment, making a small issue appear as a massive public outcry.

Screenshot Culture: Everything is permanent. Delete a tone-deaf response, and screenshots will haunt you forever.

Stakeholder Multiplier Effect: Employees, customers, investors, and media all have instant access to real-time information and platforms to share their opinions.

The Fatal Five: Crisis Accelerators That Kill Brands

Mistakes that transform manageable situations into catastrophes:

1. The Silent Treatment
The Mistake: Hoping it will blow over if you ignore it.
Why It's Fatal: Silence gets interpreted as guilt, arrogance, or indifference. Nature (and social media) abhors a vacuum.
Reality: Every minute of silence gives others the chance to control your narrative.

2. The Defensive Deflection
The Mistake: "That's not what we meant," or "You're taking it out of context."
Why It's Fatal: You're telling upset people their feelings are wrong. That never ends well.
Reality: Defensive responses get screenshot, memed, and turned into viral content mocking your brand.

3. The Legal Threat
The Mistake: Threatening to sue critics or reviewers.
Why It's Fatal: You appear to be a corporate bully targeting individuals. David vs. Goliath never ends well for Goliath.
Reality: Legal threats become rallying cries. Expect a coordinated boycott within hours.

4. The Fake Apology
The Mistake: "We're sorry you were offended" or "We're sorry you felt that way."
Why It's Fatal: Non-apologies are worse than silence. They show you still don't get it.
Reality: AI can analyze sincerity levels. Fake apologies get flagged.

5. The Delete and Deny
The Mistake: Deleting posts or blocking critics.
Why It's Fatal: Screenshots are forever, darling!
Reality: Deletion tools track what you remove. Transparency is your only option.

The RAPID Response Framework

Recognize and Respond (0-15 minutes)

Immediate acknowledgment: "We're aware of and investigating [issue]"
Show you're human: "We take this seriously and will respond properly."
Set expectation: "We'll have a detailed response by [specific time]."

Analyze and Assess (15-60 minutes)

Gather facts: What actually happened?
Identify stakeholders: Who is affected and how?
Measure impact: How far has it spread?
Determine severity: Is this a minor issue or brand-threatening crisis?

Plan and Prepare (1-3 hours)

Craft response strategy: Own it, fix it, or contextualize it?
Identify spokesperson: Who has credibility to speak on this?
Prepare multi-platform response: Different messages for different audiences
Anticipate follow-up questions: What will people ask next?

Implement and Inform (3-6 hours)

Release coordinated response: Same message, multiple platforms
Engage authentically: Respond to comments and questions
Provide updates: Keep stakeholders informed of progress
Monitor sentiment: Track how your response is being received

Deliver and Demonstrate (Ongoing)

Follow through: Do what you said you'd do
Provide evidence: Show, don't just tell
Maintain transparency: Regular updates on progress
Learn publicly: Share what you've learned and how you're changing

Your Digital Crisis Manager

Here's how to use AI for crisis management:

AI-Powered Crisis Detection

Early Warning System Prompt: "Monitor social media mentions of [brand name] and alert me to any posts that:

- Have negative sentiment above 70%
- Are gaining rapid engagement (shares, comments, likes)
- Include keywords like 'boycott,' 'terrible,' 'never again,' 'lawsuit'
- Are posted by accounts with >10K followers
- Provide a severity score (1-10) and recommend immediate action."

Sentiment Analysis

Prompt: "Analyze the sentiment of these 50 comments about [crisis situation]. Categorize them as:

- Angry/Outraged
- Disappointed/Hurt
- Confused/Seeking Information
- Supportive/Defensive
- Neutral/Observing
- Identify the main concerns and emotions driving negative sentiment."

AI-Assisted Response Drafting

Initial Response Template Prompt: "Draft an initial crisis response for [situation] that:

- Acknowledges the issue without admitting legal liability
- Shows empathy for those affected
- Commits to investigating and responding properly
- Sets a realistic timeline for detailed response
- Maintains [brand voice: professional/friendly/authoritative]
- Keep it under 100 words and suitable for all platforms."

Detailed Apology

Prompt: "Create a comprehensive apology for [specific situation] that includes:

- Acknowledgment of what went wrong
- Acceptance of responsibility
- Genuine empathy for those affected
- Specific actions we're taking to fix it
- Timeline for implementation
- Commitment to preventing recurrence
- Tone should be [sincere/humble/professional] and avoid legal-speak."

AI for Multi-Platform Adaptation

Platform-Specific Messaging Prompt: "Adapt this crisis response for different platforms:

- X: 280 characters, conversational tone
- LinkedIn: Professional, detailed, business-focused
- Instagram: Visual-friendly, authentic, personal
- TikTok: Transparent, relatable, brief
- Press release: Formal, comprehensive, quotable
- Original message: [your response]"

Apology Prompts That Work

- "Write a short apology statement addressing a tone-deaf social media post, keeping the tone sincere and brand-aligned."
- "Summarize lessons learned from a brand PR failure in 5 bullet points."

The Accountability Apology
When: You messed up and need to own it.
Template: "We messed up. [Specific description of what went wrong]. This isn't who we want to be, and it's not the experience we want for our customers. We take full responsibility.
Here's what we're doing to fix it:

- [Specific action 1 with timeline]
- [Specific action 2 with timeline]
- [Specific action 3 with timeline]

We'll share updates on our progress every [frequency] until this is resolved. To those affected: [specific remedy/compensation]. "We're sorry. We'll do better."

The Clarification Response
When: You're being misunderstood or taken out of context.
Template: "We're seeing some confusion about [issue], and we want to set the record straight
What actually happened: [clear, factual explanation]
We understand why this might have looked like [misunderstanding], and we should have been clearer from the start. Here's what we actually believe/support: [clear position]
Going forward, we'll [specific change to prevent confusion].
Thank you for giving us the chance to clarify."

The Learning Response
When: You made a mistake due to ignorance or oversight.
Template: "We got this wrong, and we're learning from it.
What happened: [brief, factual description]
What we've learned: [specific insights/education gained]
How we're changing: [concrete actions and policies]
We're grateful to those who took the time to educate us. This conversation has made us better.
We're committed to [ongoing commitment/value]."

Advanced Crisis Scenarios:

The Viral Employee Complaint

Scenario: Current or former employee posts viral video about toxic workplace culture.
Response Strategy:
Immediate: "We're aware of [employee's] concerns and are investigating."
Investigation: Review claims, interview stakeholders, gather evidence
Response: Address specific issues, announce changes, provide evidence of improvement
Follow-up: Regular updates on cultural improvements, employee satisfaction metrics

AI Prompt for This Scenario:

"An employee posted a viral TikTok claiming our work place is toxic. Draft a response that:

- Takes the concerns seriously
- Doesn't throw the employee under the bus

- Commits to investigation and improvement
- Acknowledges this isn't the culture we want
- Provides specific next steps
- Avoid defensive language or dismissing their experience."

The Influencer Partnership Gone Wrong

Scenario: Brand ambassador or sponsored creator posts problematic content while representing your brand.

Response Strategy:

Immediate: Distance from specific content while supporting the person

Assessment: Determine if this is pattern or one-time mistake

Decision: Continue, pause, or end partnership

Communication: Explain your values and how partnerships align with them

AI Prompt for This Scenario:

"Our brand partner posted controversial content. Draft a response that:

- Clarifies our values without attacking them personally
- Explains how we choose partners
- Addresses whether we're continuing the partnership
- Maintains respect for all parties involved
- Reinforces our brand values

Keep it diplomatic but clear."

The Product Safety Crisis

Scenario: Customer injury or safety concern goes viral on social media.

Response Strategy:

Immediate: Express concern for customer safety

Investigation: Work with authorities, conduct internal review

Transparency: Share findings and actions taken

Prevention: Implement safeguards and monitoring

AI Prompt for This Scenario:

"A customer was injured using our product and posted about it online. Draft a response that:

- Prioritizes customer safety above all else
- Shows genuine concern for the injured person
- Commits to thorough investigation
- Avoids admitting liability while showing empathy
- Provides clear next steps for affected customers
- Maintains trust in our brand's commitment to safety"

The Reputation Rebuild Playbook

Once you've managed the immediate crisis, the real work begins. Here's how to rebuild stronger than before:

Phase 1: Demonstrate Change (Weeks 1-4)

- Show, don't tell: Provide evidence of changes made
- Transparency reports: Regular updates on progress
- Third-party validation: Independent verification of improvements
- Employee voices: Let your team share their experiences

Phase 2: Prove Consistency (Months 2-6)

- Sustained effort: Continue improvements beyond initial response
- Measurement: Track and share relevant metrics
- Stakeholder engagement: Regular check-ins with affected parties
- Industry leadership: Become an advocate for better practices

Phase 3: Build New Reputation (Months 6-12)

- Thought leadership: Share lessons learned with industry
- Proactive initiatives: Go beyond fixing to preventing
- Community investment: Support causes related to your crisis
- Culture evolution: Make changes part of your brand identity

Crisis Prevention: The Immunity System

The best crisis management is crisis prevention. Here's how to build organizational immunity:

Early Warning Systems

- Social media monitoring: AI-powered sentiment tracking
- Employee feedback: Regular surveys and anonymous reporting
- Customer advisory boards: Direct line to customer sentiment
- Track competitors: Monitor and learn from industry crises

Cultural Antibodies

- Value-based hiring: Recruit people who align with your values
- Regular training: Keep everyone updated on brand standards
- Decision frameworks: Clear guidelines for tough choices
- Psychological safe environment: People can discuss problems

Response Preparation

- Crisis playbooks: Documented responses for common scenarios
- Trained spokespeople: Multiple people ready to respond
- Legal guidance: Know when to involve attorneys (spoiler: not immediately)
- Stakeholder maps: Know who to contact when things go wrong

The Crisis Communication Checklist

Before Crisis (Prevention):

- Social media monitoring tools active
- Crisis response team identified
- Legal and PR advisors on standby
- Employee communication channels established
- Brand values clearly documented
- Decision-making authority clarified
- Stakeholder contact lists updated

During Crisis (Response):

- Immediate acknowledgment posted within 15 minutes
- Fact-gathering initiated
- Legal team consulted (but not leading response)
- Multi-platform response coordinated
- Stakeholder communication initiated
- Media monitoring intensified
- Timeline for detailed response communicated

After Crisis (Recovery):

- Commitments fulfilled
- Progress regularly reported
- Stakeholder feedback collected
- Changes implemented and verified
- Lessons learned documented
- Systems improved for future prevention
- Brand narrative updated

Sample Crisis Responses: The Good, The Bad, The Viral

The Good: Transparency and Accountability

"We messed up. Yesterday's email contained language that doesn't reflect our values or the respect we have for our customers. We wrote it quickly during a stressful time, but that's not an excuse. We're sorry. We're reviewing our communication process to prevent this from happening again, and we'll share what we learn. Thank you for holding us accountable."

The Bad: Defensive and Dismissive

"Recent social media posts have taken our comments out of context. We stand by our original message and believe our intentions were clear. We're disappointed that some people chose to misinterpret our words. We will not be bullied into changing our position."

The Viral: Authentic and Human

"Hi everyone. I'm [Name], CEO of [Company]. I'm recording this from my kitchen at 6 AM because I couldn't sleep after seeing your messages about yesterday's event. We let you down, and I wanted to look you in the eye and say I'm sorry. Here's what happened, here's what we're doing to fix it, and here's my personal commitment to making this right."

Advanced AI Prompts for Crisis Management

Crisis Severity Assessment

"Analyze this crisis situation and provide:

- Severity score (1-10)
- Potential impact on brand reputation
- Stakeholder groups affected
- Recommended response timeline
- Similar crisis examples and outcomes
- Key risks if not handled properly
- Situation: [describe crisis]"

Stakeholder Communication Strategy

"Create different communication strategies for each stakeholder group:

- Customers: [tone and key messages]
- Employees: [internal messaging approach]
- Investors: [business impact focus]
- Media: [newsworthy angles and quotes]
- Social media: [platform-specific approaches]
- Crisis: [situation description]"

Long-term Recovery Planning

"Develop a 12-month reputation recovery plan including:

- Month-by-month milestones
- Success metrics to track
- Communication checkpoints
- Investment required
- Potential obstacles and solutions
- Brand narrative evolution strategy
- Crisis context: [situation details]"

The Golden Rule of Crisis Management

Always acknowledge any complaint with gratitude. This means:

- Thank them for caring enough to speak up
- Acknowledge their experience as valid
- Appreciate the opportunity to improve
- Recognize their patience as you work to fix things
- Every crisis is feedback. Every complaint is a gift. Every critical post is an opportunity to reveal who you truly are when things get tough.

The brands that thrive are the ones that handle mistakes with grace, authenticity, and genuine commitment to being better. Are you ready to turn criticism into an opportunity? Remember: your response to criticism often matters more than the criticism itself. Make it count.

FOUR

Bonus Prompt Vault

1. Press Releases

Sample Prompts:

"Write a press release announcing [product/book] with a punchy headline and 3 emotional hooks."

"Rewrite this release for a trade magazine with a formal tone."

"Add a quote from a founder that sounds authentic and media-ready.

2. Podcast Pitches

Sample Prompts:

"Turn this paragraph into a 60-second pitch for a podcast that covers [niche]."

"Suggest 3 warm, benefit-led intros for a relationship podcast."

"List 5 compelling interview questions for a podcast host."

3. Social Media Captions

Sample Prompts:

"Write a bold, visual Instagram caption for a product launch. Include 3 hashtags and a call to action."

"Turn this customer testimonial into a TikTok script."

"Generate a LinkedIn post using a trending topic and my book's core theme."

4. Pitching Creators & Influencers

Sample Prompts:

"Based on [creator name]'s last 10 posts, suggest a custom pitch for collaboration."

"Write a casual outreach message to a newsletter writer about covering my book."

"Create 3 email subject lines that feel platform-native and intriguing."

5. Launch Campaigns

Sample Prompts:

"Create a 5-day email campaign to launch my nonfiction book, with teasers, proof points, and urgency."

"Turn this press release into a launch-day Instagram carousel with bold headlines."

"List 3 emotional hooks I can use in pre-launch content."

6. Proof + Social Credibility

Sample Prompts:

"Summarize these 3 testimonials into a single quote card caption."

"Turn my customer success story into a short case study for media use."

"Generate 3 punchy quotes I can say in an interview to position myself as an expert."

7. Research & Customization

Sample Prompts:

"Analyze [journalist or creator]'s latest content and suggest a relevant story angle."

"What trending topics in [industry] could I hook my product to this week?"

"Summarize the top 3 media angles my competitor used, and how I can stand out."

8. Troubleshoot or Reputation Repair

Sample Prompts:

"Draft a brief, empathetic statement addressing a social media backlash."

"Create a recovery strategy email for a failed launch, using humor and transparency."

"Rewrite my apology tweet to sound sincere but not defensive."

9. Wildcard Prompts

(For fun, bold ideas or weird requests!)

"Write a tongue-in-cheek press release for a CEO in a tutu."

"Turn my FAQ into a rap battle script."

"Write a Vogue or Vanity Fair cover line about my software launch."

10. Book Launch & Marketing Funnel Prompts

Goal: Create a lead magnet, landing page, and automated email flow.

- **Create a Lead Magnet Prompt:** "Act as a nonfiction marketing expert. I've written a book titled [Book Title] for[Target Audience]. Based on this, generate 3 compelling lead magnet ideas(e.g., mini-guides, checklists, quizzes, excerpts) that I can offer for free to capture emails."
- **Prompt 2: Write My Landing Page** "Write a landing page for the lead magnet titled '[Lead Magnet Title]'. Use persuasive but friendly language, include a strong headline, subheading, short benefit-driven bullet points, and a call to action. Make it feel like a personal invitation to readers who love[genre/topic]."
- **Prompt 3: Generate the Email Sequence** "Create a 5-partemail nurture sequence for people who downloaded my free lead magnet titled'[Lead Magnet Title]'. Tone: authentic, helpful, lightly humorous. Goal: build rapport, highlight value, and softly introduce my book [Book Title] with a link to buy by email."

Optional upgrade: Ask AI to format in ConvertKit with subject lines.

- Download ***The Pitch, Publish & Pop Playbook*** here:

FIVE

Pitch, Publish & Pop!

A STEP-BY-STEP PLANNER FOR MEDIA OUTREACH

Download this workbook from carolinehurr y.com

- **Download the entire Pitch, Publish & Pop Playbook here!**

Six

Essential Tools

Must-have Platforms and AI-powered Solutions

Using these foundational tools strategically will turbocharge your media outreach, content creation, and crisis management capabilities.

1. Content Creation & Design

- Canva
  Design anything with easy drag-and-drop tools.
- Logo.com
  Create high-resolution, customizable logos quickly.
- Grammarly
  AI-powered writing assistant for grammar, style, and tone improvements.
- Jasper AI
  AI copywriting platform for releases, blogs, and social content.

- ChatGPT / Custom GPTs
  Personalized AI content generation and editing.

- Surfer SEO
  Optimize content for search engines with AI-driven keyword and structure suggestions.

- Descript
  AI-powered audio and video editing, transcription, and podcast production.

- Lumen5
  Automatically turn blog posts or press releases into engaging videos.

- Kapwing
  Easy meme and short-form video editing for viral marketing.

2. Press Release Distribution & Free Submission Platforms

- PRLog
  Free press release hosting with SEO-friendly formatting and paid upgrades.

- PRFree
  Free account for press release distribution to news outlets and social media.

- Newswire Today
  Focuses on technology, business, and industry news with a basic free option.

- Online PR News
  Freemium model offering free basic press release packages.

- PR.com
  Free submissions with distribution to search engines and third-party sites.

- Free Press Release
  Another free platform for wide press release distribution.

3. Media Monitoring & Social Listening

- Google Alerts
  Monitor online brand mentions, press releases, and keywords.

- Feedly
  News aggregator to stay current with industry trends and competitor news.

- Brandwatch
  Advanced sentiment analysis, influencer tracking, and crisis alerts.

- Mentionlytics
  Real-time brand monitoring and competitor insights.

- Meltwater / CisionOne
  Media monitoring, journalist databases, and analytics.

- Brand24
  Affordable media monitoring and influencer tracking.

4. PR & Media Relationship Management

- HARO (Help a Reporter Out)
  Connect with journalists seeking expert commentary.

- HubSpot CRM
  Organize media contacts, track communications, and manage campaigns.

- Prowly
  All-in-one PR CRM with press release distribution and analytics.

- Agility PR Solutions
  Media database, monitoring, and campaign analytics.

- BuzzSumo
  Content analysis and influencer identification for outreach.

5. Social Media Platforms & Management

- Facebook Pages
  Dedicated business pages for sharing press releases and engaging audiences.

- Instagram
  Visual storytelling to complement press releases and connect with media.

- LinkedIn
  Professional networking for sharing news and building industry relationships.

- Twitter (X)
  Engage journalists, influencers, and media outlets in real time.

- TikTok
  Short-form video content for viral marketing and brand awareness.

- Bluesky
  Emerging decentralized social platform for niche engagement.

- Hootsuite / Buffer / Sprout Social
  Schedule, manage, and analyze posts across multiple social networks.

- Later
  Instagram-focused scheduling with AI content suggestions.

6. Scheduling, Collaboration & File Sharing

- Calendly
  Schedule interviews, press briefings, and meetings seamlessly.

- Slack
  Team collaboration, file sharing, and communication.

- Zoom
  Video conferencing, webinars, and virtual press events.

- Dropbox
  Store and share press kits, multimedia, and documents securely.

7. SEO & Analytics

- Ahrefs / Semrush / Ubersuggest
  Keyword research, backlink analysis, and competitor SEO insights.

- Google Analytics 4
  AI-powered website and app analytics for tracking campaign impact.

- Tableau
  Data visualization platform for campaign performance reporting.

8. Podcasting & Audio Distribution

- Podbean
  Host and distribute podcasts to discuss press releases and industry topics.

- Spotify for Podcasters
  Record, publish, and analyze podcasts for media outreach.

- SoundCloud
  Share audio press releases, interviews, and insights in an accessible format.

9. Survey & Market Research

- SurveyMonkey
  Create surveys to gather audience feedback and market insights.

- Typeform
  Engaging, interactive surveys and forms for better response rates.

10. Specialized Tools

- Bitly / TinyURL
  Shorten and track links for press releases and social media posts.

- Universal Links (BookLinker)
  Useful for books to direct readers to country-specific retailers.

- WordPress
  Build websites or blogs to showcase press releases and attract media attention.

SEVEN

Layout Links

1. **A Collaborative Template**
2. **Proof of Participation Template**
3. **Book Launch Template**
4. **Job Opportunities Template**
5. **Airline Feature Template**
6. **Familiarization Tour Template**
7. **Introductory Proposal Zoom Zelda**
8. **Flaming Lorraine Template**
9. **CEO Template**
10. **Pitch, Publish & Pop Workbook**

Please Review

If "Splash It!" inspired creative flight

A kind rating or review would spark delight!

Thank you and best of luck with your marketing!

Pass the Pen!

Thank You!

If *The Writer's File* helped spark your next chapter, please drop a review on Amazon. Your kind words help other writers find theirs. Here's a link

www.ingramcontent.com/pod-product-compliance
Lightning Source LLC
Chambersburg PA
CBHW060018030426
42334CB00019B/2087

* 9 7 8 0 7 9 6 1 4 2 1 6 0 *